PETER FUDGE
Gardens

PETER FUDGE
Gardens

Hardie Grant Books

TO ARCHIE & LOLA

This edition published in 2007
First published in 2005
by Hardie Grant Books
85 High Street
Prahran, Victoria 3181, Australia
www.hardiegrant.com.au

All rights reserved. No part of this publication may be reproduced, stored in a retrieval system or transmitted in any form or by any means, electronic, mechanical, photocopying, recording or otherwise, without the prior written permission of the publishers and copyright holders.

The moral right of the author has been asserted.

Copyright text © Peter Fudge 2005
Copyright in the photography remains with the original photographers.

All photographs by David Matheson unless otherwise acknowledged. See page viii for a complete list of contributing photographers.

National Library of Australia
Cataloguing-in-Publication Data:

> Fudge, Peter.
> Peter Fudge gardens.
>
> Includes index.
> ISBN 978 1 74066 496 7.
> ISBN 1 74066 496 5.
>
> 1. Peter Fudge Gardens. 2. Gardens - Australia - Design. 3. Landscape architects - Australia. I. Title.
>
> 712.60994

Edited by Clare Coney
Designed by Trisha Garner
Typeset in Berthold Imago by Pauline Haas
Leaf etching by Trisha Garner
Printed and bound by SNP Leefung

10 9 8 7 6 5 4 3 2 1

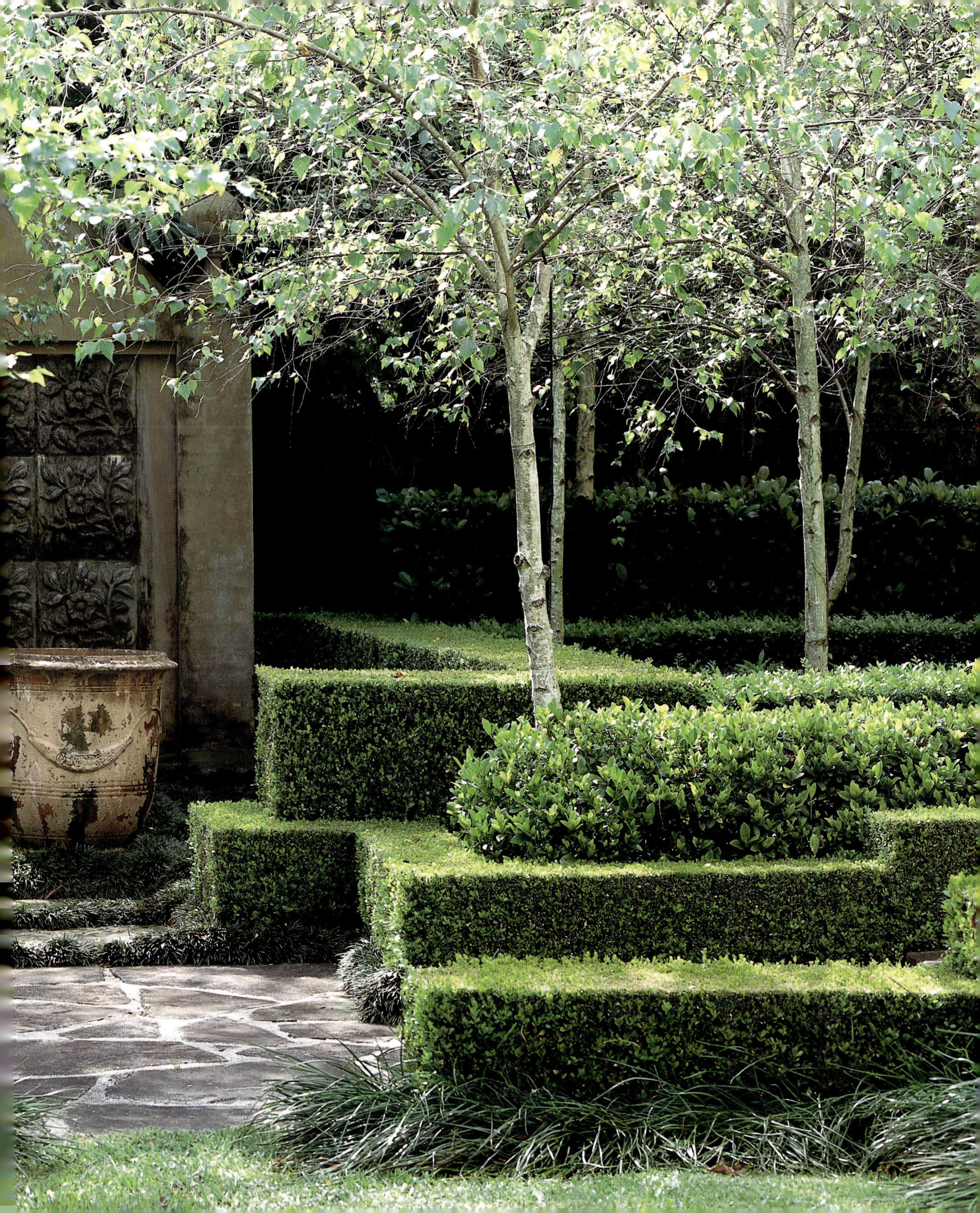

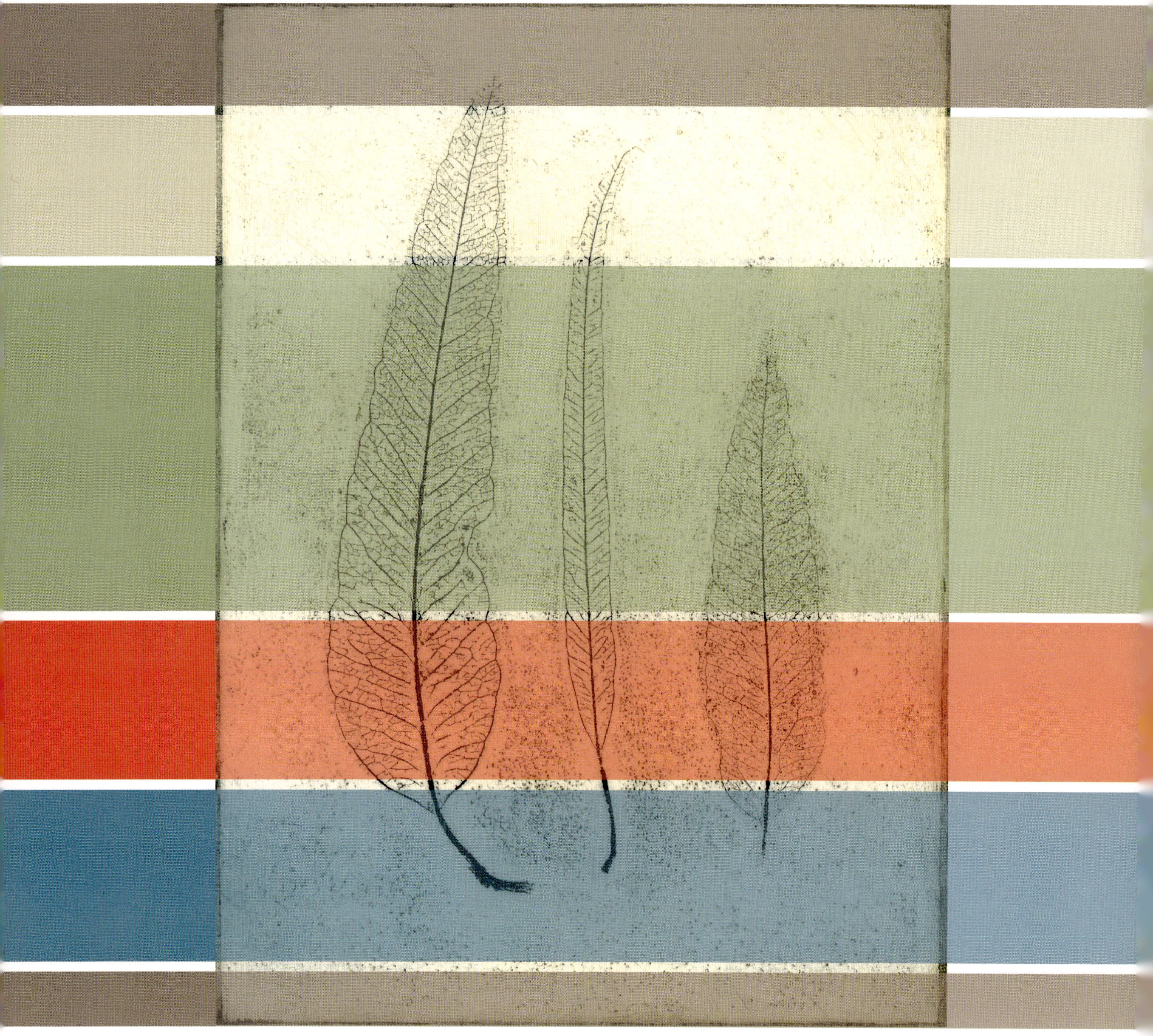

CONTENTS

Introduction	ix

COUNTRY gardens — 1

Living Symmetry	3
Wildes Meadow	
A *belle* Garden	17

URBAN gardens — 27

Contemporary Comforts	29
A Graceful Edge	35
Mission Possible	43
Naturally Distinctive	51
Urban Elegance	57
Stone and Greenery	65
Plane Sailing	73
Visual Enlightenment	79
Garden of Eden	83
Manchurian Drive	95
Integrated Living	99

COURTYARD gardens — 107

Echoes of Light	109
Sultry Fusion	113
A Classic Reflection	119
Poise and Beauty	123

CONCEPT gardens — 129

Contemporary Australian Design in a Bush Setting	131
Sydney in Bloom	
A Display Garden in Sydney's Domain	137

Index	144

ACKNOWLEDGMENTS

I would like to thank all the clients who have opened their gardens to me over the last 15 years, especially those who generously allowed us to photograph their gardens for this book.

However, none of the gardens would have been there to shoot without the staff and contractors who have worked with me during my career. To all of them I say a very grateful thank you.

I will also be eternally grateful to the publishers at Hardie Grant for giving me the opportunity to realise a dream, especially Kirsten Abbott and Julie Pinkham for their belief and enthusiasm with the entire process. This book wouldn't be in your hands now if it wasn't for the amazing ability of Jasmin Chua, who picked up the project halfway, and patiently led me through the publishing maze. Thank you very much. A special thank you to Clare Coney for her invaluable assistance and patience in editing the book, and to Trisha Garner for her inspired book design.

I would like to thank Helen Fitter for her inspiration and friendship early in my career and her continued support now.

Thank you to Steve and Gilly Bibb for their friendship and faith, and mostly for the motivation in making this book happen.

Thanks to Gen Antill for her creative inspiration and willingness to help me with this project.

Thank you to my parents for their love and support.

To the many suppliers who have helped me over the years and, in particular, those that have helped make my visions become a reality in this book: eco concepts, FY2K, Ici et la, Spence and Lyda, and Andre.

To David Matheson – what can I say? It has been an incredible experience for me to have worked with someone so talented. I would like to thank David for being positive about my design approach and being able to capture it so beautifully.

And last, but not least by any means, thank you to my wonderful wife, Brigitte, for her patience, encouragement, enthusiasm and hard work on this and all the other projects we have worked on.

PHOTOGRAPHY CREDITS

All photographs by David Matheson, with the exception of the following:

Leigh Clapp: 95, 97; Dan Freene: ii, 98, 99, 100 (both), 101, 102, 103, 104 (both), 105; Sam McAdam: 16, 17, 18, 19, 20, 21 (both), 23, 24–5, 122, 123, 124 (both), 125, 126 (both), 127, 129, 130, 131, 132, 133, 134 (both), 135, 136, 137, 138 (both), 139, 140 (both), 141; Rob Tuckwell: 94, 96.

INTRODUCTION

My initial attraction for things external started at a young age, when I seemed to pass more time outdoors than indoors.

Between the ages of four and eight I spent a great deal of time with a childless elderly couple who lived on an acreage behind our house in the northern suburbs of Sydney. For me their property contained a collection of the most fascinating things. Mr and Mrs Mac, as I called them, were a retired couple from New Zealand and Mr Mac was the most capable and informative person. When he wasn't trying to drum into me the major successes the New Zealand rugby team had had over the Australians, he was explaining the many wonders of his garden and its inhabitants.

Mr Mac was really a farmer in denial. He had massive shadehouses full of award-winning orchids, highly intricate and efficient composting systems, different breeds of pedigree ducks and chickens, aviaries full of exotic and native finches and ground birds, and he would lovingly tend his expansive and very productive veggie beds. To walk through his garden was like walking through the film set of *The Lord of the Rings* – native and exotic trees and shrubs (many from New Zealand) were all thriving within a series of garden rooms. And all the while, as he tended his plots, he would answer my persistent questions with facts that left me in awe and asking more.

As my home was also 200 metres from bush land, I spent much time exploring it. This too was to be a formative experience for my later work – although of course at the time I had no idea how much this wandering in the bush would affect me.

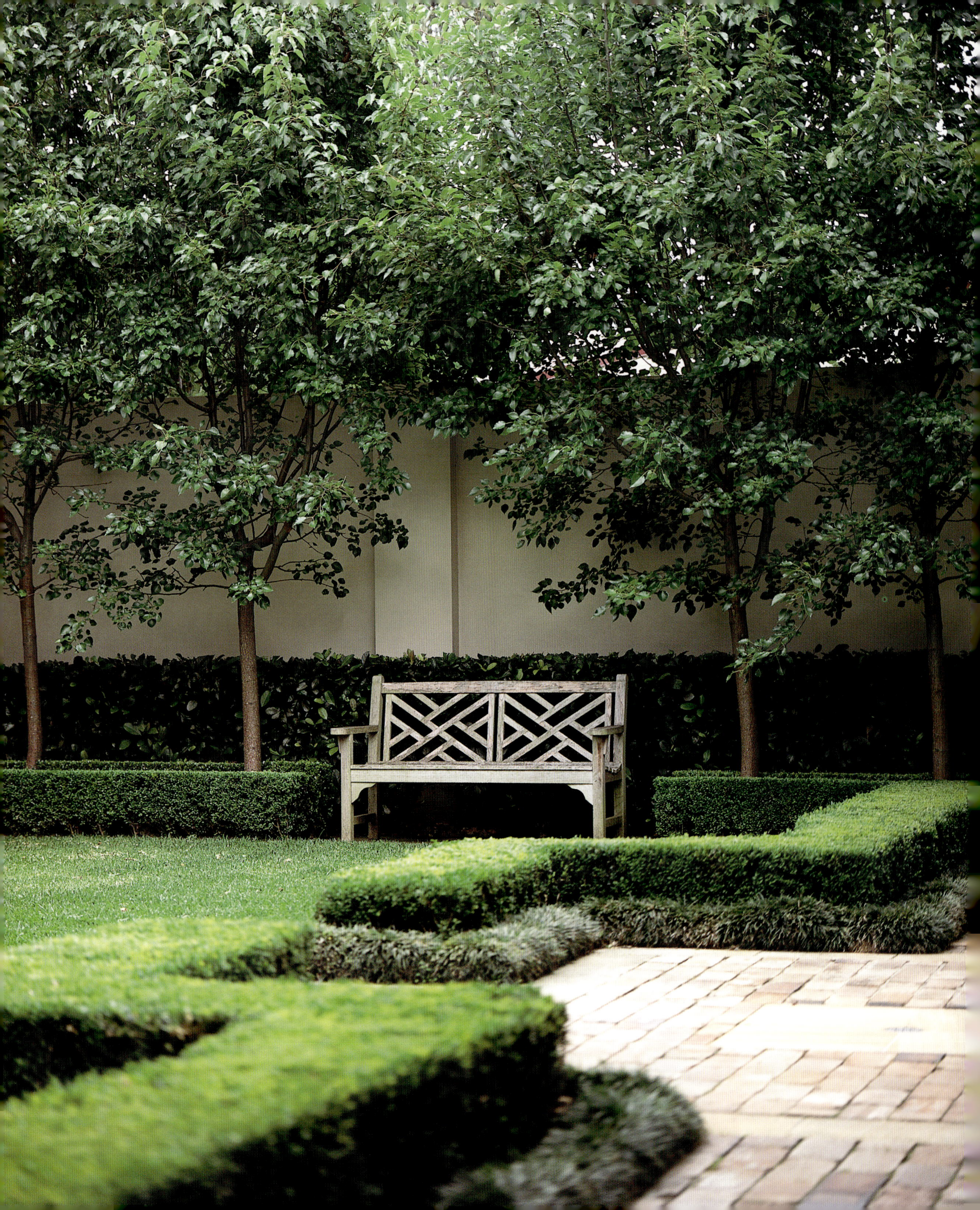

These heady and dreamlike days soon gave way to the serious business of school and after-school sport. However, I kept up my friendship with the Macs until their deaths and tucked away those earlier bedazzling and informative years somewhere in my mind.

After school I enrolled in a landscape design course. I gained solid practical experience with the leading residential landscape company of that time and managed to fly through my course. On completing it I wanted to see the world so, like almost every young Australian in their early twenties, I travelled to Europe.

I guess I was drawn to Europe because of my English heritage, as well as an appreciation for the simplicity, balance and scale of European garden design that I had come to appreciate through my course. My passion for gardens took me to some remote and beautiful destinations throughout Europe, and it was reassuring to be equipped with a reason for my wanderings – my sense of direction took me to far-flung gardens – as curious as this was to my fellow backpackers.

I travelled to all the major gardens – Sissinghurst and Hidcote, Versailles and Villandry, among many others – absorbing as much as I could, taking roll after roll of film. More than anything I tried to imagine the manual labour involved; those people without machinery who moved mountains to create grand gardens. Gardens that were extensions to grand palaces, chateaus and homes.

The garden that probably had the greatest impact on me was the Alhambra in Granada, Spain. This late medieval Moorish garden captivated me. It has stunning garden rooms with beautifully simple water features and plantings that create enclosed oases, a tranquil space away from the city outside. The most intriguing thing for me was the gravity-fed water features and fountains. Today I know that elements of this garden have been instilled within my philosophy.

Since then I have travelled the United States of America and New Zealand, even dragging my new wife around wonderful public and private gardens on our honeymoon in New England, North America. This continues to give me inspiration, seeing how other garden designers have been influenced by classic European gardens and how they then interpret them.

I returned from Europe in 1988 and have operated a landscape design and installation company ever since. I was fortunate enough to start my career on the Upper North Shore of Sydney, working on the gardens of many grand old Victorian and Federation homes, whose architectural symmetry suited my balanced garden design philosophy. House sites on the North Shore are generally larger than elsewhere in Sydney and this gave me the opportunity to exercise some of the major design principles – such as scale, symmetry and proportion – that I had observed in Europe. It also reinforced for me the vital influence that architecture has on garden design and how intrinsically the two are linked.

Nowadays I am lucky enough to work not just on the North Shore, but all over Sydney, regularly in the Southern Highlands and other parts of Australia, and even overseas. However, my travels now are not my source of inspiration. While I truly believe that travelling to foreign countries and absorbing those countries' cultures is a fantastic way to become inspired, it is not always practical and, moreover, it is not always relevant to what is current in one's own environment. And although I have purchased hundreds of garden design books (which I keep promising myself I'll read when I retire!) over the years, my inspiration these days comes from different sources.

Over the last ten years Australian residential architecture has developed into a movement I believe is not only unique but is of a world-class quality. More and more I think Australian architects are creating houses that fit their particular environments. The architect's approach is subtle and sensitive to the surrounds, whether the house's setting is rural, bush land or in the city. Don't get me wrong, I still see plenty of homes that are bloody awful, but on the whole I think we no longer need to look overseas for ideas about modern home design.

I draw enormous inspiration from the clean lines of good modern architecture. I love the use of glass, steel and stone in today's homes, just as I can still appreciate the elegance and beauty of traditional houses. I have learnt from working with a lot of contemporary architects to design asymmetrically when producing a garden that will complement their houses, whereas at one time I designed only symmetrically. Now, with the bones of French classic garden design that I absorbed on my travels and the recent lessons from modern architecture, I am able to do both.

Another source of inspiration in my garden design, along with terrific architecture, has been the recent developments in plant breeding. It's always stimulating to be able to incorporate a new plant into a scheme and many once humdrum plant species have been enlivened with new and exciting cultivars and hybrids. Now landscape designers have a huge range of plants with excellent form and colour to choose from. Whether the plants are native or exotic, there has also been a recent emphasis on breeding varieties that are less reliant on water than older specimens. This is a direction that I very much support.

The enormous growth in landscape products and materials, such as paving, cladding, walling and even furniture, has also given all designers more versatility than ever before. All these make today a very exciting time to be involved in the landscaping industry.

Whether I am designing a contemporary garden or a more classic garden – projects which I approach very differently – my years spent exploring the Australian bush have given me another resource, that of restraint. Wherever I travel throughout Australia I have come to respect the way nature organises its elements. Whatever the situation, our native plant communities seem to display so many principles that can be drawn from when designing a garden, whether it be the layering of vegetation in a rainforest or the simplicity and restraint seen in so many eucalyptus woodlands, with an understorey of textured grasses massed beneath the trees.

The final source of inspiration I wanted to mention is that given to me by my clients. The longer I remain in this industry the more I realise how critical it is to listen properly to the clients and to gain an understanding of what really excites them about a garden – whether I agree with it or not. Of course, I never lose sight of the fact that they have employed me to give them direction – to bring their garden wishes into fruition. But for me the role of a good landscape designer or architect is to get inside the client's head, understand their wishes, and then design for that client's lifestyle. After all, every one is different. This is what keeps me inspired.

Pete

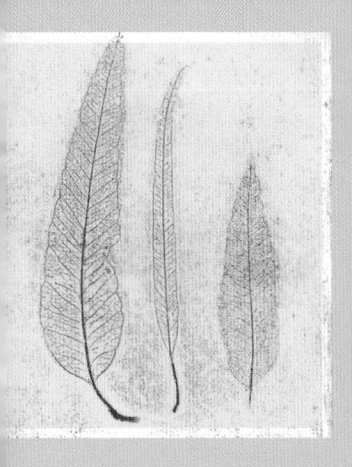

COUNTRY gardens

For me, exercising restraint to achieve continuity is the secret to designing large gardens.

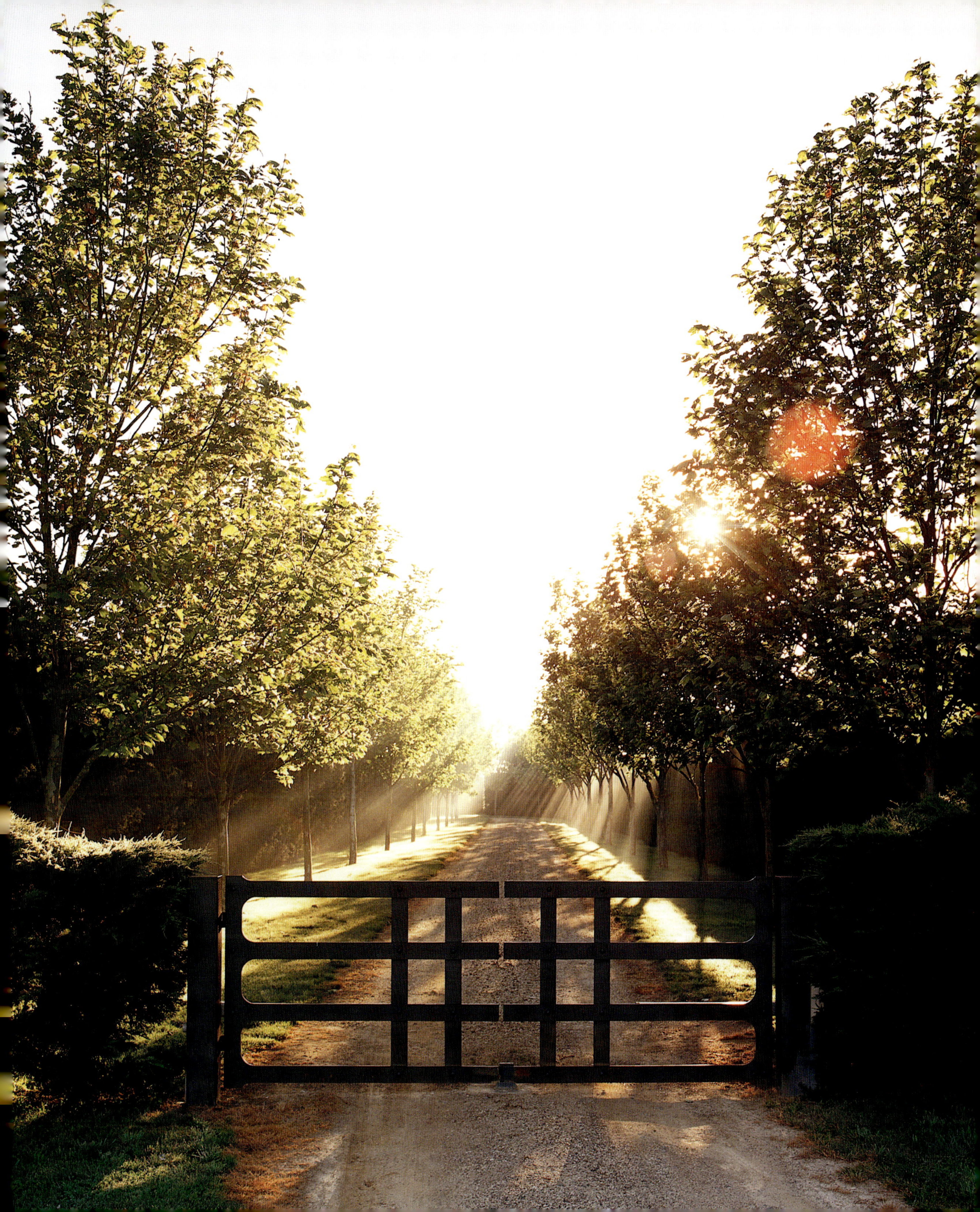

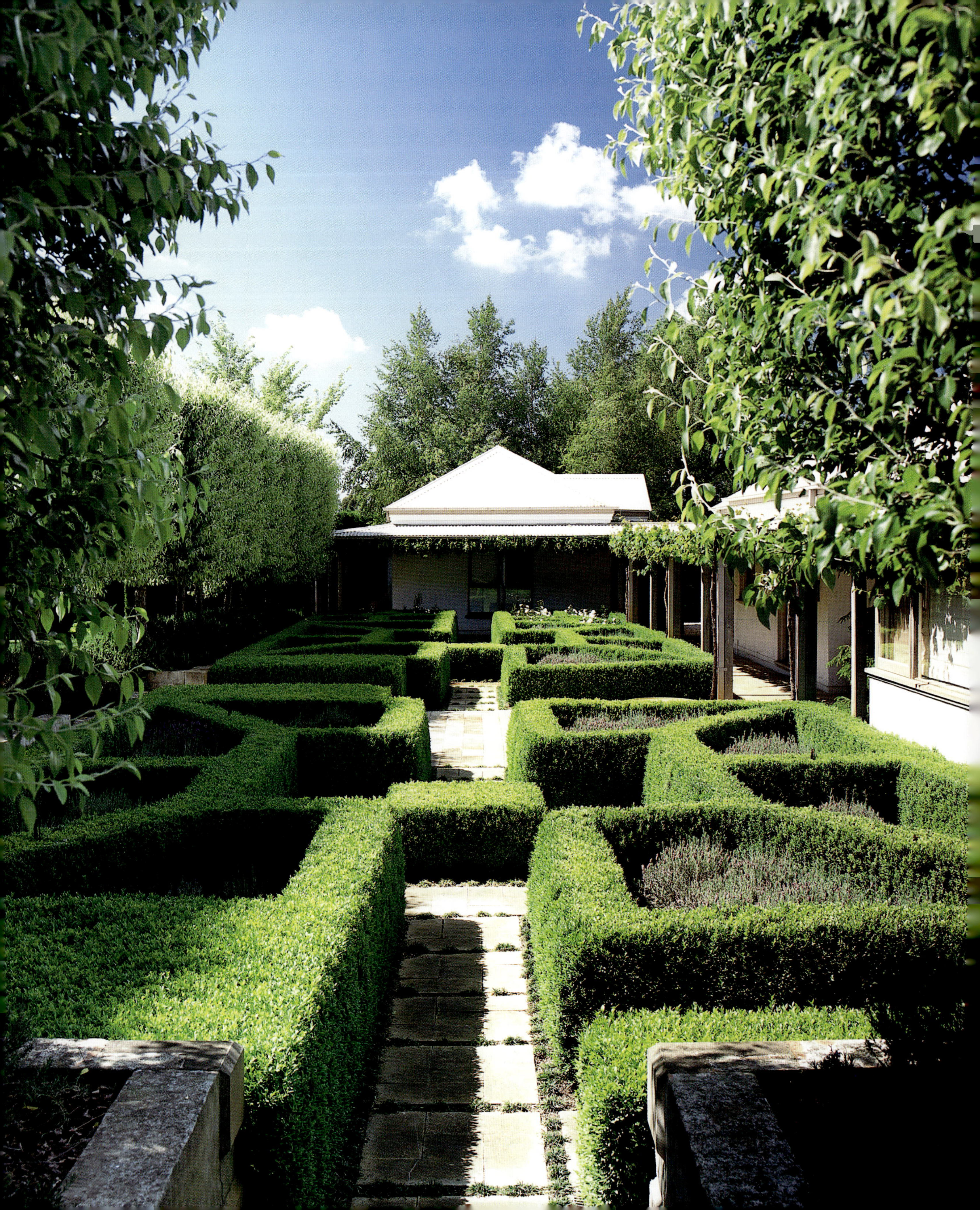

LIVING SYMMETRY

THE SETTING
'Tobermory' is a 2 hectare (5 acre) property in the Southern Highlands of New South Wales, near Moss Vale. Eight years ago, when I made my first visit, the clients had moved into a modern cream-rendered brick residence with an iron roof. The site was part of a subdivision of a larger farming property, and even though there were pleasant views of the surrounding countryside, any newly planted vegetation would need protection from strong seasonal winds.

THE BRIEF
The clients initially wished me to design the land immediately around the house as a formal garden, leaving much of the block as pasture. Only once these more formal zones were planned, constructed and planted did I develop complementary ideas for the whole property. Over the past eight years all the property has become garden, and it is still evolving – and improving.

THE DESIGN
My initial impression was that the home was placed awkwardly on the property, as it was not lying parallel to any of the boundaries. The garden design, therefore, would have to attempt to correct any feeling of imbalance. I believed this could be achieved by forming clear and distinctive garden lines emanating from the home. This would help focus the eye on the harmony between house and garden.

Moss Vale is about 680 metres above sea level and the climate is much cooler than on the New South Wales coast. There are four distinct seasons, with heavy frosts in winter, which can occur as late as November, and there is sometimes even snow – all the plantings in the garden therefore had to be hardy, withstanding temperatures below 0° Celsius – while the average maximum temperature in January and February is only 25° Celsius. The land is fertile and about 700 millimetres of rain falls annually. Thus the Southern Highlands is an excellent area for gardening and is home to some of

OPPOSITE Diverging axes are commonplace in this garden.
ABOVE Morning sunlight drenches the long drive lined with London plane trees.

ABOVE *The white landscaper roses and the* Echeveria *provide colour in the garden all year round.*

the most beautiful gardens in New South Wales, such as Kennerton Green in Mittagong.

The original garden design brief concentrated on the areas immediately surrounding the home. I began by envisioning a series of formal 'garden rooms' around the house. These are all connected with stepping stones that are edged with mini mondo grass, *Ophiopogon japonicus* 'Nana'. Originally I used thyme – which looked absolutely beautiful, but it died off and so the switch was made. Today, every square metre of the 2 hectares has been carefully designed, and the garden comprises fifteen separate rooms, including a golden ash walk, a contemporary Japanese courtyard, a lavender parterre, a poplar plantation, *Populus deltoides*, and a sunken garden. This description may suggest a 'busy' garden, but for me 'Tobermory' is a tranquil place.

The sense of peace I feel there arises from the numerous rooms being unified by several intentional design elements. The foundation or underlying skeleton of the garden is deliberately strong and simple. All lines of sight connect with the house, forming linear perspectives that, I think, lend a quality of unaffected beauty to the garden. Indeed, I love 'Tobermory' in mid-winter when the drama and simplicity of the garden is emphasised.

The attraction of 'Tobermory' comes, too, by restricting the number of varieties of plants. The use of too many different plants in one design can lead to a confusion of the senses and a shapeless quality to the garden. At 'Tobermory' each garden room relies on massed arrangements of one featured plant with a few selections, most notably 'Leighton Green' cypress hedges (x *Cupressocyparis leylandii*), used more widely to create harmony between the separate rooms and to form the walls.

In addition, the 'Tobermory' garden – like many of my designs – has a natural and free-flowing relationship with the home. Courtyards, paths, garden beds, hedges and rows of trees are used to merge the living and entertaining areas of the residence with the garden settings. When the owners are inside the house, my intention is that their eyes should be drawn continually outward, whether through a doorway or window, to a particular point or vista beyond. I really wanted them to feel that they could not wait to get out in the garden again, that they would look out and then be physically drawn outside. This was done by creating gaps in hedges that led to views beyond or to a strategically placed recessed focal point.

In planning the garden at 'Tobermory' I was also acutely aware of not wanting to lose the sense of intimacy that I love in smaller gardens.

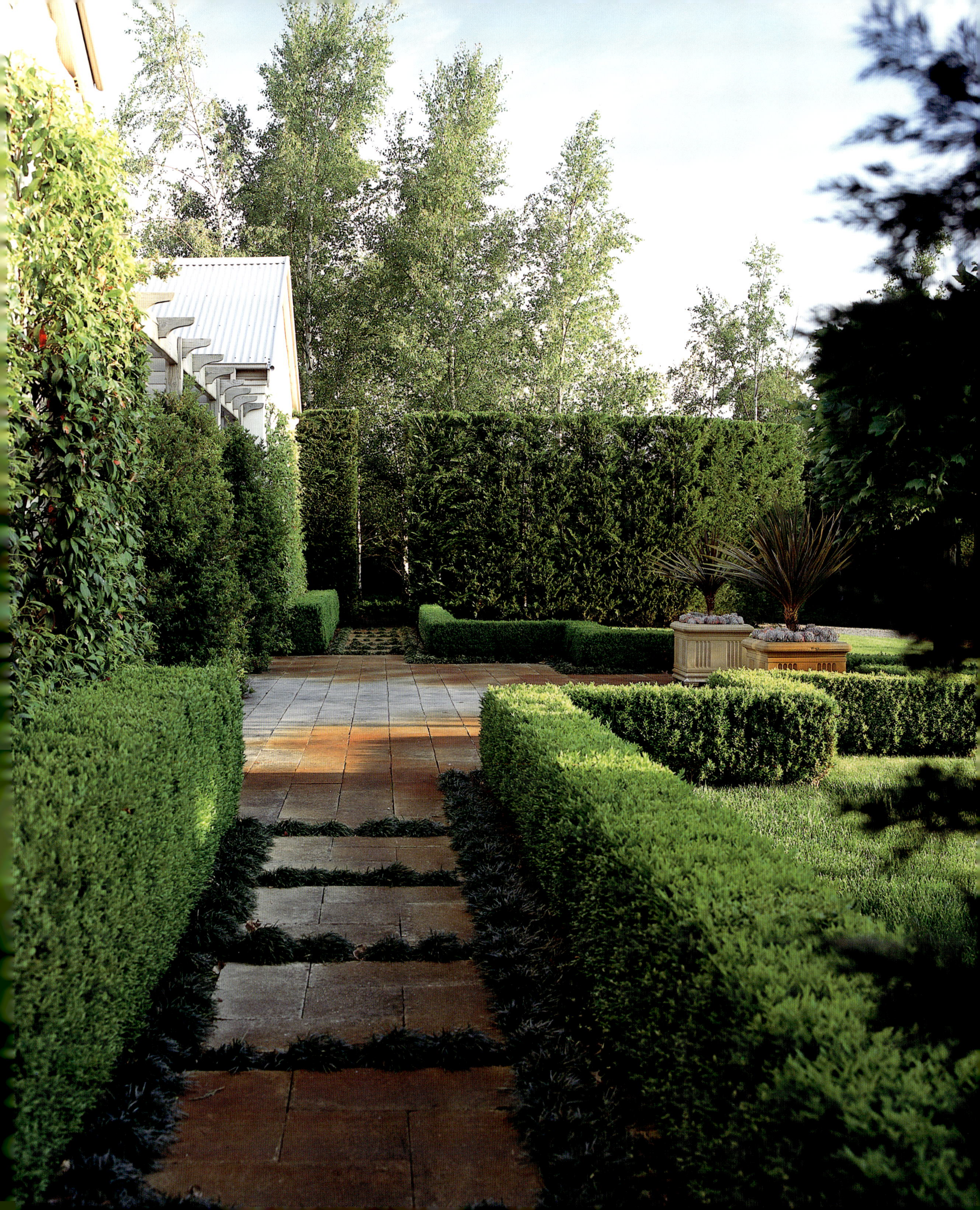

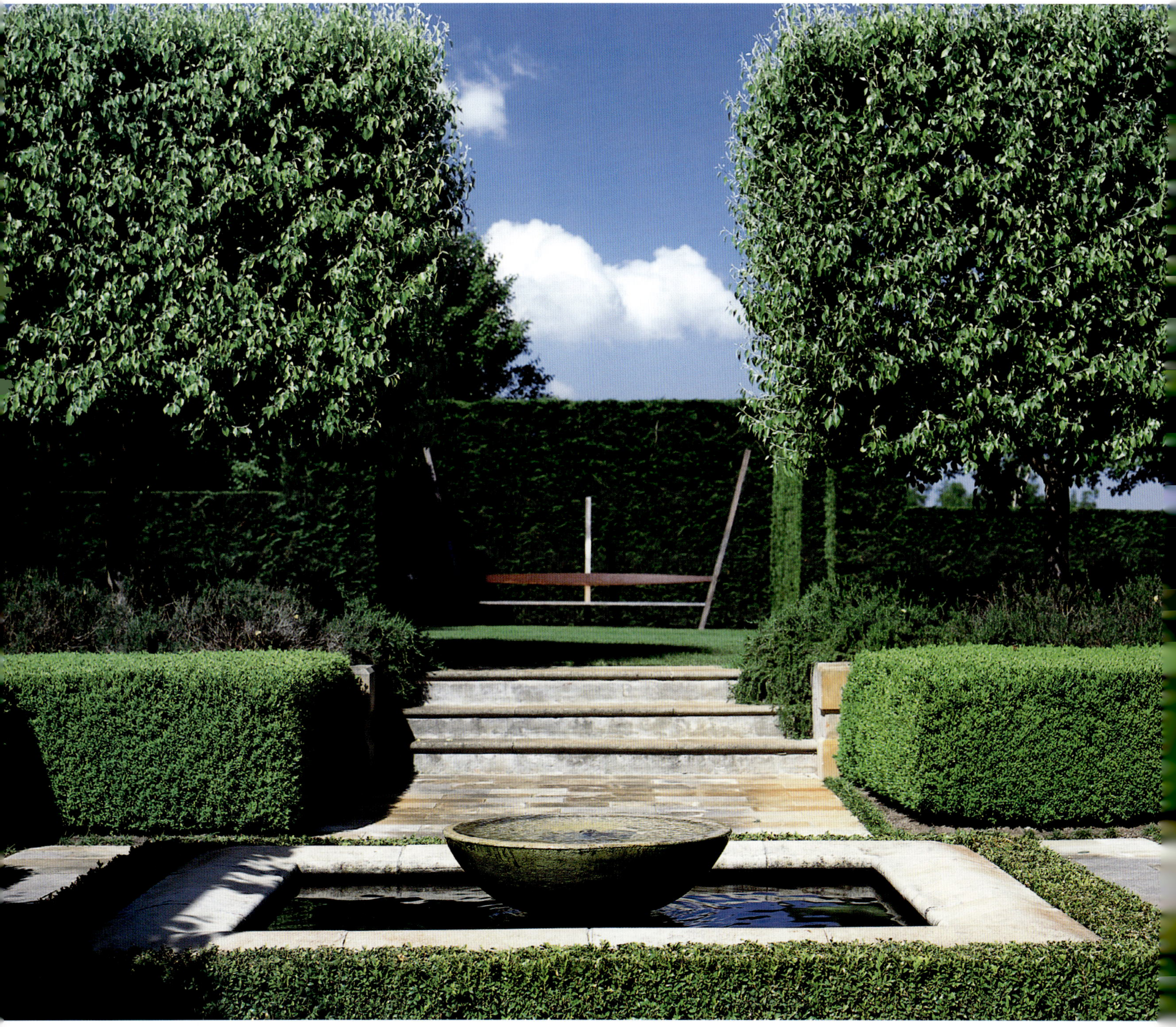

I wanted to balance the need to make each garden room enticing, distinctive and secretive, yet still be part of the one garden experience. The extensive hedging of closely planted and clipped 'Leighton Green' cypresses, which surrounds the separate rooms, unites each part to the whole while enticing one to explore further. These wonderful thick green walls also provide practical windbreaks – necessary to ensure more delicate plants within the rooms do not suffer wind damage – and their own micro-climates.

The first room I designed was the parterre. It is 8 metres wide by 25 metres long and is situated directly outside the rear of the house. When I began work it had views beyond it to the paddocks of the neighbours. The parterre consists of massed Italian lavender, *Lavandula stoechas*, contained by clipped English box, *Buxus sempervirens* borders. At one end of the parterre, closest to the guest quarters and outside the owners' office, the two end compartments were planted with white landscaper roses. This was to keep the number of lavender compartments either side of the central axis equal. I also chose the landscaper rose as it is a plant, like lavender, that I associate with a Mediterranean-style garden.

When viewed from the kitchen at the back of the house, a low pond centrally placed in the parterre forms an axis from the house to the garden beyond. Within the parterre there is a diagonal axis through each planted compartment, forming symmetrical patterns. Compared to the surrounding garden – which was just lawn at this stage – the parterre was at the level of the house and a few feet below the level of the lawn. Therefore the parterre could be appreciated as one walked around the grounds, looking back at the house and down onto the parterre. In the higher garden, there are strategically placed gaps in the planting in line with the central and diagonal garden axes, through which one can look back onto the parterre and neighbouring sunken garden. Thus the full grandeur of this very large parterre can be enjoyed from above.

Around the higher garden above the parterre, I planted a pleached snow pear hedge (*Pyrus nivalis*). It is pruned so that the trees have 2 metre tall, straight, clear trunks, and the elevated continual canopy on top of the stems is approximately 1 metre wide by 2.5 metres tall. The pear trees are underplanted by *Rosmarinus officinalis* 'Blue Lagoon', a rosemary with intense blue flowers, forming a continuous avenue at the back of the house and to the side. I created a gap in the pear hedge to frame the view beyond, as you look out over the central axis from the kitchen.

From the kitchen one's eye is drawn over the pond, through the gap in the pear hedge to the surrounding raised garden and on over a 30 metre lawn. The focal point of this axis is a contemporary bench, which also acts as a form of modern sculpture; because it's not obvious that this object is a bench seat, once again the viewer is drawn out of the house.

From the parterre the mondo grass-lined stepping stones lead along the north side of the house to an octagonal paved area. Beside these stepping stones, in a bed next to the house, bay tree cones are planted, under which originally a herb garden was planned. On arriving at the octagonal garden through the cypress hedge one can view the ash walk.

OPPOSITE The magnificent view from the kitchen window; a distinctive bench also acts as a form of contemporary sculpture in the garden.

LEFT A 1.5 metre tall Turkish olive jar makes a simple statement on the northern side lawn. OPPOSITE My favourite part of the garden; this magical pathway, lined with golden ash, is just wide enough for two people to walk down side by side.

The golden ash (*Fraxinus excelsior* 'Aurea') walk is backed by the cypress hedges, which form a 3 metre wide and 13 metre long tunnel, giving the walk a strong sense of perspective. The pleached golden ash are planted approximately 1.5 metres apart, inside the cypress tunnel, either side of a fescue lawn 'path' about 1.3 metres wide. The ash trees are underplanted with a double *Buxus sempervirens* (English box) hedge: the back hedge is 80 centimetres high and 40 centimetres wide, while the front hedge is 50 centimetres high and 40 centimetres wide. The pleached ash form a high continuous 'hedge' pruned to 80 centimetres wide by 1.2 metres high, above 2.2 metres high clear, straight trunks. In this way pedestrians can walk without being obstructed by the low limbs of the trees.

In summer the delicate yellow ash leaves form a shady canopy that ensures the walk remains cool. The leaflets turn a wonderful deep gold in autumn before they fall, and in winter there is additional interest as the yellow of the smaller branches contrasts strongly with the black leaf buds they carry. The pathway itself is wide enough for two people to walk down side by side. The grass under foot here is velvet green and soft – a green so intense that in combination with the yellow of the trees traversing the ash walk becomes an almost surreal experience.

I really enjoy creating smaller, narrower spaces when designing large gardens as a contrast to experiences elsewhere in the garden. This dramatic alley is lined centrally with the owners' bedroom window and at any time of the day – though it is especially stunning in the early dawn or at dusk – the eye drawn down the long alley to a simple two-tiered iron fountain sitting in a 3 metre diameter pond at the end, flush with the lawn path.

Access from the garden to rooms either side of this alley is gained by gaps at the end of the walk but before the pond. A semi-circular cypress hedge skirts and backs the pond.

Between the bedroom windows and the alley I designed an octagonal flower garden. A stone urn planted with trailing *Echeveria* succulents sits centrally within the octagonal planting and lines up directly with the fountain and the window. Between the paving and the octagonal framework of a cypress hedge, I designed ascending layers of flowering shrubs, the like of which is not found elsewhere in the garden. First there is a low hedge of English box, *Buxus sempervirens*, then a layer of blue iris, a layer of *Hebe* 'Lake' and then a band of single white rugosa roses and, finally, in front of the 'Leighton Green' hedge a layer of *Teucrium fruticans*, bush germander. This makes it the softest part of the whole garden. Two columns either side of the bedroom windows frame this intimate but extensive view. We covered the columns with *Rosa bracteata*, the beautiful, evergreen Macartney rose.

From the octagonal garden room more stepping stones lead to the front of the house and the 7 metre central circular drive. We relocated a London plane tree, *Platanus* x *acerifolia*, from elsewhere in the garden and set it in the centre, then massed *Ophiopogon jaburan* beneath to soften the drive. We elevated the canopy of the plane tree so that views from the living room down the drive, under the plane tree, are not interrupted.

Surrounding the outside edges of the drive we created a beautifully contoured, 4 metre wide fescue lawn and planted a pleached plane tree avenue in its centre. The trees are pruned to form a continuous circular canopy 1 metre wide by 2 metres high above straight, smooth trunks 2.5 metres high. The trees really complement the circular drive. Naturally the all-connecting and unifying cypress 'Leighton Green' is planted behind the plane trees, enclosing this large entry garden.

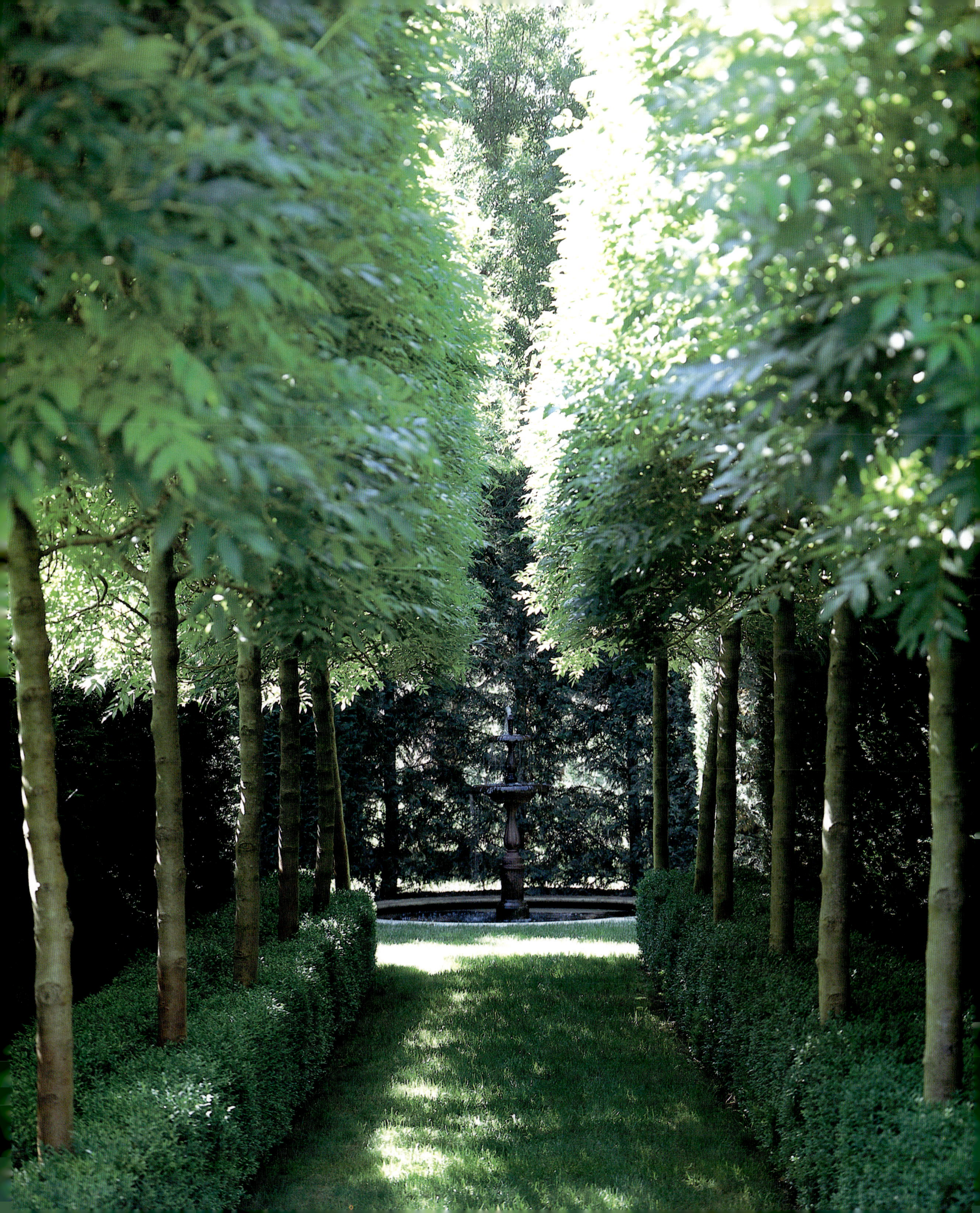

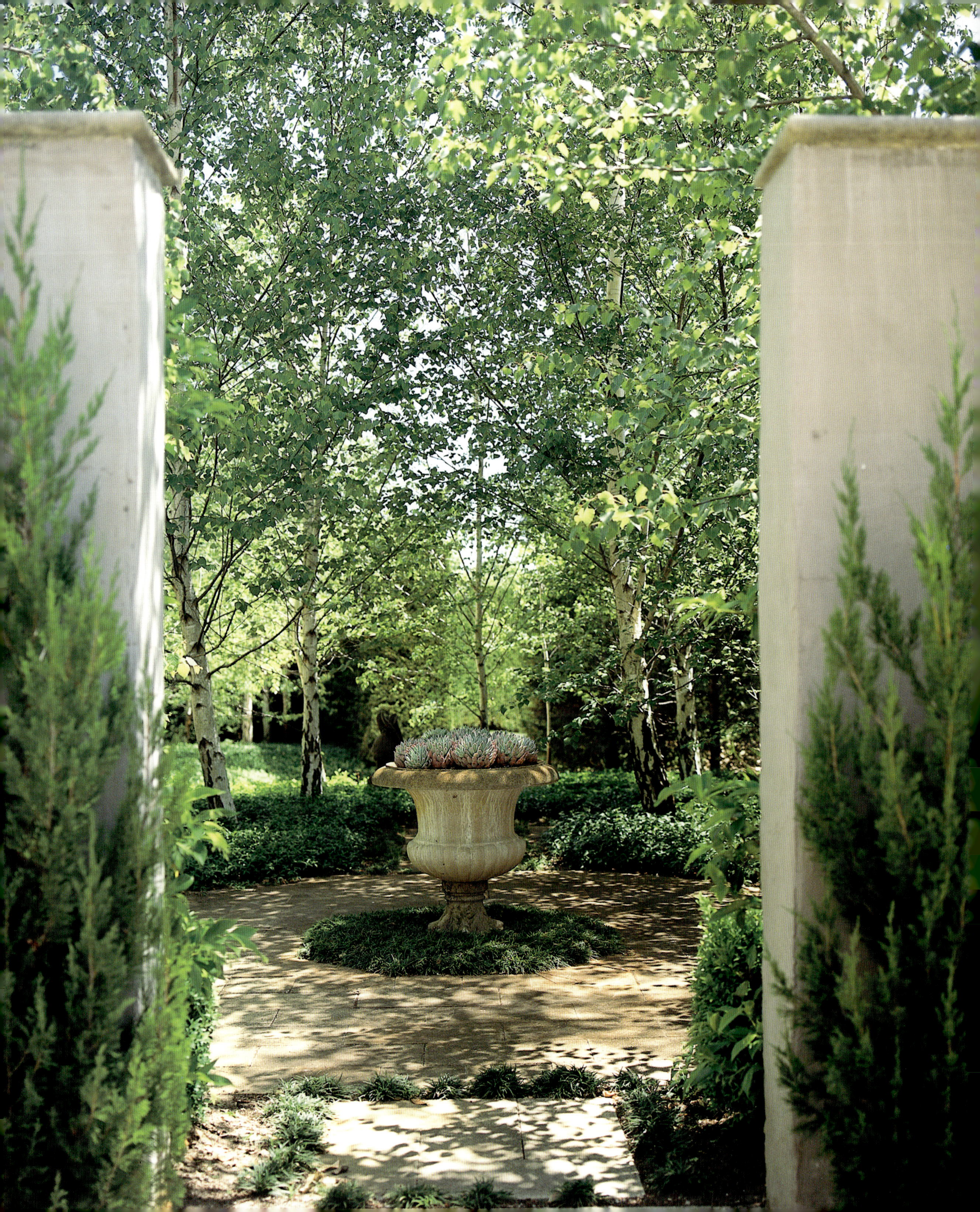

A 3 metre wide gap in the cypress hedge lines up directly square with the living room doors at the front of the house. This powerful axis draws the eye from the living room over the centrally planted plane tree and through the gap to a large pond and the garden beyond.

The doors from the living room open onto a generously paved entry terrace reached by steps from the drive and lined with timber columns which are planted with *Rosa bracteata* to continue the theme. These rose-clad columns soften the large paved area and frame the view beyond. Square pots planted with spiky *Cordyline* 'Red Sensation' and *Echeveria* succulents accentuate the steps from the gravel drive.

The stepping stones continue around the south side of the house to a Japanese courtyard. On the journey to the courtyard many scores of silver birches, *Betula pendula*, line the drive which leads to the garage. The birches hug the drive beautifully and the drive disappears through contoured beds raised higher than the drive. These beds are massed with periwinkle *Vinca minor* 'Alba', forming a velvet-green carpet under the white-stemmed birch, all of which is stunning in winter.

Before entering the Japanese courtyard, a second octagonal paved area – matching the octagonal paved area on the north side – houses a stone urn again planted with *Echeveria* and underplanted with mini mondo grass. The birch and periwinkle lining the drive also surround this paved area, creating a beautiful, dapple-shaded space.

OPPOSITE Betula pendula *grows beautifully in this climate; groves of silver birch hug the last part of the drive.*

The Japanese courtyard is very simple and lies outside generous dining room doors from the house. The 5 metre by 4 metre area is paved with the same reconstituted stone pavers that are used all over the garden. The courtyard walls are 2 metres high and are rendered white. Surrounding the paving at the base of the wall is *Juniperus virginiana* 'Spartan', forming a dark green hedge around the courtyard, stopping on the back feature wall to allow for a handmade cantilevered hardwood timber bench. The wall behind the bench has been painted in a green–grey colour for contrast. In the centre of the courtyard sits a pebble pond, flush with the paving.

At the top of the pond a grate lies only 10 centimetres below the surface. Quartz-coloured translucent pebbles sit flush with the coping of the pond. A copper tube connected to a pump feeds up through the grate and the pebbles, forming a bubbling fountain. I laid a pebble band inlay around the pond between the coping and the paving to extend the pebble look. A light within the pond plays with the water, pebbles and foliage, making it a beautiful sight at night.

Nearer to the doors of the dining room, two *Acer palmatum* 'Sango Kaku', coral bark maples, break up the paving. They are underplanted with *Acorus gramineus* 'Variegata', Japanese sweet flag, to keep up the Japanese theme. The pink bark of the maples is highlighted against the green conifers and grey wall. I wanted this 'room' to be an unexpected surprise, contrasting with the themes of the rest of the garden.

The garden outside the guest cottage situated at the end of the parterre is probably the most used garden room of the house. To change the feel I decided to create steps from the paved verandah

ABOVE The sunken garden next to the guesthouse: the cypress hedges are deliberately angled down so that you can capture views of the paddocks beyond.
OPPOSITE What was once a horse paddock is now a woodland garden with a reflective dam.

down to a sunken garden, which is how we refer to this area. The outdoor furniture here was handmade and when sitting in it there is one of the few views to the 'outside' allowed in the design, as the cypress hedges that enclose this room are angled down to capture the view of the paddocks. We have enjoyed many a beautiful lunch here as the owner is a magnificent cook. The planting within the sunken garden is simple and architectural and follows on from the formality of the parterre: contrasting *Buxus sempervirens* and *Buxus microphylla* var. *japonica* hedges surround the paving and are defined by a clip gap of 5 centimetres. In the corners of the garden four variegated elms (*Ulmus variegata*) form slender, arching canopies over the paving. This is one of my favourite places in the garden.

The sunken garden has two exits – one leads to the large grassed area behind the parterre garden and the other leads to the south, to a larger level area screened with cypress hedges and intended for a pool. At one end of this space we cut views through the hedge, battlement like, forming 'windows' that frame views of pasture beyond.

The garden spaces beyond these immediate green 'rooms' surrounding the house become larger and looser and yet are still contained by cypress hedges.

At the front of the property I designed a straight gravel drive 300 metres long flanked by plane trees and backed by a 4 metre high cypress hedge. Simple and dramatic! I also designed steel gates and an intercom post inspired by classic rural style but with a contemporary edge. As the gates open you are surrounded immediately by the garden and have a sense of being at home.

As one is moving along the long drive, windows cut into the northern cypress hedge afford views of the dam, which I extended and changed in shape from the original circle to a more natural form. I wanted to elongate it so that it could be seen from the house.

In this large 'front paddock' the beautifully clipped cypress hedges form a stunning backdrop to groves of *Ulmus parvifolia*, Chinese elm, and *Fraxinus angustifolia* 'Raywood', the Raywood ash, which has rich burgundy foliage in autumn. This is a wonderful area of woodland/parkland – a great place for picnics – interrupted by a central avenue of *Poplar deltoides* halfway up the woodland, whose white trunks form an avenue leading one into a poplar plantation which is surrounded by scalloped cypress hedges. In the plantation itself the hundreds of trees are symmetrically placed so that no matter where you are, the trunks always line up.

THE RESULT

'Tobermory' owes much to the tenacity, encouragement and inspiration of the clients. I may feel I have concluded my ideas on their garden, yet it has not finished with me. It continues to mature and surprise me anew. It was certainly one of the most fulfilling garden design projects of my career.

For me the garden holds so much magic. It changes hour by hour and season by season – I never tire of it. I am still enticed to walk around corners, through alleys and tunnels, into woodlands and secret nooks and I still have a feeling of anticipation. This is garden magic.

It was achieved using a select number of species and shapes. For interest it relies on changes of scale, shades of green, restraint, simple ornamentation; David Mabberley wrote in *Vogue Living*, 'this minimalist and almost urban approach gives to this country garden a sense of serenity through a clinically pared down simplicity'.

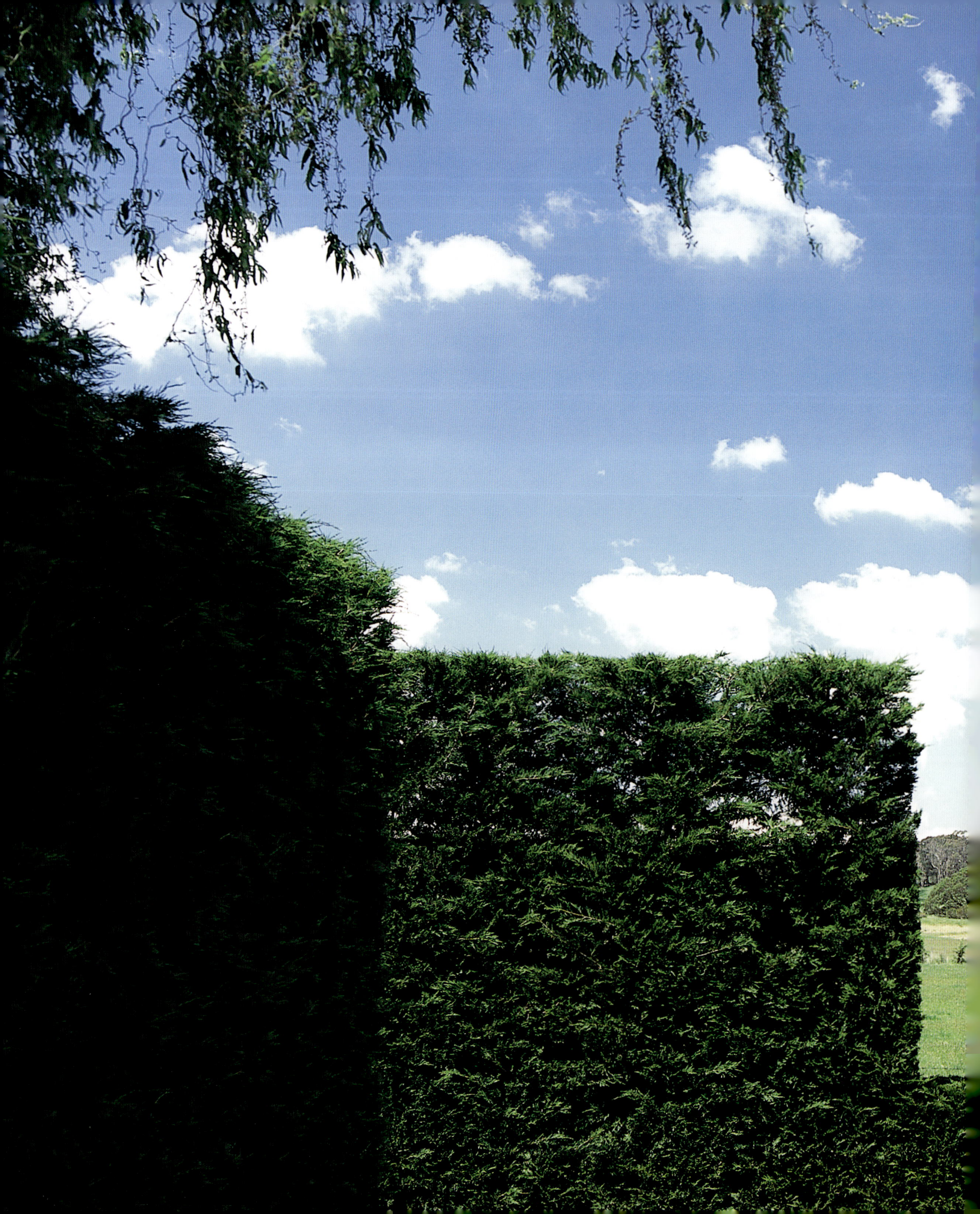

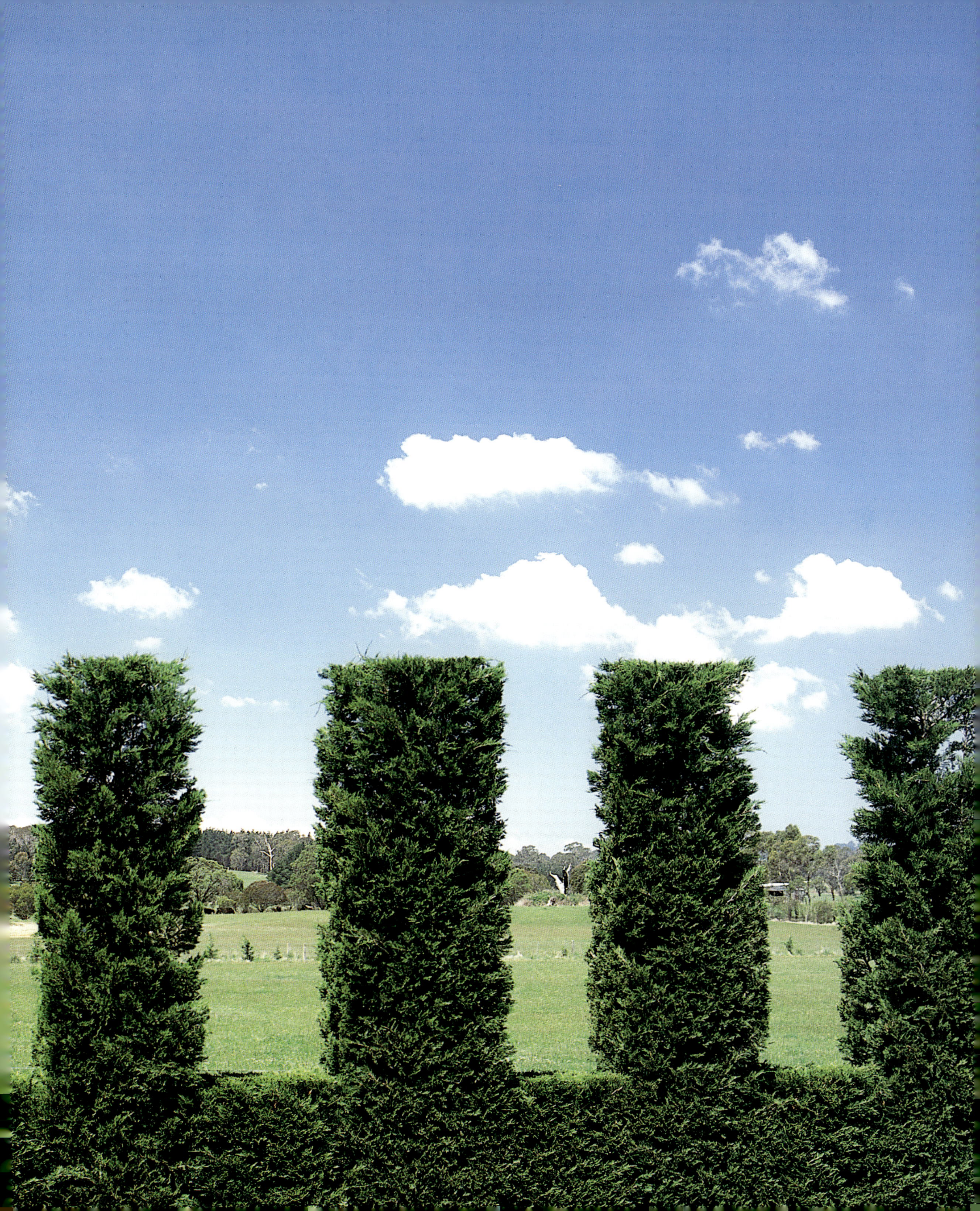

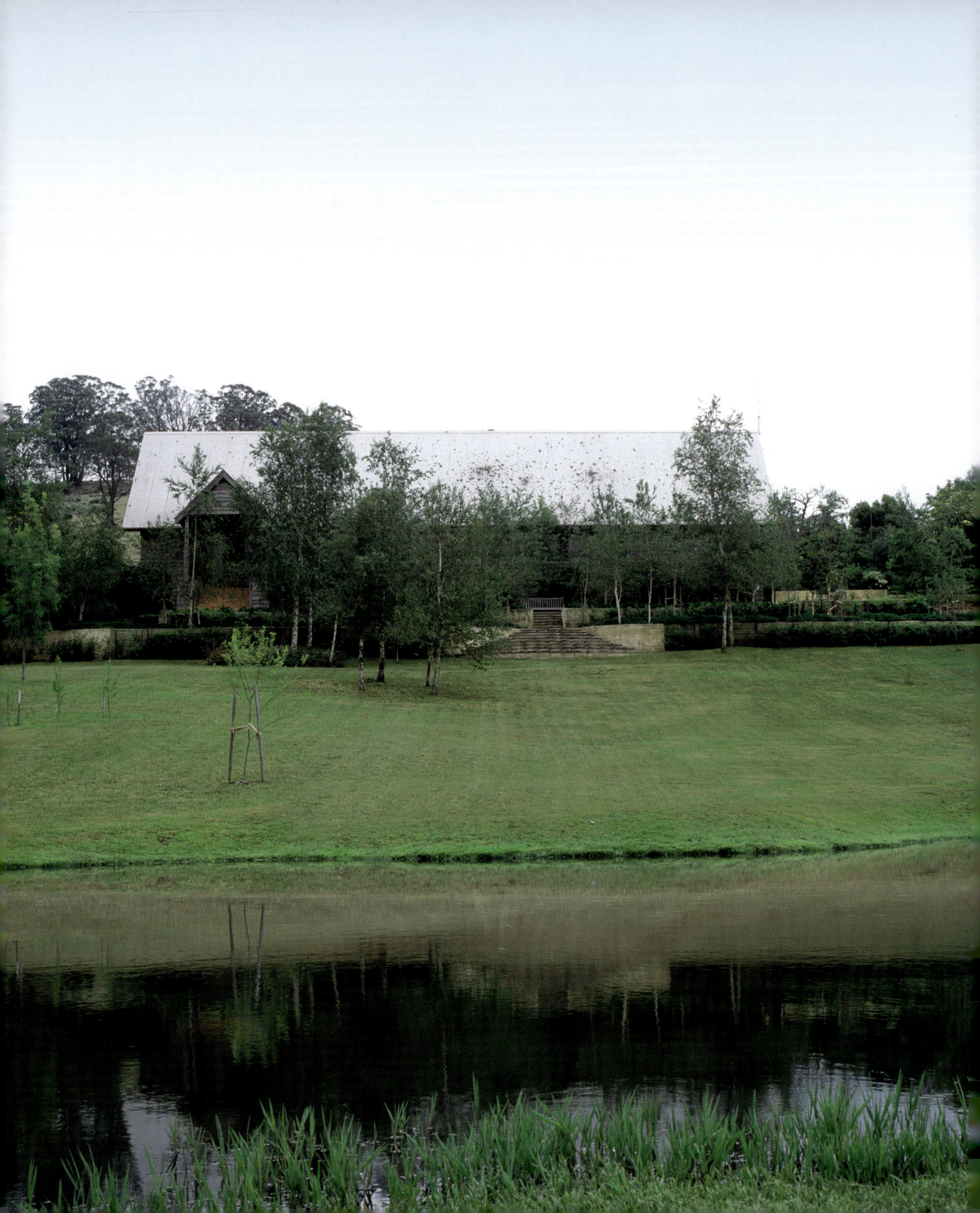

WILDES MEADOW
A *belle* GARDEN

THE SETTING
A country property in New South Wales's Southern Highlands, about 2 hectares (5 acres) in area. It was a wonderful cedar home set amongst a semi-established garden on volcanic soil.

THE BRIEF
Although I had no way of realising it initially, this was to be one of the most challenging briefs I have ever had. First, a confession: this was in fact my parents' property, which they had moved to from the upper North Shore in Sydney. My parents trustingly gave me total freedom to design whatever I wanted in the garden. However, as the project unfolded over several years, I always kept at the back of my mind the fact that my mother has a true passion for a more flowery garden than I would ever want.

THE DESIGN
The first issue to be resolved in planning for the garden's design was wind. If the garden was to succeed this issue had to be immediately addressed, as strong winds that could last for up to 10 days at a time and blow from any direction seemed to be fairly usual conditions. Even the cattle in surrounding paddocks would go crazy for a while.

So we planted a dense x *Cupressocyparis leylandii* 'Leighton Green' screen around the entire perimeter, a plant that people in warmer climates have an aversion to, owing to its high maintenance requirements – it needs constant trimming. In this windswept environment it is the perfect choice for a substantial windbreak as it is naturally pruned and controlled by the elements.

OPPOSITE From the winding tree-lined drive, we are offered glimpses of the simple front garden layout, which belies the surprise of the elaborate garden rooms behind the house.

ABOVE The shape and form of Cynara scolymus, *the globe artichoke, is visually impressive. OPPOSITE Shrubs and perennials wrap around the house – the relaxed arrangement and variety of plants delighted my mother.*

Once we had established protection from the winds, planting of the garden could begin. I assessed the semi-established garden my parents had inherited and found that I was able to totally rework the front of the garden. However, I tried to incorporate much of the established ground levels and existing layout in the back garden.

In the back garden I formalised what was the main lawn area, planted with a fescue grass (*Festuca* sp.). Some insignificant trees were removed and the edge of the lawn was surrounded with a pleached hedge of the double crab apple, *Malus ioensis* 'Plena', and thus a perfect croquet ground was created! The crab apples were pleached to form 2 metre high single straight stems with a continuous elevated canopy, clipped 60 centimetres wide by 2 metres high.

Malus ioensis 'Plena' is a very attractive apple, sometimes called Bechtel's crab. Its bark is silvery, so is pretty in winter when the tree is bare, while the flowers and foliage are features at other seasons of the year. In late spring the tree bears clusters of pale pink, double blooms which have a delightful fragrance. In autumn the bright green leaves turn into a spectrum of red, orange and yellow colours before they fall.

Apples have traditionally been pruned and trained to suit various situations and to improve their yield of fruit. Espaliered trees set against walls were a common sight in northern Europe for centuries. By pruning an apple tree to grow in two dimensions, flat against the wall, the tree's energy goes into producing fruiting spurs rather than in outward growth. Therefore the idea of turning crab apples into a pleached hedge was not an outlandish one. This particular crab apple would also delight my mother with its pretty blossom.

These crab apple trees also frame the main central axis as seen from the back of the house, highlighting a stunning view of forested hills beyond. To accentuate this optical perspective, a moss-covered teak bench was placed on the boundary of the garden. For fun I dotted an avenue of English box (*Buxus sempervirens*) on the slope of the hill above the croquet lawn, towards the bench. English box is long-lived and slow-growing, but eventually these will be circular balls about 1 metre in diameter. My aim was that at this stage they should look as if they wanted to roll down the slope, but are stuck on to the hill – in suspended animation!

I have always enjoyed creating 'rooms' within a garden and this is particularly important with large gardens. Small garden 'rooms' are easier for the viewer to relate to the human scale, and they create a sense of intimacy whilst people in the garden are still able to appreciate its greater expanse. Another part of my design philosophy is to give structure to gardens; this was done here by creating hedges within the garden to act as the walls of each room.

Along the north-facing back of the house I decided to create a softer look that I knew my mother would appreciate, which was a mixture of groupings of perennials with a mauve and white theme. The garden beds consisted of a collection of plants which we thought were both pretty or had a good leaf form. A couple of Japanese box balls (*Buxus microphylla* var. *japonica*) and an *Eriostemon myoporoides*, long-leaf wax flower, clipped into a huge

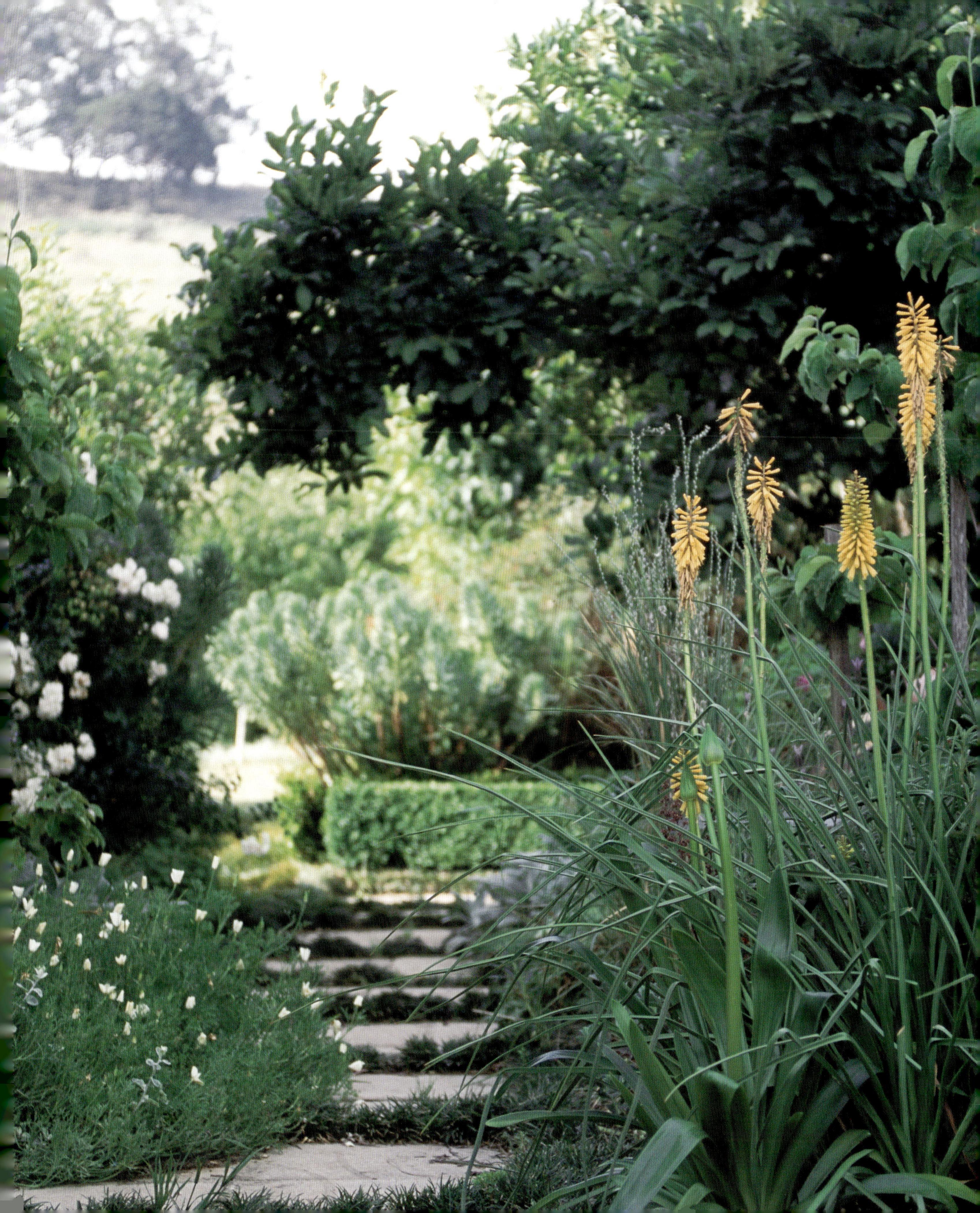

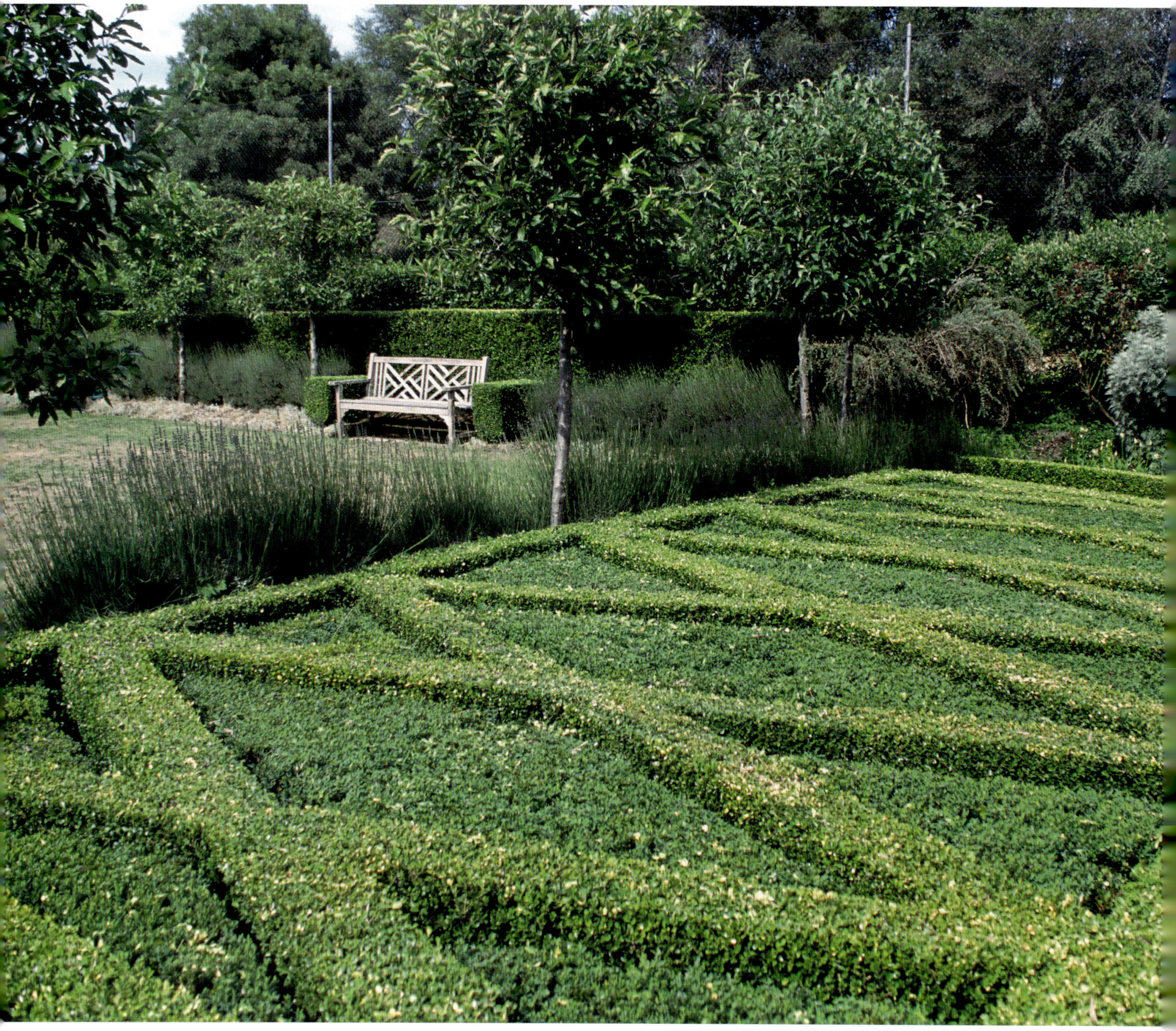

ball – all three inherited from the previous owners – gave this area my necessary structure! As the garden grew over the eight years my parents owned it, I would alter these beds, lastly giving the whole area a more contemporary edge by using a mixture of architectural plants such as the colourful New Zealand flax, *Phormium*, and native grasses alongside traditional favourites such as French lavender, *Lavandula dentata*, roses and salvias.

Between this garden and the croquet lawn I designed a diagonal box parterre which is so visually powerful it complemented the more rambling style of the garden next to the house. Diagonal hedges of *Buxus microphylla* var. *japonica* form a frame for massed triangles of *Buxus sempervirens*. Both varieties are clipped to 35 centimetres high, the two box hedges being separated by a 5 centimetre-wide void.

OPPOSITE It may look like a tranquil setting; however, this is where many games of highly competitive croquet took place.

Below the croquet lawn/crab apple garden, and probably my most favourite area of this garden, is the dramatic silver pear walk. This consists of a 40 metre long alley with a wall of x *Cupressocyparis leylandii* 'Leighton Green' on one side and sweet viburnum, *Viburnum odoratissimum*, on the other. In front of these is a double box hedge: two *Buxus microphylla* var. *japonica* hedges, with a space between them. The front one is clipped to 30 centimetres, while the rear is 80 centimetres high. Silver pears, *Pyrus salicifolia*, were planted along the avenue between the double hedges, while underneath their canopy a hundred white Monet tulips were planted to produce sensational seasonal interest. At the end of the avenue we constructed a rendered wall with a mirror that reflects the whole pear walk, making it seem about 100 metres long.

Silver pears are deciduous, and their branches have a drooping quality. The small narrow leaves are silver. They form mound-like canopies, and will grow to about 5 metres high. Their silver foliage will visually complement the white tulips in spring.

Behind the 'Leighton Green' hedge that borders this avenue is the luxury of a huge vegetable garden where my father can reap the rewards of his hard labour. A vegetable garden was very important to him – and to the rest of the family, who were all supplied with armfuls of fresh produce on every visit!

At the front of the house I defined the 500 metre driveway with an avenue of linden trees, *Tilia cordata*. On either side I placed two large dams, shaped to look like natural lakes; they were surrounded by Chinese elms, *Ulmus parvifolia*, chosen for their graceful broad-dome habit, and *Eucalpytus mannifera*, red-spotted gums, to unify the surrounding area with the structured spaces. The gums' common name comes from their bark – the new bark is coloured bright pink or red.

The house is set high on a hill and overlooks the front garden, where the softly curving tree-lined drive winds up between the two dams to the house. The lindens have now grown so that they hide the house on approach, which adds to the anticipation of entering the home.

Against the house I created a level garden with stepping stones and broad stone sweeping stairs leading the visitor into the paddock. The planting scheme for this south-facing area was extremely minimal, with massed *Juniperus horizontalis*, creeping juniper, as a groundcover and a hundred or so silver birch trees, *Betula pendula*, in groves, positioned to frame views from within the house. Being on the south side of the house, this garden was never used in winter although it is viewed from the kitchen every day of the year. So the position of the dams and the placement of the birches were orchestrated from the kitchen, where I knew most of the enjoyment of this view would be had.

Creeping juniper is a spreading, prostrate plant that will eventually form mats up to 50 centimetres thick. Its leaves are needle-like and aromatic. There are a number of different cultivars, whose foliage turns shades of purple and mauve in winter.

Off to one side of the driveway, behind a Western red cedar, *Thuja plicata*, hedge, I allowed my mother her last say – a tank garden! Literally surrounding the water tank and septic tank she was able to plant any perennial that she liked for cutting and using in the house – out of the view from the rest of the garden.

The final garden we created was an alley to the west of the house. A 30 metre path of white gravel and stepping stones leads the eye to a focal point. We lined one side with an avenue of tulip trees (*Liriodendron tulipera*) forming a pleached hedge. Along the other we massed evergreen dogwoods and effectively screened the tennis court behind.

THE RESULT

Designing this garden was a wonderful experience for me, as I was able to experiment a lot. I never tired of walking through the different garden rooms – some were simple, formal and dramatic while others were relaxed and rambling. In this garden contemporary meets classic, but the entire garden gave me lessons in building a strong foundation to protect the new gardens and working to a master plan.

The garden was awarded the accolade of *belle* magazine's 'Garden of the Year' in 2003. I was certainly pleased with this result, and I know my parents were also.

OPPOSITE The view from this bench gives the most spectacular views of the entire garden, with each room clearly defined and 360° views of the surrounding countryside. OVERLEAF This enchanting garden avenue, lined with silver pears, has a mirror at the end, which reflects the whole pear walk and makes it seem about 100 metres long.

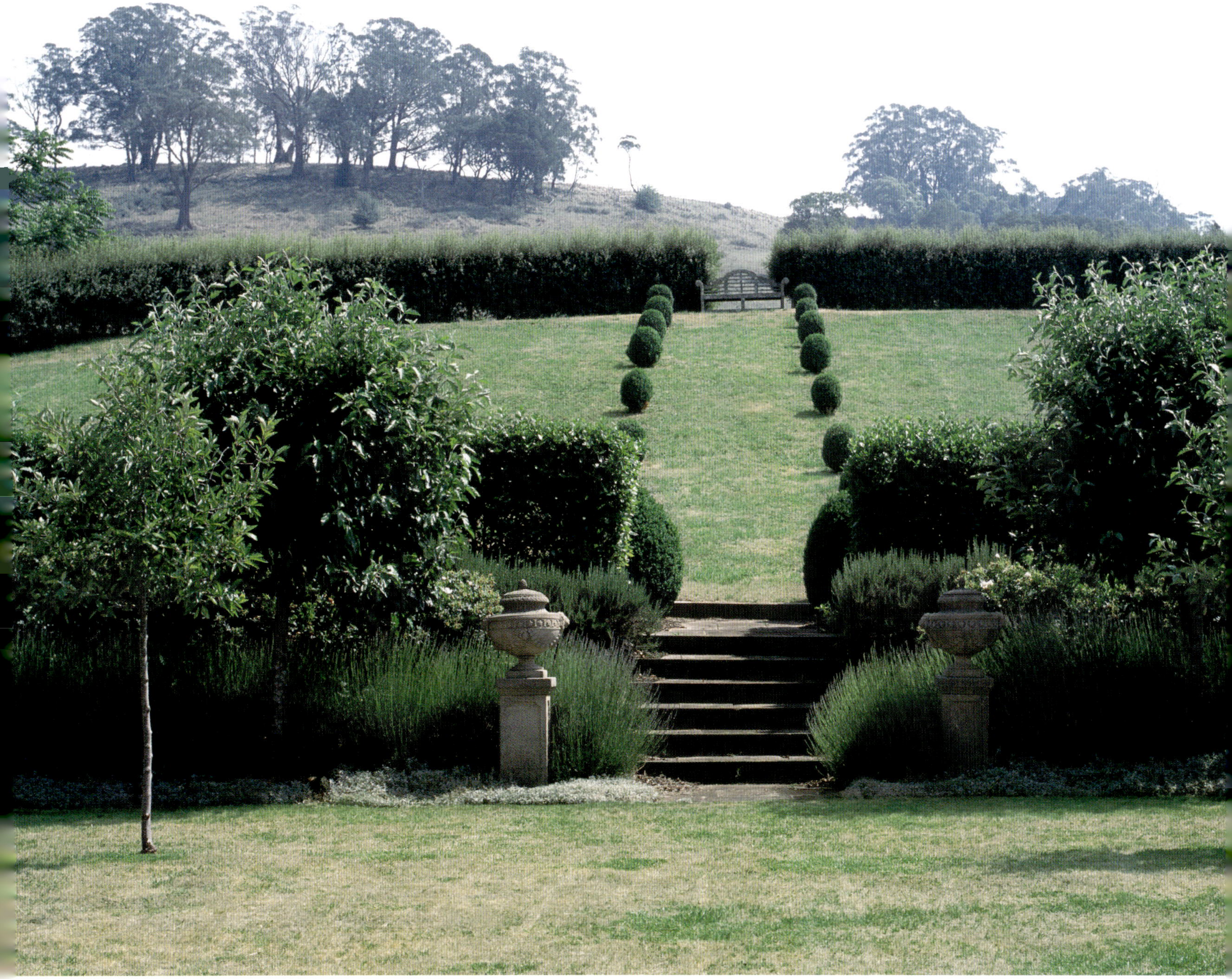

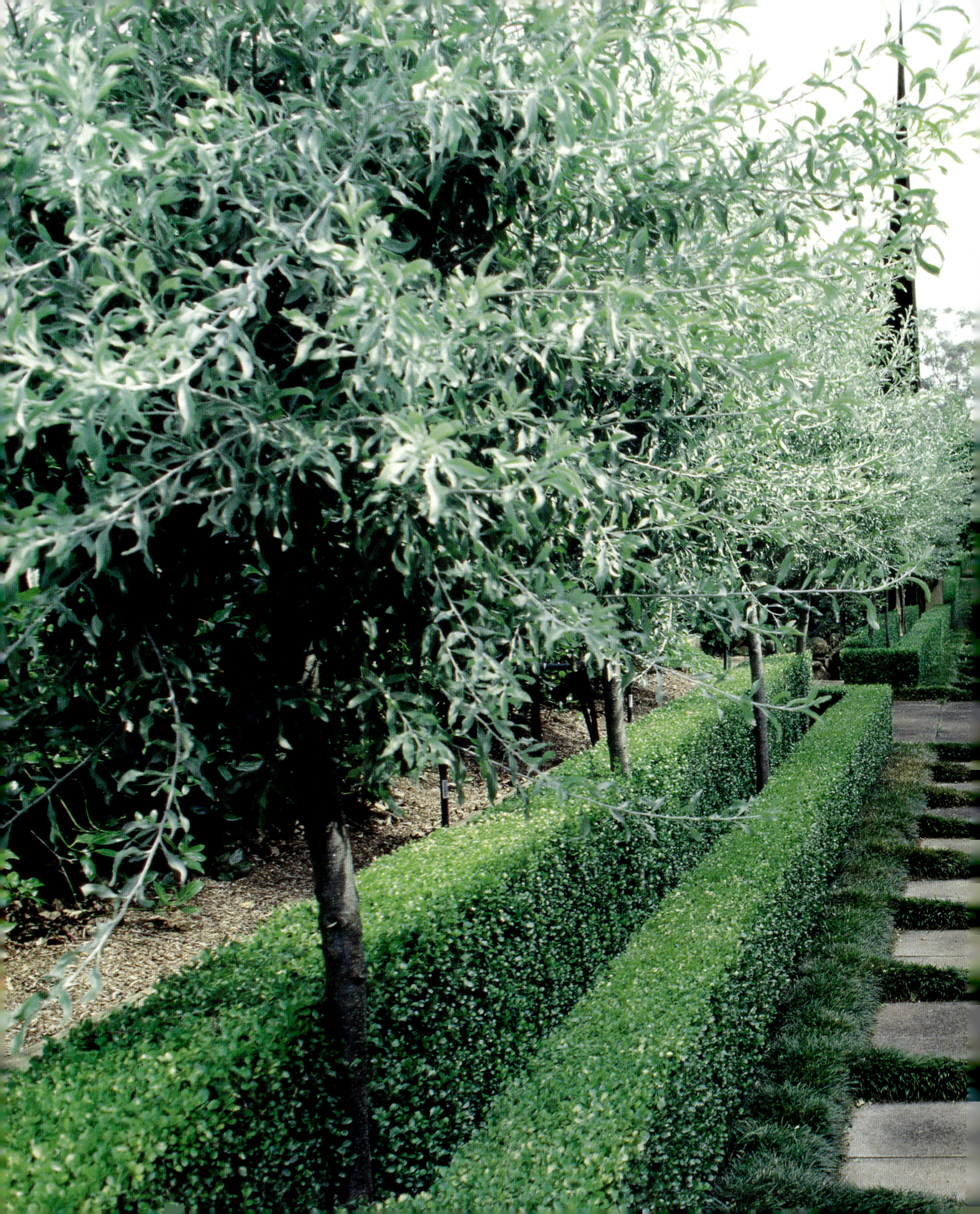

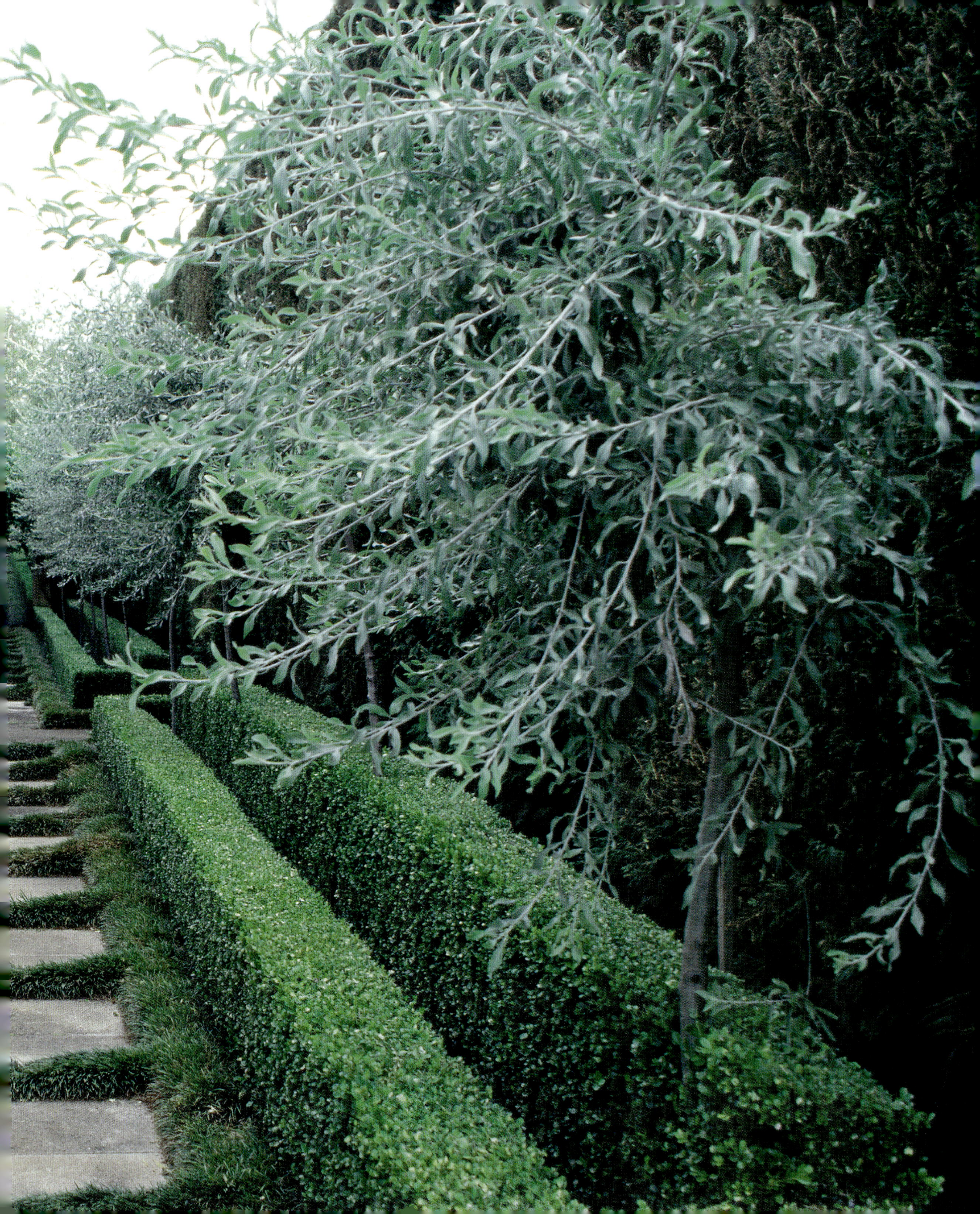

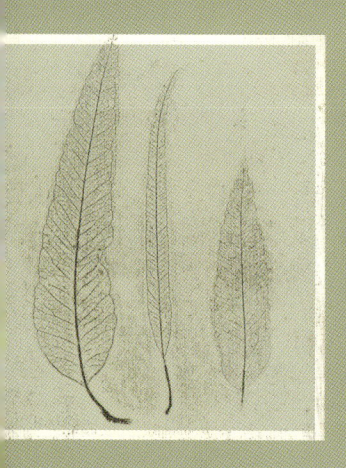

URBAN gardens

The combination of functionality and aesthetics drives
the design of the urban garden.

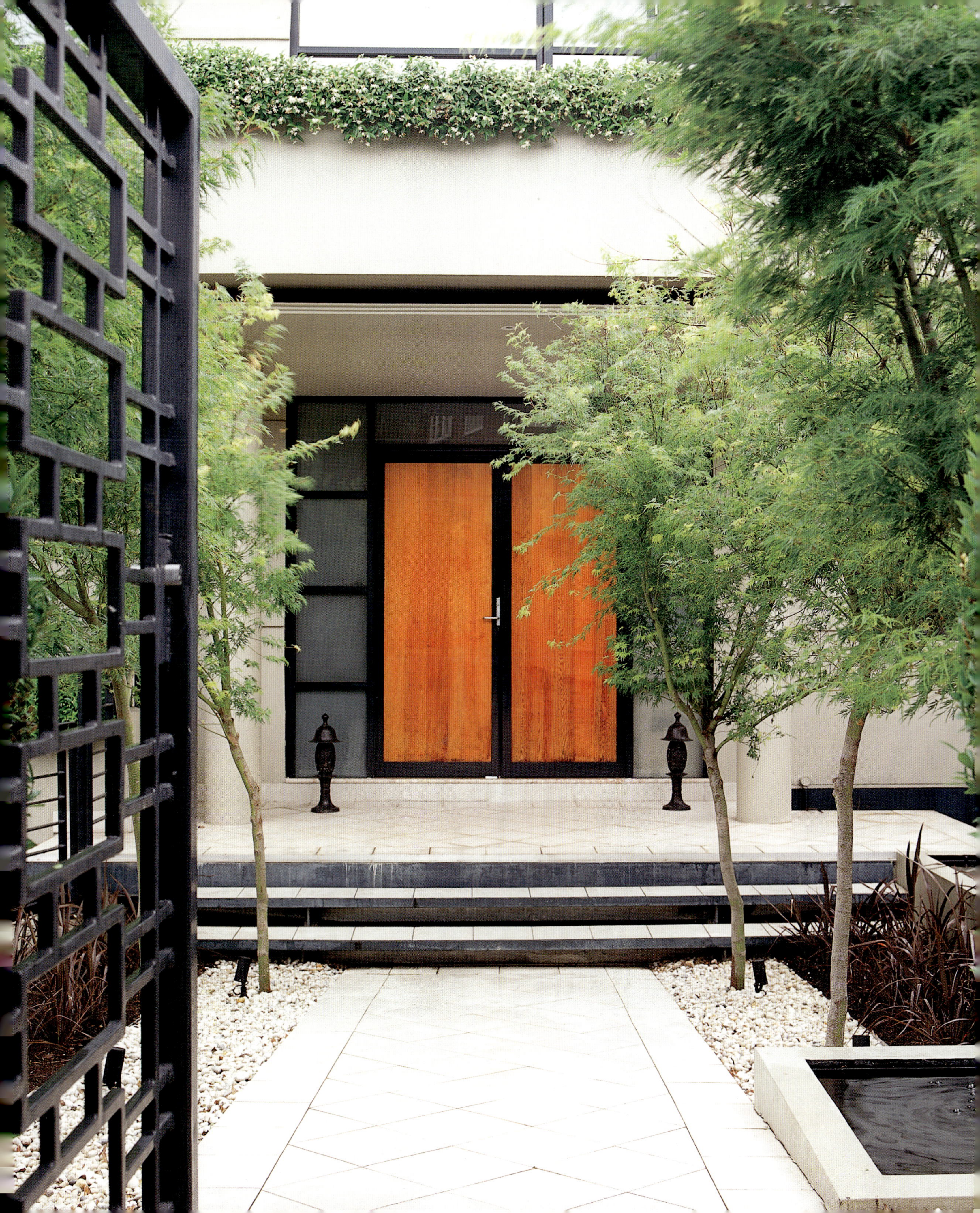

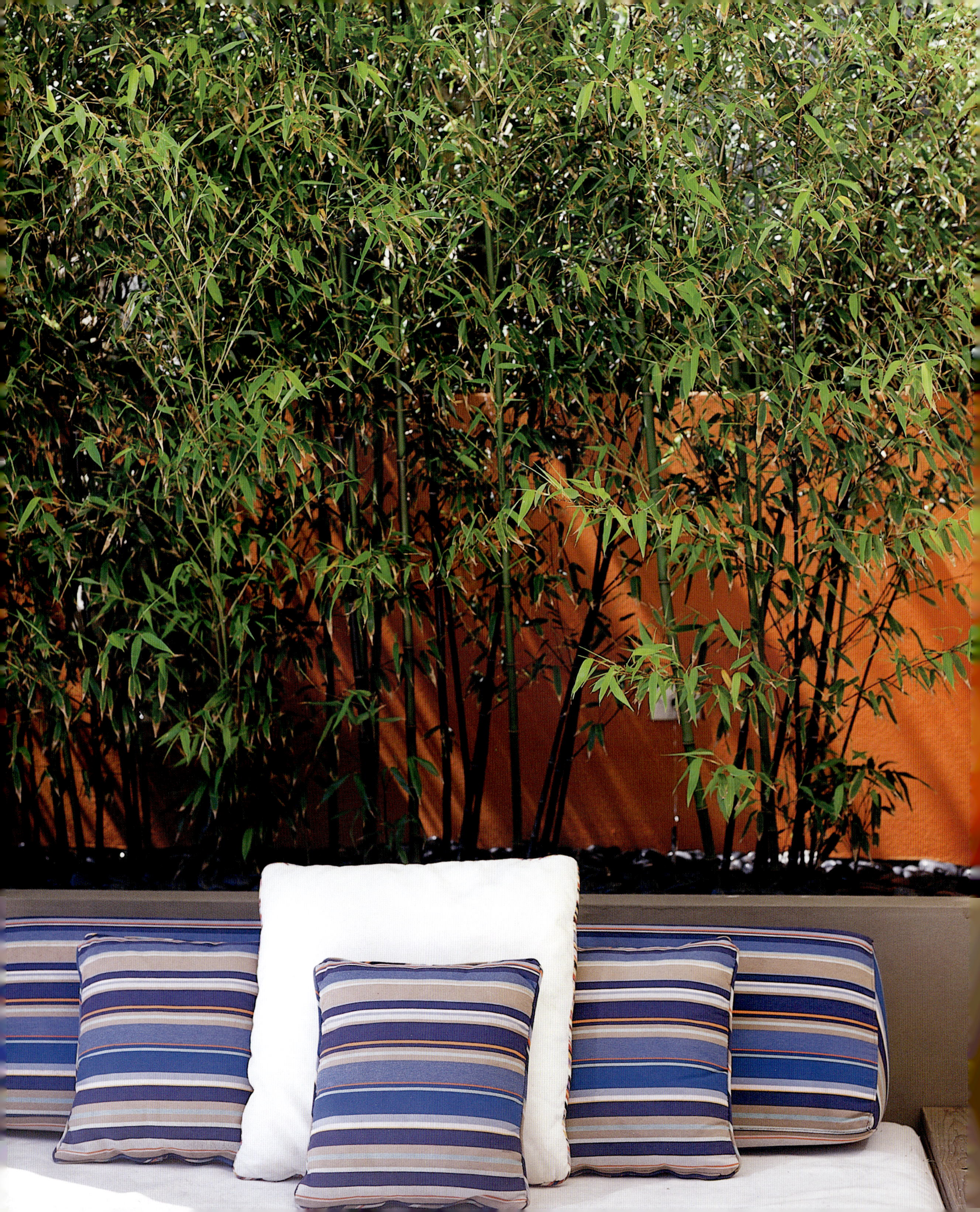

CONTEMPORARY COMFORTS

THE SETTING
A contemporary house close to the beach on the northern peninsula of Sydney, with a courtyard area leading off the ground floor that was used for utility and storage.

THE BRIEF
To transform the under-utilised storage area into an extra 'room' that flowed effortlessly between house and garden. The space was to fulfil more than one function – it was to be used as a place to gather, to entertain and also to relax, while at the same time retaining some storage facilities for beach equipment. Perhaps most importantly, the redesigned area was to possess an aesthetic beauty, as it was often viewed from the upper level terrace of the house above.

THE DESIGN
Perched on the uppermost ridge of Sydney's northern peninsula, with panoramas of both Pittwater to the west and the Pacific Ocean to the east, the house is in a breathtaking location. Due to the wonderful views on both sides and the contemporary style of the house's architecture, the garden was clearly in need of a more intimate space. An important part of the challenge was the creation of visual interest.

Although this area had been very much under-utilised, it is an important space within the design of house and garden, as it can be viewed from many angles. With the above criteria in mind, the design created a courtyard that is both functional and aesthetically pleasing from what had been a dumping ground for surfboards and other beach paraphernalia.

It is now an intimate, decked area with a comfortable daybed – a double bed, with a fitted, firm mattress that slots inside a timber frame – and benches covered with colourful cushions, surrounded

OPPOSITE Soft furnishings are a great way to introduce colour into a garden; a vibrant burnt orange wall complements the contemporary architecture of this urban retreat.

by water and the rustling of bamboo leaves in the sea breeze. Flowing from a downstairs entertaining area, it is used as a seating area by day by the owner's teenage children. On balmy summer nights the parents can be found sleeping out on the bed beneath the stars – under a mosquito net canopy, of course!

To begin, a high neighbouring wall was rendered and painted in a radiant burnt orange to complement and add to the lightness of the contemporary architecture. In front of it a 6 metre long, raised planter box, made of rendered masonry and containing a clump-forming bamboo, *Bambusa lako*, Timor black bamboo, was created to screen the wall.

ABOVE The candy-striped deck chairs enhance the relaxed, modern and easy-going feel of the garden. OPPOSITE The stainless steel emitters are a modern day version of a Romanesque concept.

The planter box itself has dual functions: as a visual water feature, resembling a trough, and as a garden bed to grow the bamboo in. To achieve this dual effect, it was necessary to build the planter box with smaller, isolated planter boxes inside it for the bamboo.

Bamboo is a grass, and different species can grow from less than 1 metre high – which are used as groundcovers – to giants of up to 40 metres. This species will grow to 8–10 metres if unchecked, but as the bamboo is intended to form an informal screen between the neighbours and this courtyard and become a backdrop to the setting, the 'hedge' will be kept at 4 metres in height. This will be done by irregular removal of larger stems from the base of the clump and younger shoots will be pruned to 4 metres tall.

The stems, or culms, of *Bambusa lako* are spectacular, being purple–black with fine vertical green stripes. There is year-round shedding of old leaves as new leaves emerge, in a stunning bright green contrast to the black stems.

Bamboo likes water, and many species are able to withstand wet conditions around their roots. However, they cannot be grown in water alone – although I wanted to produce that illusion. Thus the large planter box appears to be a pond through which the shielding bamboo grows. To create this illusion the entire planter box has been mulched with charcoal-coloured pebbles, 7 centimetres in diameter, so that the eye believes the bamboo is growing straight from the water, which is not possible!

Bamboo also has a reputation for spreading with intensity and being difficult to control. By planting it within confined boxes, this undesirable feature has been prevented.

Bamboo prefers a sheltered position in sun or part shade and will grow well in most soils provided they are free draining. This bamboo was planted in organic potting mix, an ideal medium as it is both free draining and nutrient rich. Bamboo requires regular moisture and fertilising, and mulching to keep the roots cool will always benefit it. It should be fed every five weeks from September to April with an all-round fertiliser.

Behind the bamboo, attached to the wall, are stainless steel emitters, taking water from the trough – which acts as a reservoir for the recycling water wall feature – and sending it back down to the

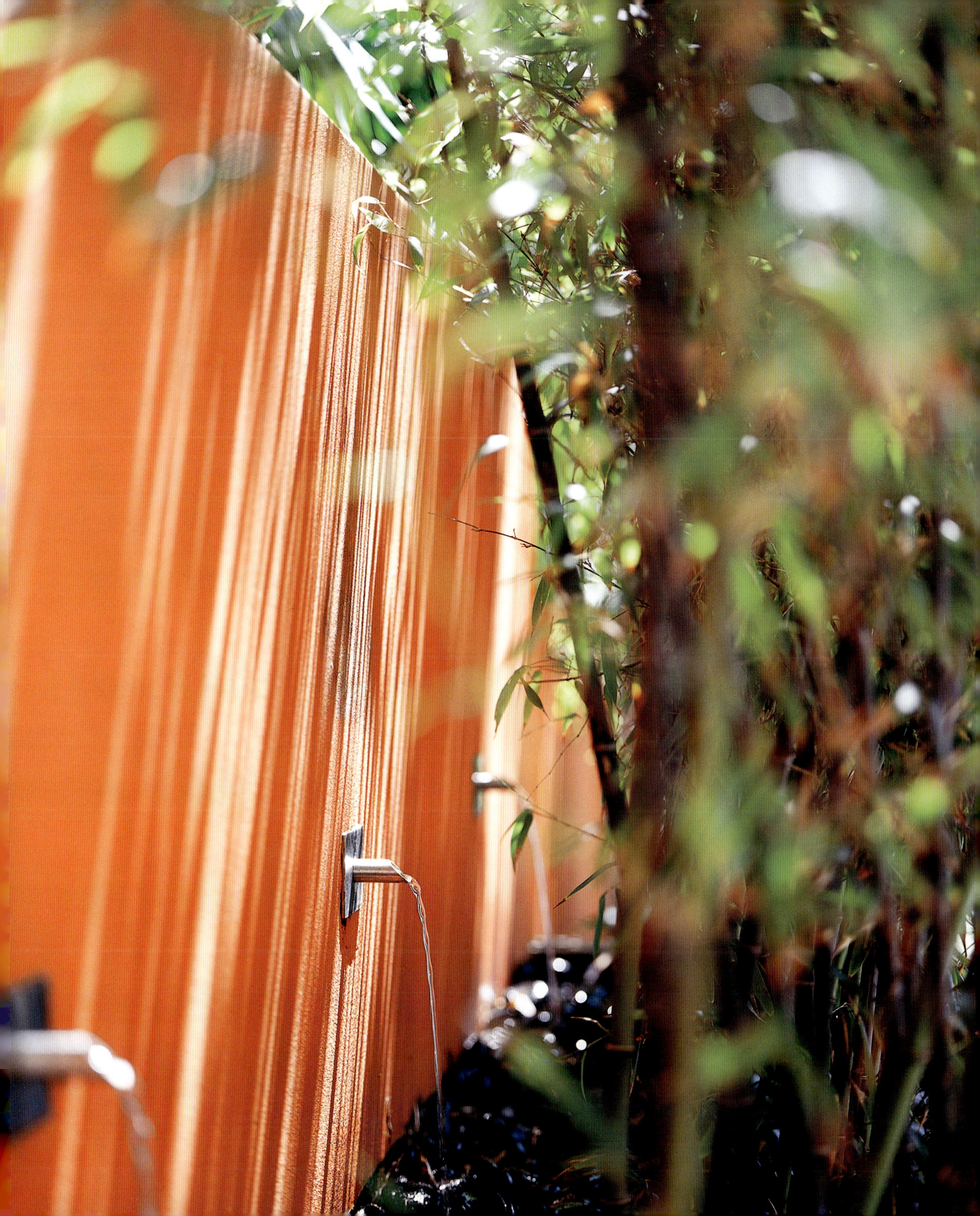

trough's pebbles in pleasant streams. All this adds to the relaxing ambience of the courtyard, as the soothing splashing of water is a faint background noise.

To add subtle interest the existing deck was extended and a reflective pond was installed, wrapping around the end of the deck, which gave the new courtyard a unique sense of floating. The pond also provides a closure of the courtyard on one side, as well as a sense of unification; although the two water features are not connected, to a viewer they appear to be.

In the pond, 'floating' on the top of the water surface, is a stepping stone which gives access from the deck to the lawn. It highlights the seamlessness and simplicity of the design. I wanted the stepping stone to look light rather than bulky as it adds to the illusion that the deck is floating and surrounded by water.

All the materials used in the construction of the new courtyard – such as the timber for the decking and benches and stainless steel in the water feature – were chosen as they already existed in the architecture and thereby gave a sense of connection to the house. The decking and benches are made of treated pine to match the rest of the house's decking. It is not stained but once a year the client applies a natural oil to it to reduce cracking and premature ageing.

The final touches were to blend indoors with out. Colourful striped fabric was chosen to make cushions for the daybed and seating for the benches, and a canopy was made from a retractable sail to provide shade – and to visually become a 'ceiling'. All these elements make this courtyard feel like another room of the house.

The daybed is not only for lounging, as it also provides a practical space for hiding any beach gear. Underneath the mattress there is a hinged lid covering a useful storage compartment.

BELOW AND OPPOSITE This striking urban oasis is now enjoyed by everyone in the family; in the pond, a 'floating' stepping stone provides access from the deck to the lawn.

THE RESULT
What was once a 'non-area' has been transformed into a visually tantalising space that is also practical, being used by the family for a variety of functions. The courtyard conjures up images of an oasis of peace amongst rustling, tropical bamboo leaves, and its overall feel is relaxing, contemporary, easy-living and casual.

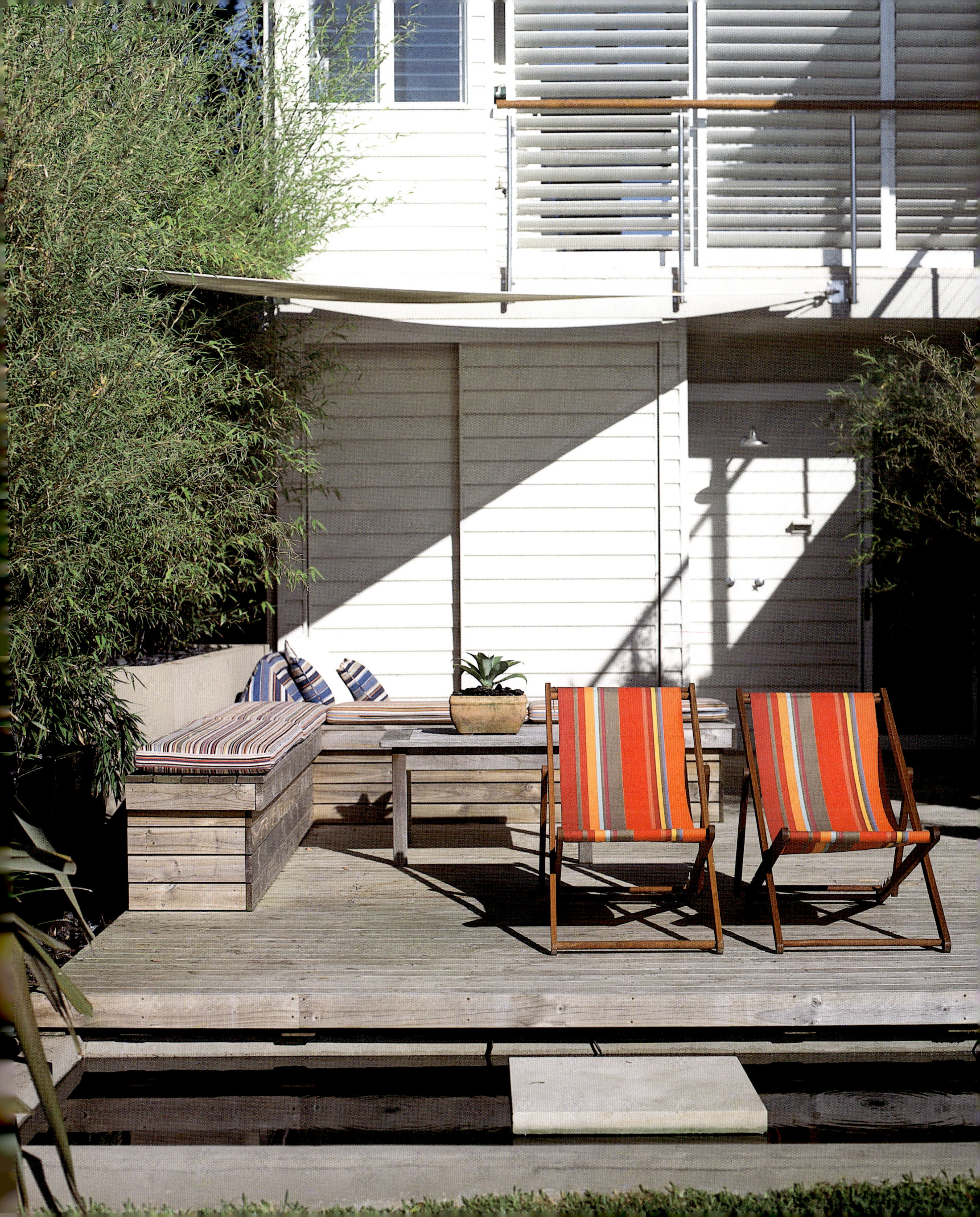

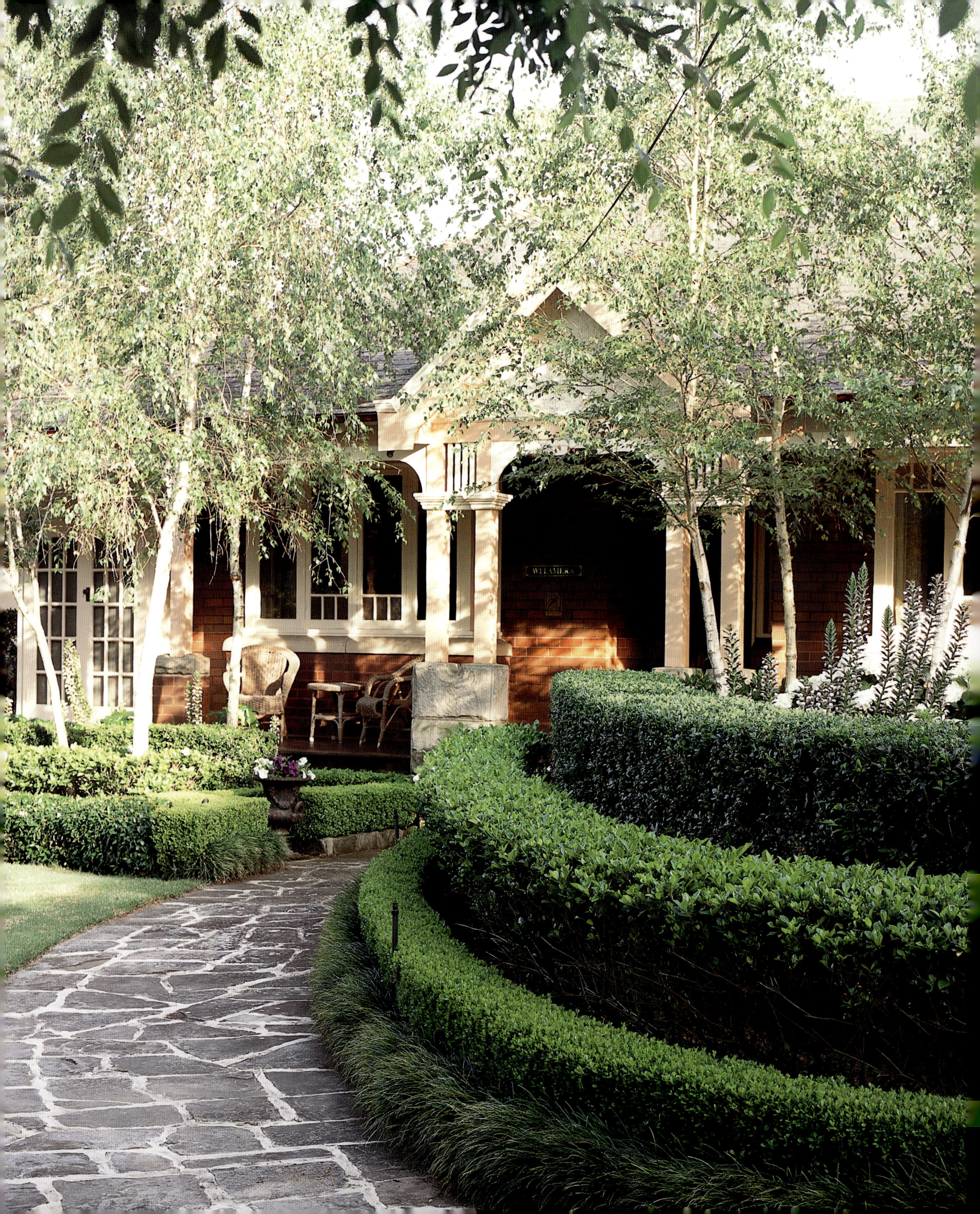

A GRACEFUL EDGE

THE SETTING
A lovely Federation house in a classic garden setting, in a northern suburb of Sydney.

THE BRIEF
To overhaul the existing garden. The owners, keen gardeners, enjoyed the floral elements of the garden although they thought it needed more visual impact. It also required a lot of work to keep it looking good: they wanted a design that would result in a lower maintenance schedule.

THE DESIGN
When I first arrived at this beautiful Federation home I realised I was going to be fortunate: there were a number of established trees in the garden and, to my delight, all were in locations I could work with. This doesn't happen very often. Two crab apples, *Malus* sp., a Chinese weeping elm, *Ulmus parvifolia*, a Japanese maple, *Acer palmatum*, and a crepe myrtle, *Lagerstroemia indica*, had been planted towards the front and side boundaries, creating their own microclimates within the garden.

Even though the house was designed and built in a more formal era it has a really relaxed and inviting feeling – no doubt due in part to the charming couple who live within it. Together we decided the look of the garden should be casual though semi-structured, with more formal sections offsetting looser plantings. It would result in a semi-formal look that the clients could dabble with, such as by changing the seasonal colour of the annuals in urns. The input of the clients was critical: both were happy to spend many hours in the garden so therefore I knew I could include more variety in the plantings than I would normally, and that the garden would still receive the attention it required.

The front garden is all about soft, romantic curves. A wide cream sandstone path leaves the drive and gradually leads through the lawn and garden to the front door. On the left of the path a gently sloping, curved lawn meets a border of dwarf star jasmine, *Trachelospermum asiaticum*, which defines the slow lawn curves. Instead of being allowed to run freely as a mat, which is how I have used this plant in other gardens, here the jasmine is mounded into a soft border about 20 centimetres high by about 60 centimetres wide. The variety we used has a more prostrate habit than many, so is less inclined to grow upwards. As a result, it doesn't need constant cutting back.

Within the main garden and at its widest parts are three self-contained 'rooms'. The first one is a two-tiered rusty fountain in

OPPOSITE Full, gentle curves entice the visitor to the front door.
ABOVE This ornate, two-tiered fountain was deliberately positioned opposite the front door and can be viewed from the long hall inside the house.

ABOVE AND OPPOSITE The formal and informal plantings give this Federation-style garden a sense of balance.

a raised pond, which sits at the front of the garden but lines up opposite the front door and can be viewed from the long hall inside the house. The second is a sandstone-paved area approximately 4 metres in diameter, with a curved stone bench offering pleasant views from the garden back to the house. The third garden room sits below the front verandah and consists of a large reconstituted stone urn, which is planted seasonally with annuals.

To add reinforcement to the idea of small garden rooms, the small box *Buxus microphylla* var. *japonica* was used to help define their boundaries, being trimmed into tight bands around the paving or pond. I also used this boxwood along the verandah, forming a consistent foundation to the varied planting in front.

Creating rooms within a garden helps maintain interest and intrigue in the garden, even for those who live with them every day of the year. These points of interest should be carefully balanced throughout the garden and not overdone. Their content should be different.

The entire front garden is tied together by bold bands of planting in layers. These layers provide the garden with its structure and behind the layers I planted different plants in accented groups. So, behind the dwarf star jasmine border are ascending layers of the 'Florida' variety of gardenia, *Gardenia augusta*, clipped into a continuous rounded mound about 50 centimetres high, and then *Murraya paniculata*, hedged to 1 metre. Behind the *Murraya* I planted bold groups of white hydrangea, *Hydrangea macrophylla*; silver plectranthus, *Plectranthus argentatus*; hellebores, *Helleborus orientalis*; *Acanthus mollis*; sweet-smelling *Daphne odora*; azalea *Rhododendron* 'Alba Magna'; Japanese windflowers, *Anemone* x *hybrida*; and arum lily, *Zantedeschia aethiopica*. All these plants thrive in the shaded environment towards the back of the garden and also serve to lift the shade with their white flowers or light foliage. They were chosen to some extent to create seasonal interest: the daphne and hellebores will flower in winter, the arum lilies in early spring, the hydrangeas in summer. White-flowering *Camellia sasanqua* 'Setsugekka' has been planted on the boundaries to provide a lush backdrop and screen; sasanqua camellias flower profusely in autumn and early winter.

Groves of *Betula pendula*, silver birch, have been planted near the house to soften its outline, and give the garden a sense of depth. Their silvery white stems form a nice contrast with the green foliage below. Silver birches grow in a variety of soils and will tolerate highly acidic conditions; they will also flourish in both full sun and

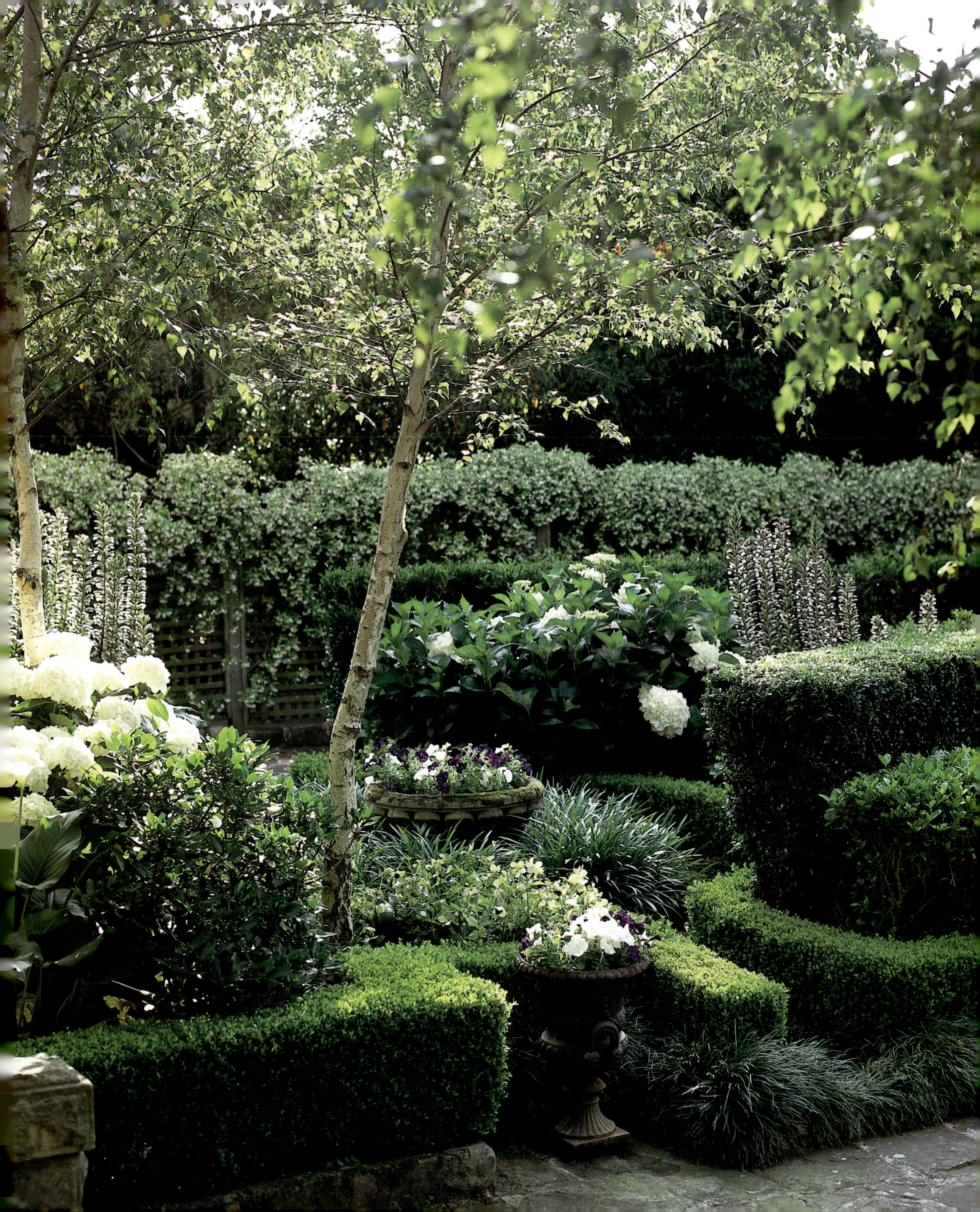

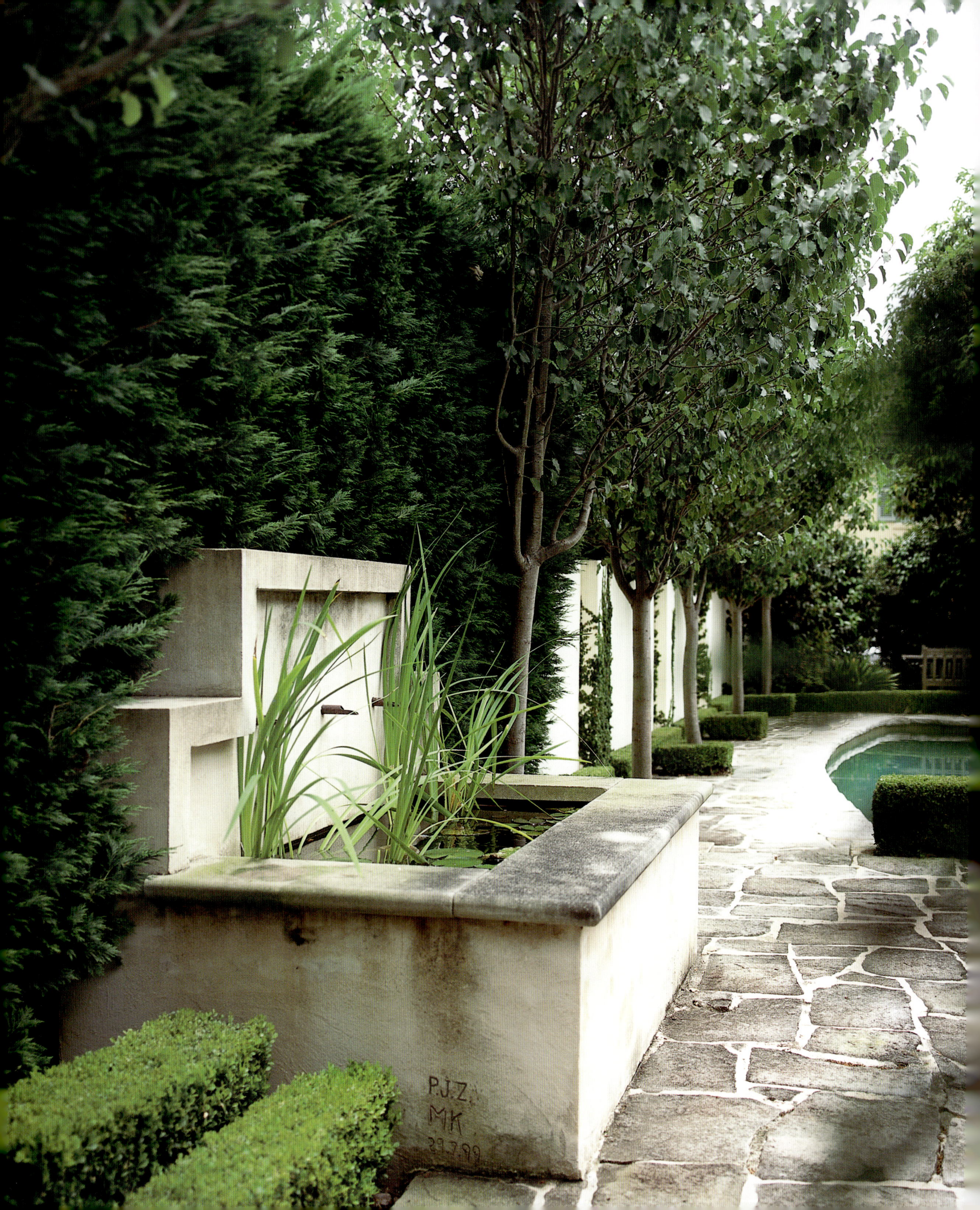
P.J.Z.
MK
29.7.99

partial shade. They grow fast for the first twenty years or so but are reasonably short-lived, often living only to sixty or seventy years. In spring they bear yellow catkins that swish like little tails in the breeze, and in autumn their leaves turn an attractive yellow before falling. The elegant droop of the branches ensures that even in winter they are delightful to look at in the garden.

The back garden needed some interest added to an existing pool and paved entertaining area. In the entertainment area a masonry water feature now doubles as a seat, the front of the trough having been extended into a seating surface. Subtle sound is created by three copper spouts positioned on the back wall of the trough, circulating water, while the trough is planted with strappy yellow Japanese iris, *Iris ensata*, which thrives in water. This feature provides the entertaining area with greater intimacy and interest, as well as giving a feeling of coolness in summer.

The water feature is flanked by two Manchurian pears, which are underplanted once more with low *Buxus microphylla* var. *japonica* hedges. On the boundary, a x *Cupressocyparis leylandii* 'Leighton Green', hedge, holds the whole scene together. I used it to form a narrow screen from the neighbours and a complementary contrast to the boxwood and pear trees.

At the rear of the house there was a lot of hard paving due to the expected traffic around the pool and to the entertaining area, so the garden beds are narrow here. To balance this and to take the garden right up to the house, star jasmine, *Trachelospermum jasminoides*, covers all the masonry walls of the house, framing windows and doors. There are also roses climbing up pillars.

To make the most of the awkward area between the pool and the boundary (which was too narrow to use as a functional space) I continued the Manchurian pear planting even though the pool is one step lower than the entertaining area. The pear trees are planted in 60 centimetre square pockets of soil in sandstone paving and underplanted with boxes of *Buxus microphylla* var. *japonica*. These pears are the variety 'Bradford', a taller and more narrow type

OPPOSITE Sandstone flagging creates a relaxed and unified theme throughout the entire garden. ABOVE LEFT Single, white anemones will flower in autumn when the garden is usually lacking in flowers. ABOVE RIGHT The flower head of the oyster plant, which grows well in the shade and has great foliage.

than the usual Manuchurian pear species – almost a columnar shape. Their dramatic forms provide the pool area with interest – since it was an old pool we wanted it to give it a lift while still relating it to the rest of the garden. In autumn their foliage turns an attractive red.

Manchurian pears are a tree grown for their blossoms rather than fruit which is small and unpalatable. For decades the tree planted in Australia as the Manchurian pear was known as *Pyrus ussuriensis*. However, a few years ago a sharp-eyed botanist, Jill Kellow, at Burnley College, part of the University of Melbourne, noticed that the leaves of all the Manchurian pears she saw in cultivation did not appear to conform to the species description. She investigated further and established that whoever had originally imported a 'Manchurian pear' to Australia in the 1960s and propagated it had brought in the wrong species, the related *Pyrus calleryana*, whose blossoms are not as large as the true Manchurian pear. The nursery business in Australia continues to sell Manchurian pears, but they should now all be identified as *P. calleryana*.

OPPOSITE At the rear of the house star jasmine flourishes and covers the masonry wall, framing the window.

THE RESULT

By placing classic plants in bold bands I have ignored the traditional expectation that viewers have of how a Federation-style garden should look. However, tradition has not been completely disregarded: to complement the Federation-style house, there are massed annuals in pots, which creates a link with expectations. My philosophy when it comes to Federation houses is that they are bold examples of architecture and that their gardens should also be bold. Following this vision, the garden now gives this home a more contemporary edge.

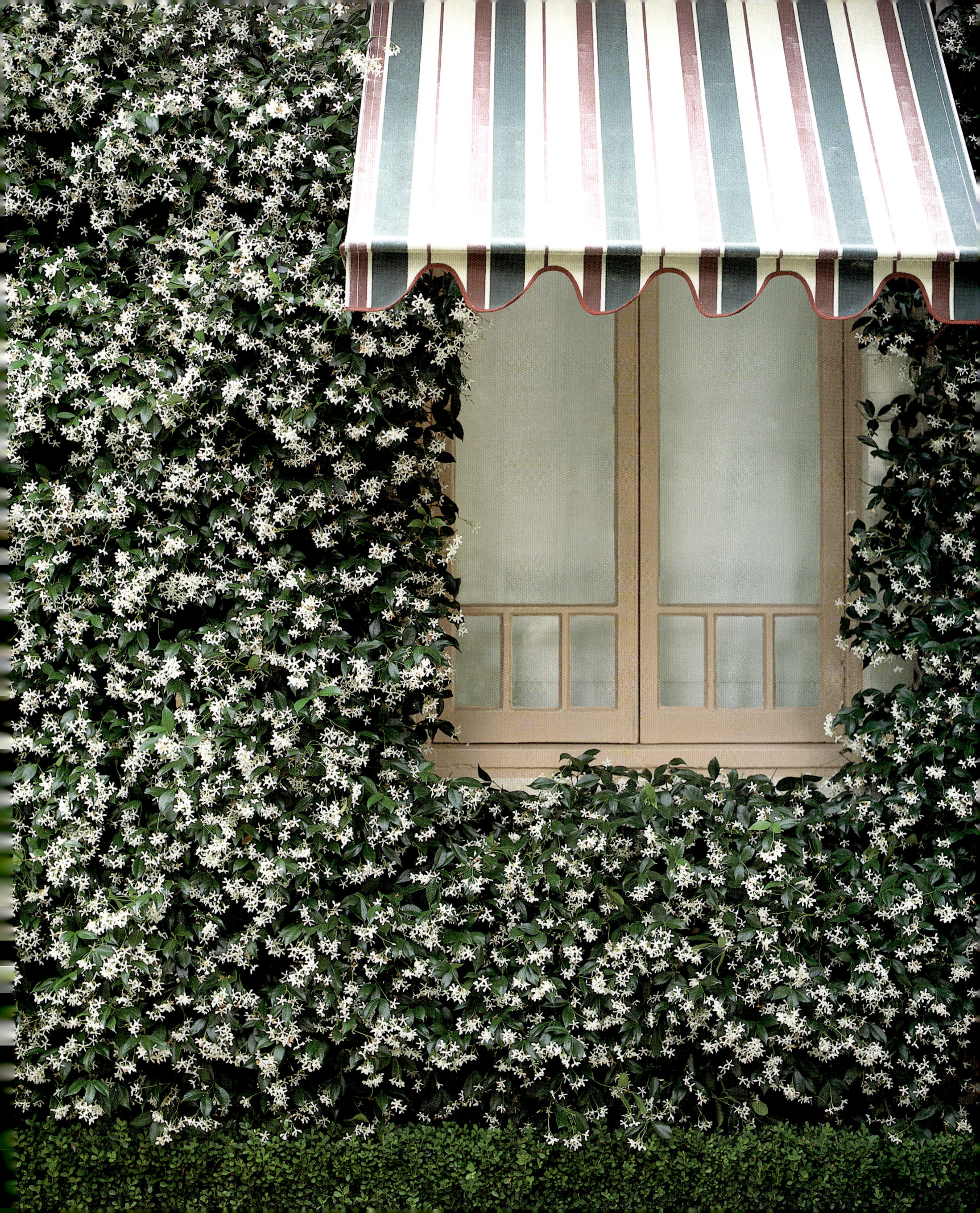

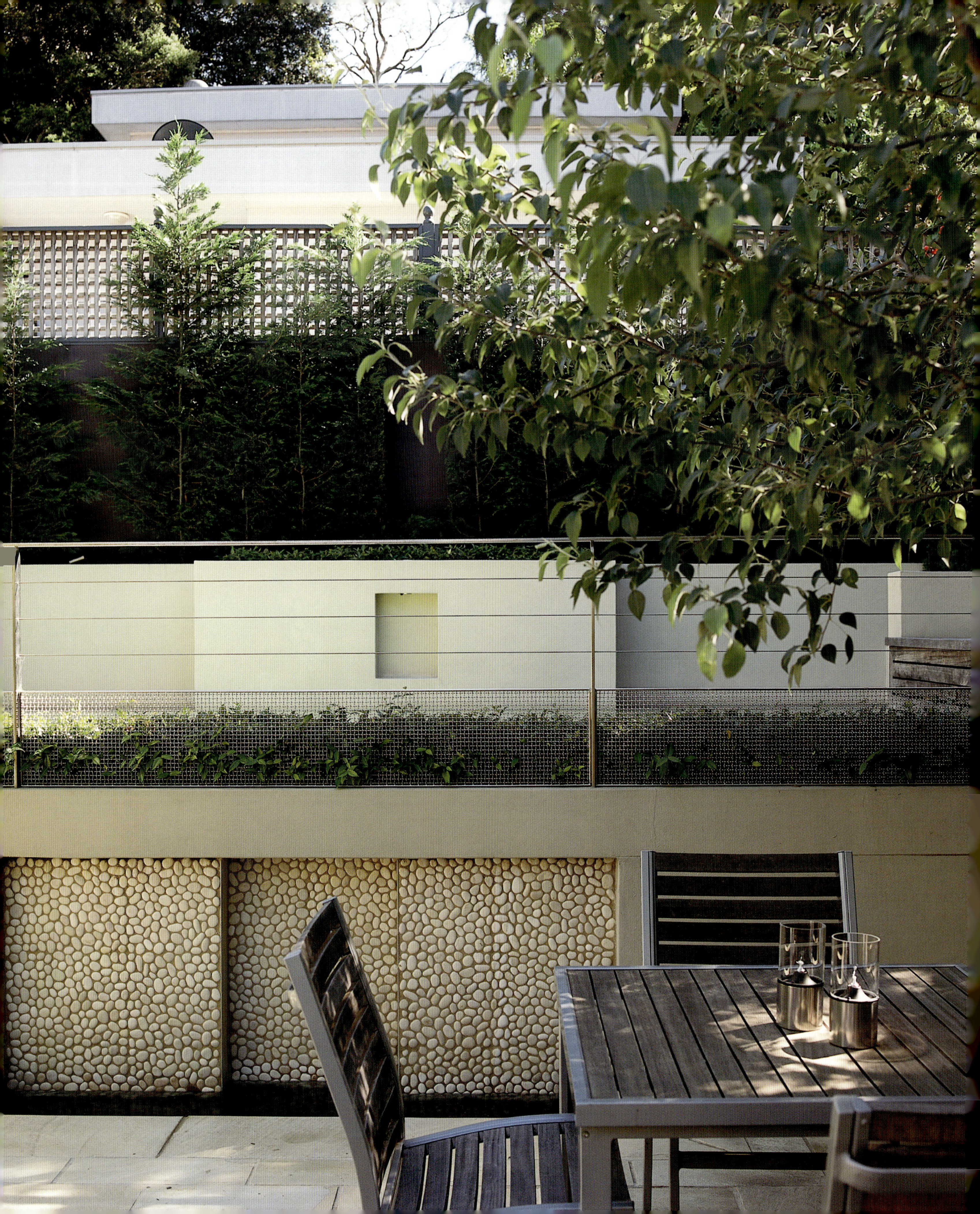

MISSION POSSIBLE

THE SETTING
The house was an older-style building, set on a steep hill in Northbridge, a suburb in Sydney that abuts Middle Harbour. The block itself was not large and the backyard rose very steeply behind the house, almost overhanging it.

THE BRIEF
The clients wished to transform their totally unusable backyard into a contemporary, streamlined, functional space with a pool and entertainment area. They also required privacy from the house directly behind: there was an existing trellis along the back and side walls, but this was not sufficient to shield properly. This job was going to be a major challenge!

THE DESIGN
Before I first viewed this site I thought I had seen every challenge a garden designer could face. However, even with my vast experience I was scratching my head – what lay before me looked like a disused quarry, but it was in fact a large piece of rock. The back garden consisted of one enormous stone with a few scant pockets of soil around it which rose intimidatingly above the house.

The backyard was relatively small, but due to the steepness of the slope it was raised above the living area at the rear of the house. It was difficult to reach without clambering. It was, in reality, not really able to be used because of the problems of access from the house.

The entire site was basically bedrock, with a little garden at the front on a thin layer of soil, but there was insufficient soil to do any large planting. There were also problems with drainage: the rock platform at the back of the block would channel water from above down towards the house.

OPPOSITE This cool and shady urban pad is screened from overlooking houses; screening is one of the first aspects I'm asked to address when designing a city garden. ABOVE The glossy leaves of the fragrant dwarf star jasmine.

OPPOSITE The dual function of the bench is to maximise space within a small area and hide the pool equipment underneath it.

The brief was so clear that it seemed to add to the complexity of the issues. The clients said they wanted a swimming pool and an entertaining area that flowed from the back of the house and that was screened from the overlooking houses. Although the house was a Californian bungalow originally built between the two world wars, the owners' taste was contemporary and casual.

Working with what we had, at the back of the property we first painted the rendered wall on the fence line an aubergine colour – a browny purple. We were then able to achieve a degree of privacy by constructing a deep planter box along the back fence line. Within the planter box is a row of 'Leighton Green' cypresses (x *Cupressocyparis leylandii*) and we continued planting it along the side walls also. This species was chosen as the planter box was only a narrow garden bed and we needed plants that would attain height without taking up much width. x *Cupressocyparis leylandii* is a columnar shape, tapering at the top. As a conifer, it will remain evergreen throughout the year, and thus give good screening. It is a fast grower, but upwards rather than outwards, and in ideal conditions it may grow as much as 1 metre per year, finally reaching a height of over 25 metres; however, in a planter box on top of solid rock such a height would not be achieved, but the trees will anyway be kept severely pruned to a hedge 4 metres high. x *Cupressocyparis leylandii* is extremely hardy, likes well-drained soil and full sun, so was well suited to the fence line, which caught more sunlight than the rest of the backyard closer to the house.

At a level below the back wall the swimming pool was constructed. Stone had to be cut away to accommodate it, and at the same time drainage work was carried out, agricultural pipes being laid throughout the areas of the garden that were to become beds and a large grate inserted near the house to drain surface water.

The planter box forms a back wall to the pool, reaching down the water's surface. The pool takes up almost the width of the backyard, and in front of it stone steps lead down the next level. The machinery associated with the pool, such as the pump and filter box, has been concealed: at one side of the decking there is a daybed/bench with cushions that hide a hinged lid and the equipment is hidden underneath it. The timber of the decking was chosen to soften the look of the hard materials – steel and stone – that were used to construct the pool and entertaining area below it.

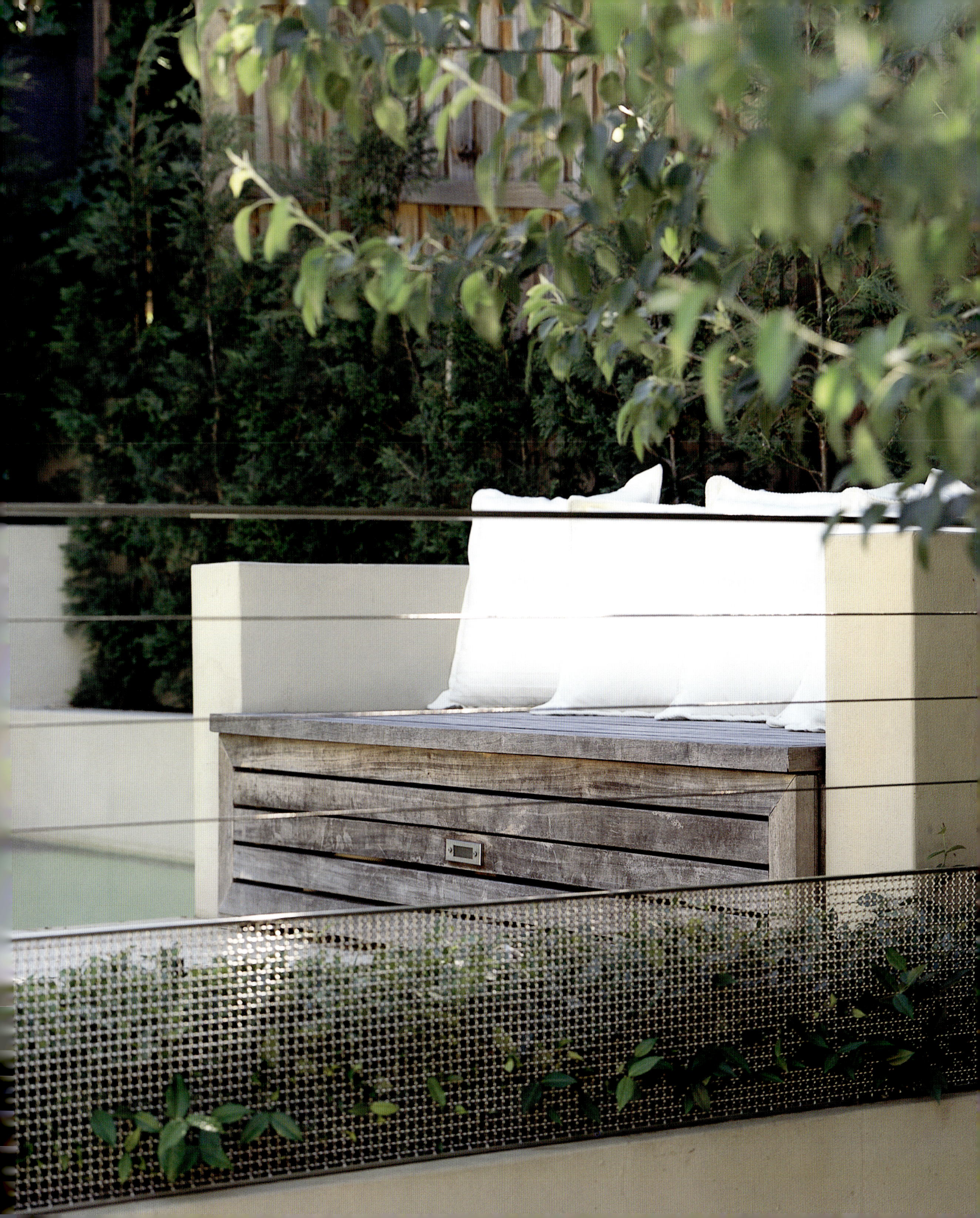

The ground below the pool level was to form the main entertaining area. First it was levelled to form a terrace, which was then laid with large sandstone pavers. Two advanced snow pears (*Pyrus nivalis*) were planted either side of the entertaining area in potting mix imported to form beds, providing a casual and deciduous natural canopy with winter sun and summer shade over the entertaining area. I used potting mix instead of soil as it has better drainage and aeration qualities than ordinary soil – and hence the pears have flourished.

Snow pears are native to southern and eastern Europe, but are extremely hardy, surviving winter temperatures of –15° Celsius. They prefer good well-drained loamy soil in full sun but will also grow well in heavy clay and will tolerate both light shade and atmospheric pollution. The trees flower in spring, but unless they are in full sun will not set fruit well – the fruit is sour rather than sweet, so this is not a great loss. Once established they are drought tolerant. Their shape is attractive and ornamental, and they can grow as high as 10 metres, but once again, we do not anticipate that they will reach such a height in this backyard, expecting 7 metres at most.

The back of the house has sliding doors and from these wide sandstone steps were built to lead up to the entertaining level. The deliberate width of the steps was to suggest an easy flowing route from the back of the house to the entertainment area, which is furnished with a timber table and chairs.

BELOW Timber tables and chairs add to the garden's relaxed and comfortable ambience   OPPOSITE By concealing the steps around the corner, the garden remains uncluttered.

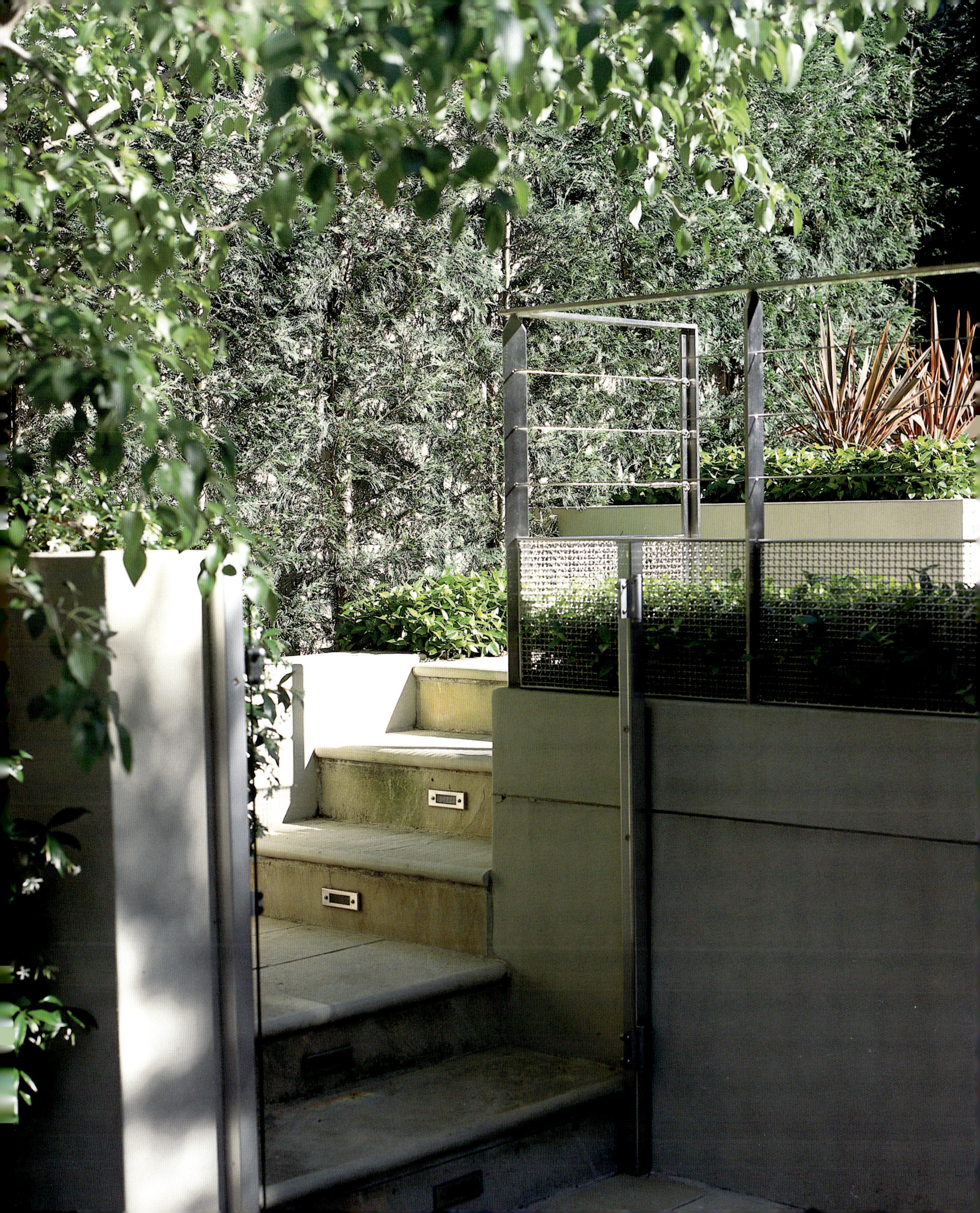

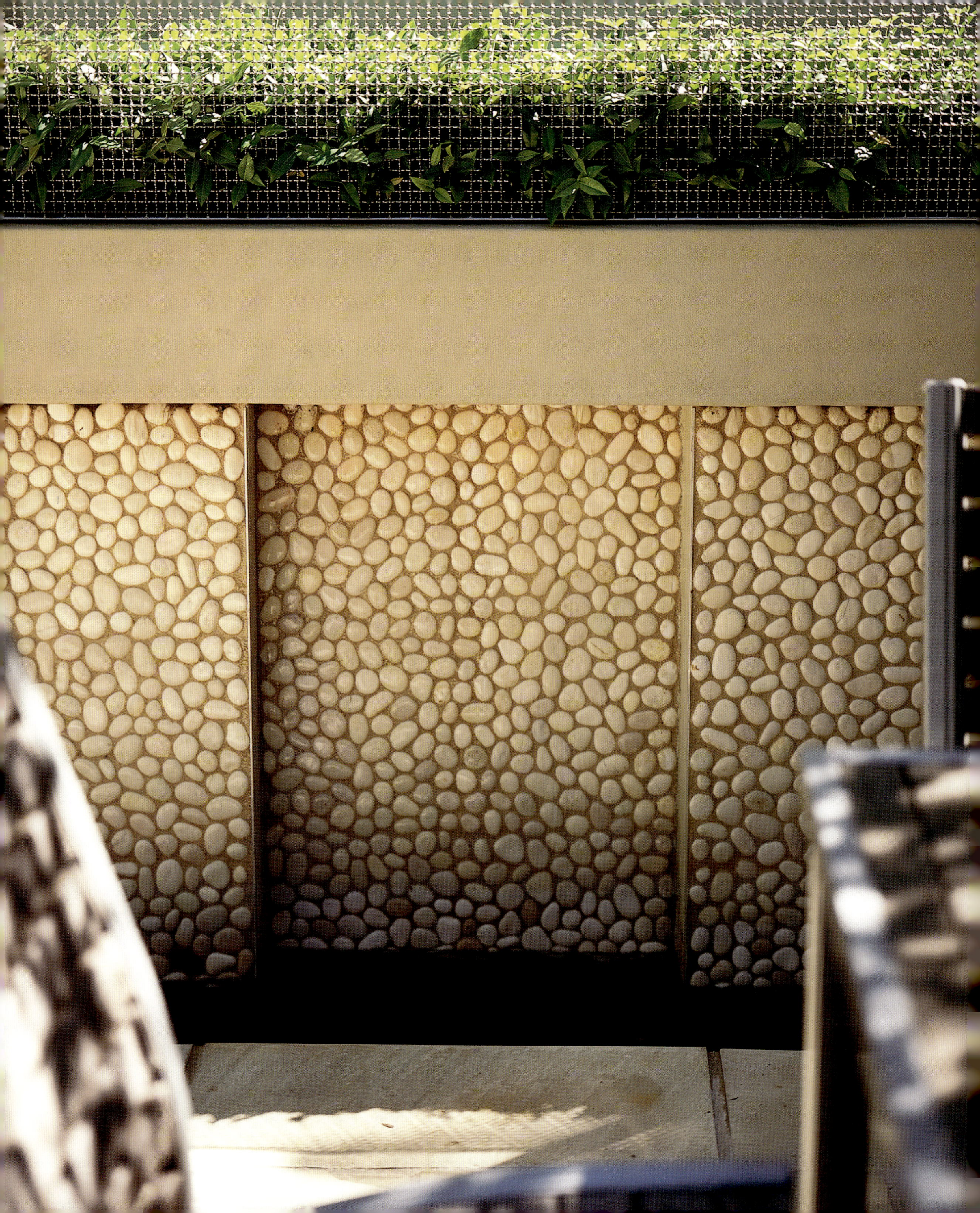

Because of the complexities of the levels in the new garden I felt I needed to reinforce the connection between the garden design and the house, so I created a strong line of sight running through the centre of the entire garden. When viewed from the house the eye is drawn to a central water feature at the entertainment level on the front retaining wall of the pool. It consists of three panels of pebbles, with water running down the central panel.

On the pool level, directly in line with the pebble wall, we stepped the planter box wall back and thus created a niche in its centre, which I purposefully downplayed so that it wouldn't take all the limelight. To reinforce the idea of the niche in the pool wall we will eventually prune several tall narrow windows within the 'Leighton Green' cypress hedge to reveal the dramatic aubergine colour of the back wall. The steel and stone of the lower garden give the whole a contemporary and streamlined look, but I chose the warm hue of the purple paint to soften the overall look produced by the harder materials.

When designing such a simple outdoor space it can be easy to overlook points of interest, but a subtle illusion is created within this space, as the water running down the central pebbled panel is perceived to have its source from the pool above. In this way the pebbled water wall remains the main feature but the viewer's eye is also drawn further into the garden.

A number of sweet viburnums, *Viburnum odoratissimum*, were planted as a hedge around the snow pear trees at the entertainment level. These will be pruned to be kept low, but for a viewer, they will produce a dramatic, contrasting double hedge with the 'Leighton Green' cypresses behind. Sweet viburnum can grow tall, but responds well to hedging. It has masses of delightfully fragrant white panicles in spring, which are followed by berries in autumn.

OPPOSITE The pebbles, stone and wall were deliberately designed in similar tones to unify the space.

Finally, dwarf star jasmine (*Trachelospermum asiaticum*) – sometimes known as Asian jasmine – was planted as a border around all the garden beds. With its dark green, glossy leaves it also creates a dramatic contrast with the cream-coloured sandstone. It is not a true jasmine, but does have fragrant flowers. It also will grow well in shade, a bonus in this garden, and forms a dense mat that prevents weeds growing.

THE RESULT
This unpromising backyard has now been transformed into an easily accessible and functional garden with points of interest. It is low maintenance, cool and shady, and reflects the owners' lifestyle.

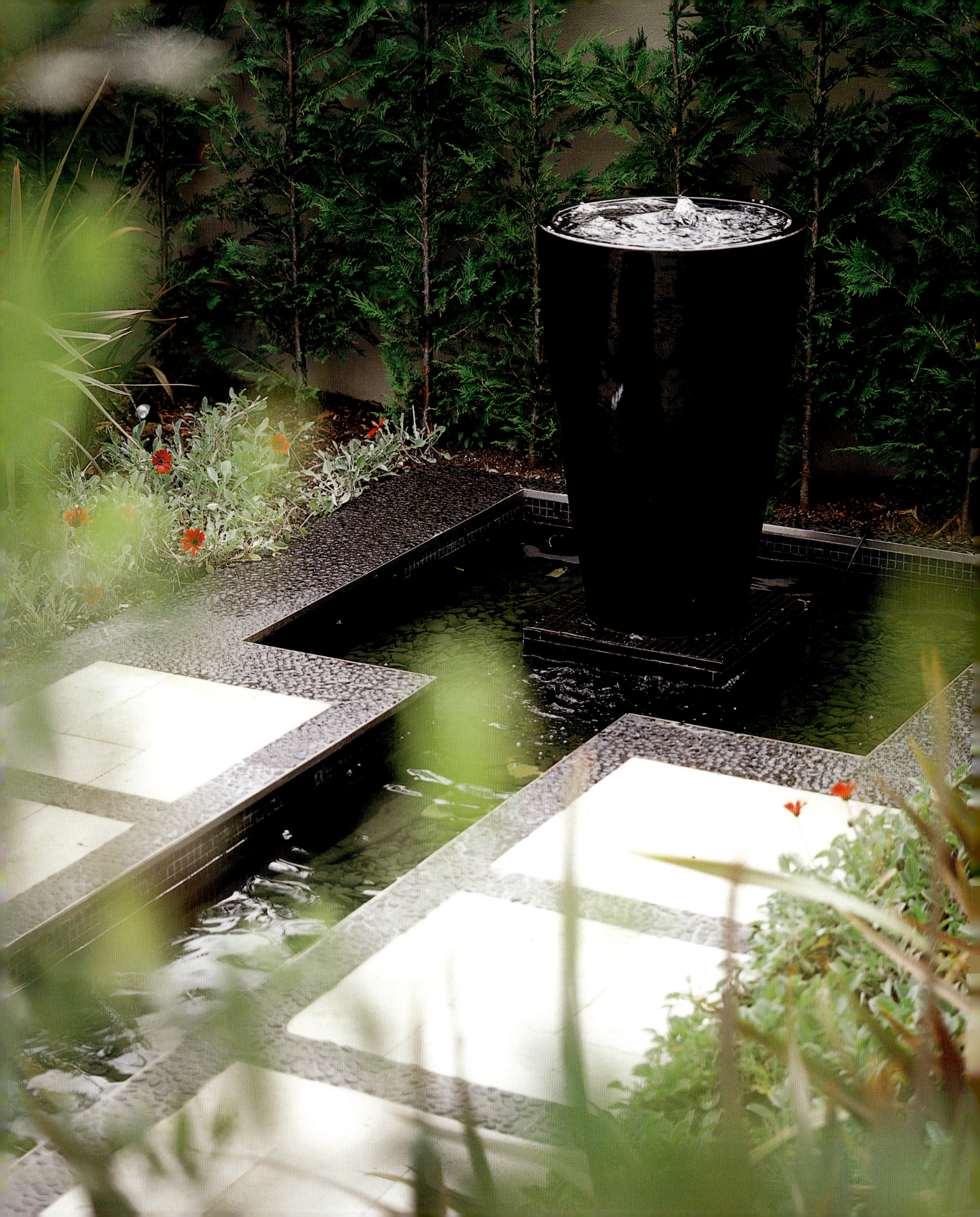

NATURALLY DISTINCTIVE

THE SETTING
This was a contemporary house in a beachside suburb of Sydney. In fact, the house was almost on the beach, and the soil was both shallow and sandy – not a fertile situation. In addition, the site was exposed and was extremely windy; this was a problem, as very few plants can survive constant salt-laden winds.

THE BRIEF
The clients asked me to design a contemporary garden that would suit the modern architecture of the house and could withstand the brutal winds. There was an existing pool in the backyard which required renovation and they wanted the design to entice people from the house into the pool area and also to create a feature with 'wow' factor in the entry garden at the front of the house.

THE DESIGN
When I arrived at this site for my initial meeting with the clients I almost got blown away, literally, and at the meeting they confirmed that this was quite normal – the house was situated in one of Sydney's windiest locations. So I immediately started to visualise a succulent garden, as my first impression is that it might be the only thing that would work.

Good design is about plant selection just as much as spatial design. The reason I say this is because I have used 'Leighton Green' cypresses, x *Cupressocyparis leylandii*, again in this design. I placed them around the perimeter of the garden in order to give protection from the winds, as they tolerate coastal conditions, and they will be pruned to a height of 2.5 metres.

The front garden was only small – approximately 9 metres of street frontage with a depth of 3 metres, and there was an entry path from the gate to the front door at one end of it. The 'wow' feature the

OPPOSITE In spring and summer the brilliant red of the Arctotis flower forms a dramatic contrast with the black pebbles surrounding the pond.
ABOVE The bold burgundy leaves of the New Zealand flax border the entrance to the house; these hardy perennials can withstand windy and harsh conditions.

clients had requested had to draw the eye as people entered at the gate. I designed a geometric pond at the far end of the garden with a contemporary fountain – an elegant black pot on a square plinth, with water from it spilling into a dark pond around it, about 1.2 metres square.

The pond is made of concrete and is lined with glass mosaic tiles in a slate colour, the dark interior making it more reflective than light tiles would have done. Dark pebbles also add to the mystery of the pond. A channel of water extended from this pond to the main entry path.

As the front garden was not somewhere for the family to play in I was able to design it as a visual appealing space. I wanted the eye to be drawn deep into the garden and I knew I could make the small space seem larger by doing that. The water channel makes the garden look longer, as it seems to disappear at the end into the pond. In fact, the channel was about 500 millimetres wide and 4.5 metres long.

The edge of the pond coping is metal, which makes the combination of water, paving and garden more seamless. To reinforce this 'perspective orientation of design', limestone stepping stones surrounded by borders of dark pebbles line the pond, defining its narrow width – the limestone in the garden echoes the use of limestone internally. Definition to the design has also been achieved by layering plants either side of the path and pond, giving the garden a greater sense of depth.

The colour scheme for this contemporary garden consisted of reds, burgundys and silver greens and all the plants were chosen for their tolerance to the strong salt-laden winds. Bordering the path are red *Arctotis* x *hybrida*, often called African daisy, or aurora daisy; the next layer is the dramatic *Phormium* 'Bronze Baby'; finally there is *Metrosideros thomasii*, New Zealand Christmas bush, with its wonderful silver leaves and red flowers. I planted the *Metrosideros* as a 1 metre high hedge along the front boundary of the house and behind the *Phormium*.

Arctotis is a hardy perennial that grows to about 20 centimetres high, although its flowers are held higher on stems. The flowers are borne singly, first appearing in winter and continuing until late summer; they may be pink, yellow, orange or white, as well as

OPPOSITE Olive trees provide accent at the entrance of the house.

red, depending on the variety. It needs very little care apart from deadheading the old flowers and an annual application of fertiliser. *Phormium*, New Zealand flax, is a similarly hardy perennial. The variety I planted will grow to about 60 centimetres high and its architectural, bold red leaves give a very contemporary look to the garden. It is grown for its foliage as it only produces its reddish flowers infrequently. *Metrosideros thomasii* will grow to 4 metres high and spread to about 2 metres in diameter, although it can be pruned. It will produce its flamboyant red flowers through spring and summer and attracts birds and butterflies.

To soften and highlight the entry path and slightly soften the house lines, I planted four olive trees, *Olea europea*, to form a light silver canopy over the entry. The limestone used internally was used once more for the entry path. The *Metrosideros thomasii* also lines the front path under the olive trees, forming a hedge, and helps to screen the driveway at one side from the entrance. I love its cool-coloured leaves and contrasting red flowers.

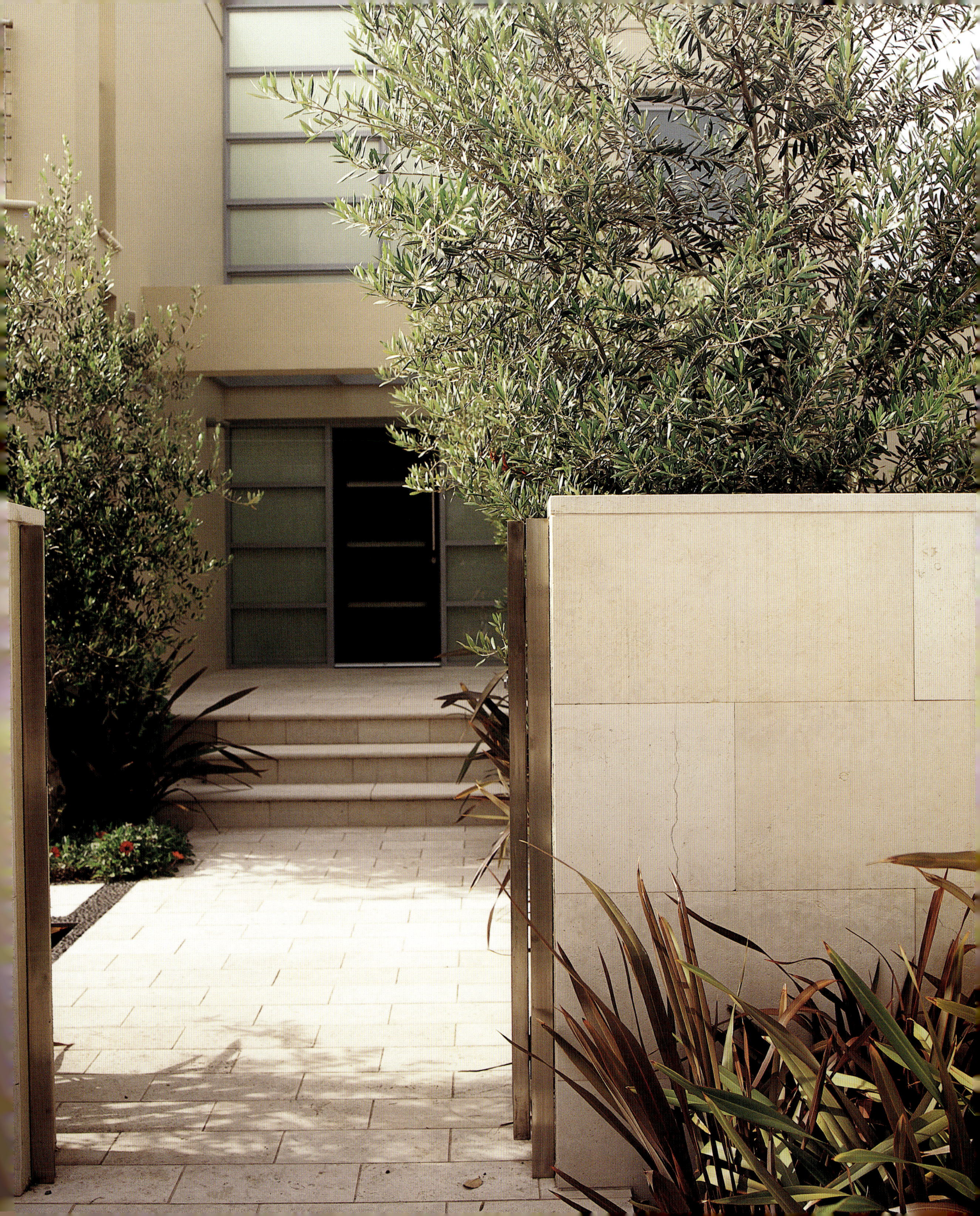

At the back of the house a terrace overlooks the ocean, perhaps the most exposed area of the brief. It features a gravel area with four large stone pots planted with the succulent *Agave attenuata*, a native of central Mexico; its thick stem is topped by a rosette of pale green leaves. This is framed by planter boxes consisting of a hedge of *Metrosideros thomasii* for protection and *Phormium* 'Dwarf Burgundy' in front of this. Through repeating the planting of the *Metrosideros thomasii* hedges I was able to connect the main garden with the entry garden.

At the garden level the existing pool shape was retained but the pool made more contemporary by using slate-coloured mosaic tiles which form a wonderful contrast with the limestone pavers. To soften the entire area a series of rendered masonry planter boxes were placed around the pool and these continued the same planting scheme of *Metrosideros* and *Phormium* as the terrace above. In planter boxes on the side boundaries x *Cupressocyparis leylandii* 'Leighton Green' hedges were planted to provide a much-needed screen. Finally, around the pool black planters were filled with dwarf red bougainvillea, which will give colour.

Limestone pavers were also used to floor an outdoor eating area under a pergola, to make an attractive setting for a meal. A built-in barbecue was constructed and the area was covered with a frosted glass roof.

RIGHT TOP AND BOTTOM Two beauties in bloom: the dwarf red bouganvillea and the Arctotis. OPPOSITE The raised entertaining area is protected from strong winds, and overlooks the pool and garden.

THE RESULT
Clean lines form the basis of this contemporary home, and they were also the basis of the garden design. The extensive use of glass and steel in the architecture contrasts with the more organic textures of pebbles and limestone outside; this creates an exciting fusion of elements. The plants' forms reinforce the strong architectural elements, while their dramatic colour offers a contrast to the cold glass and steel. Most importantly, they will withstand the challenging natural elements.

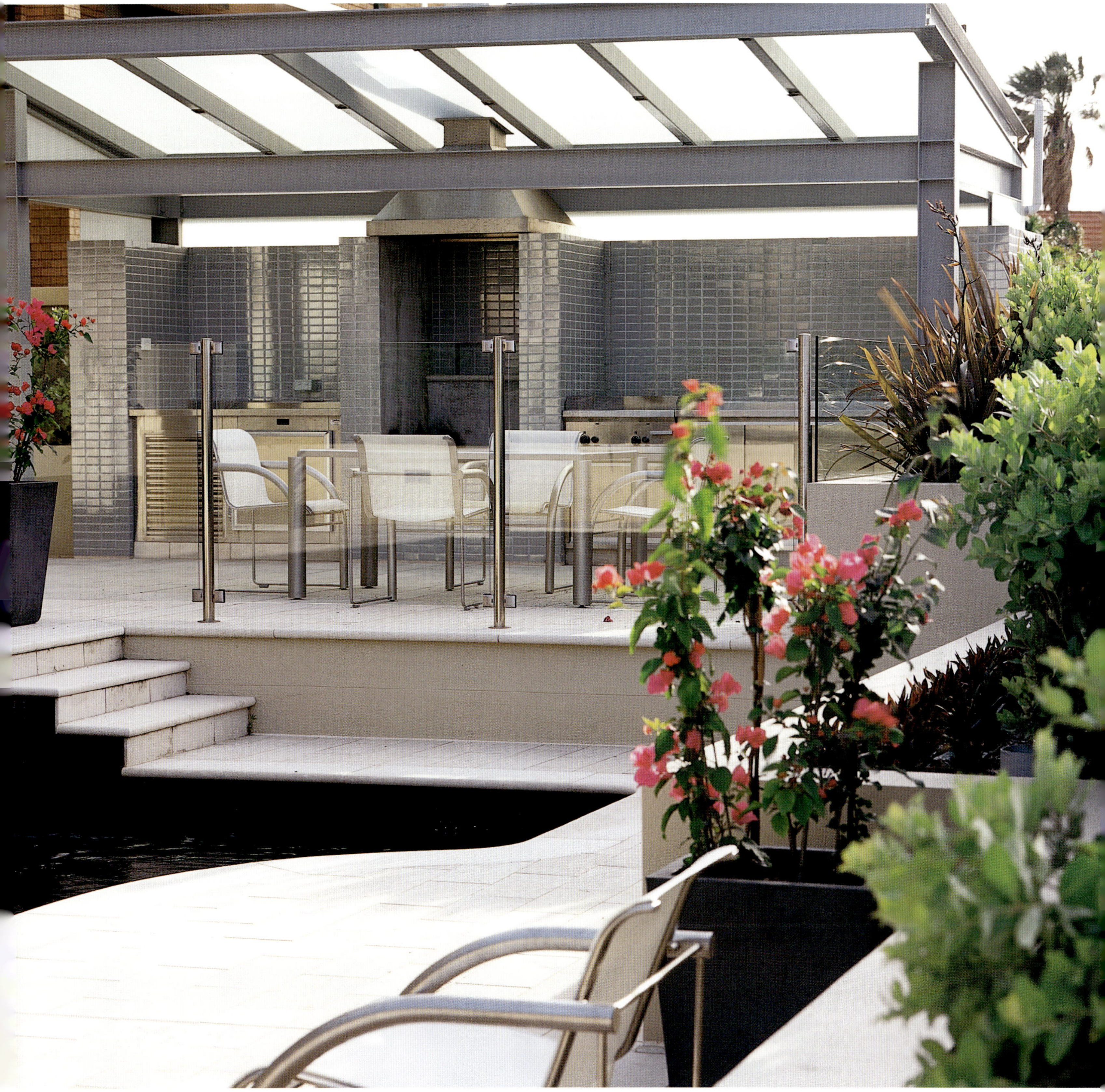

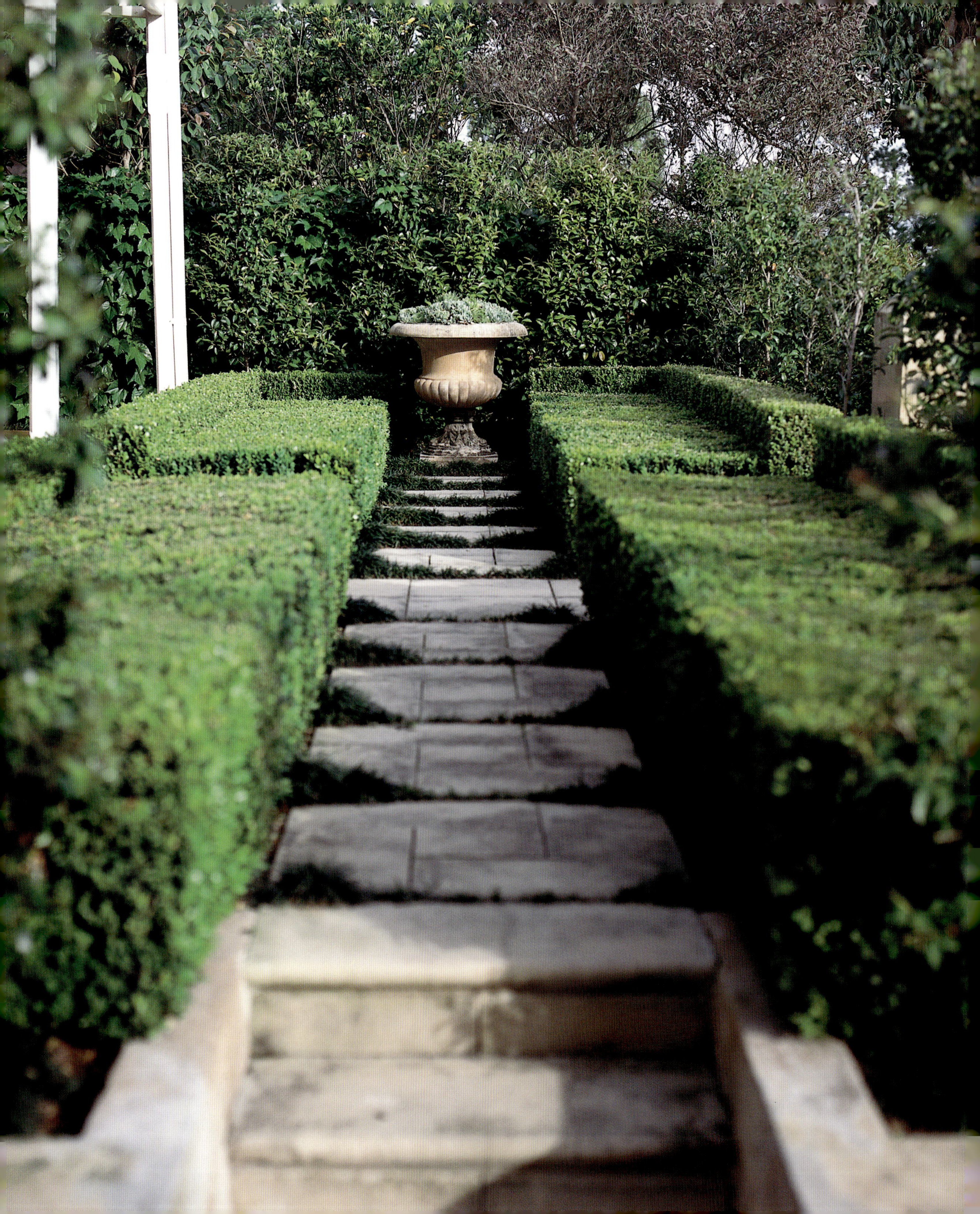

URBAN ELEGANCE

THE SETTING
This was a weatherboard house in Longueville, a harbourside suburb on Sydney's North Shore, that had been elegantly renovated. The existing garden had suffered from the building works at the front; there was also a gently sloping traditional back garden and a tiny, internal secluded courtyard surprise.

THE BRIEF
The clients wished to have an entirely new garden surrounding the newly renovated house. As they had three children, the design had to be an open and functional space suitable for a large family; there was to be an emphasis on casual outdoor entertaining but in a very stylised way, to suit the house. The front garden was to be in keeping with the traditional façade of the house.

THE DESIGN
The clients at this property had renovated an old weatherboard cottage. The small front garden measured approximately 8 metres wide by 2.5 metres in depth. There was a medium-sized back garden, plus a small courtyard halfway down the house. On entering the house I realised the style of the garden would need to reflect in some way not only the period of the house but also the clients' contemporary, elegant interiors.

Despite the fact that the period of the house lends itself to a cottage-style garden I chose to ignore this. The reasons being that, firstly, the clients – as busy parents of three young children – did not have the time to look after a cottage garden and, secondly, I wanted to create a design that would have much higher visual impact.

For the front, which is slightly raised above the access from the street at the side of the block, I massed two narrow box hedges either side of stepping stones, and produced a parterre. The hedge is the

OPPOSITE The stepping stone path bordered by dark green hedges leads to a stone urn with succulents; this combination makes a dramatic impression at the front of the house.

dark green English box, *Buxus sempervirens*, but through the centre I introduced diagonal blades of Japanese box, *Buxus microphylla* var. *japonica*, whose foliage produces a striking contrast. When viewed from one end of the garden the diagonal pattern created by the Japanese box through the hedge, together with the stepping stones – which are surrounded by dwarf mondo grass, *Ophiopogon japonicus* 'Nana' – forms an axis that appears longer than it really is. The eye is led to a stone urn at the far end massed with succulents, *Echeveria* species, which provide a unique blue shade to this green garden and will eventually hang over the urn, softening its form. The entire front garden is surrounded by a white-flowering *Camellia sasanqua* hedge, which creates a backdrop to the box and thus completes this garden room.

The house façade is pretty and I did not want the garden to detract from it, so therefore the parterre suited my intentions. The parterre gives the house breathing space, because it is lower than the building. The sasanqua hedge helps to provide intimacy, enclosing the space just enough to make it a garden room.

On walking through the house, approximately halfway down the hallway one discovers a courtyard about 4 metres square. It is viewed through ceiling to floor glass walls. As the courtyard was not large enough to work as a functional area, I was able to create a purely visual space within it. In order to achieve the greatest visual impact here I decided to restrict the number of elements and focus on three contrasting elements – water, stone and greenery.

First, the courtyard was paved with the same reconstituted stone that was used for the stepping stones in the front garden. A broad, low *Buxus microphylla* var. *japonica* hedge forms a continuous border around the courtyard, even extending against the risers of the steps. When viewed from the house a green couch stands boldly against the boundary – it is a stone bench enveloped by the boxwood. The centre of the courtyard is a simple water feature consisting of a pond that is flush with the stone paving and a small Anduze urn that has been turned into a fountain. Behind the bench a strict but narrow *Juniperus virginiana* 'Spartan' hedge forms a screen on the boundary.

LEFT Mini mondo grass forms a tight mass around the stepping stones.
OPPOSITE A sense of fun has been created within the courtyard with the inclusion of a green couch.

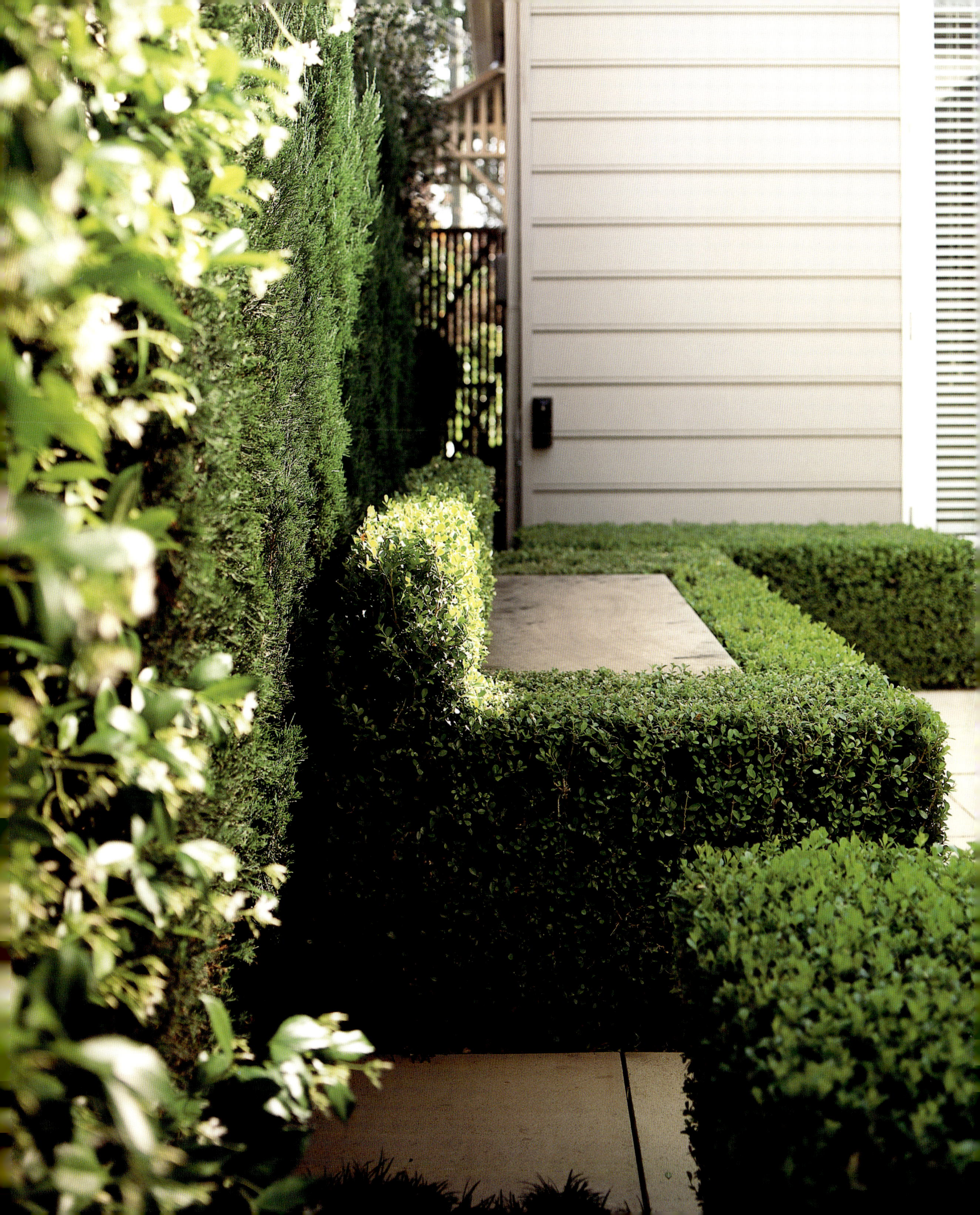

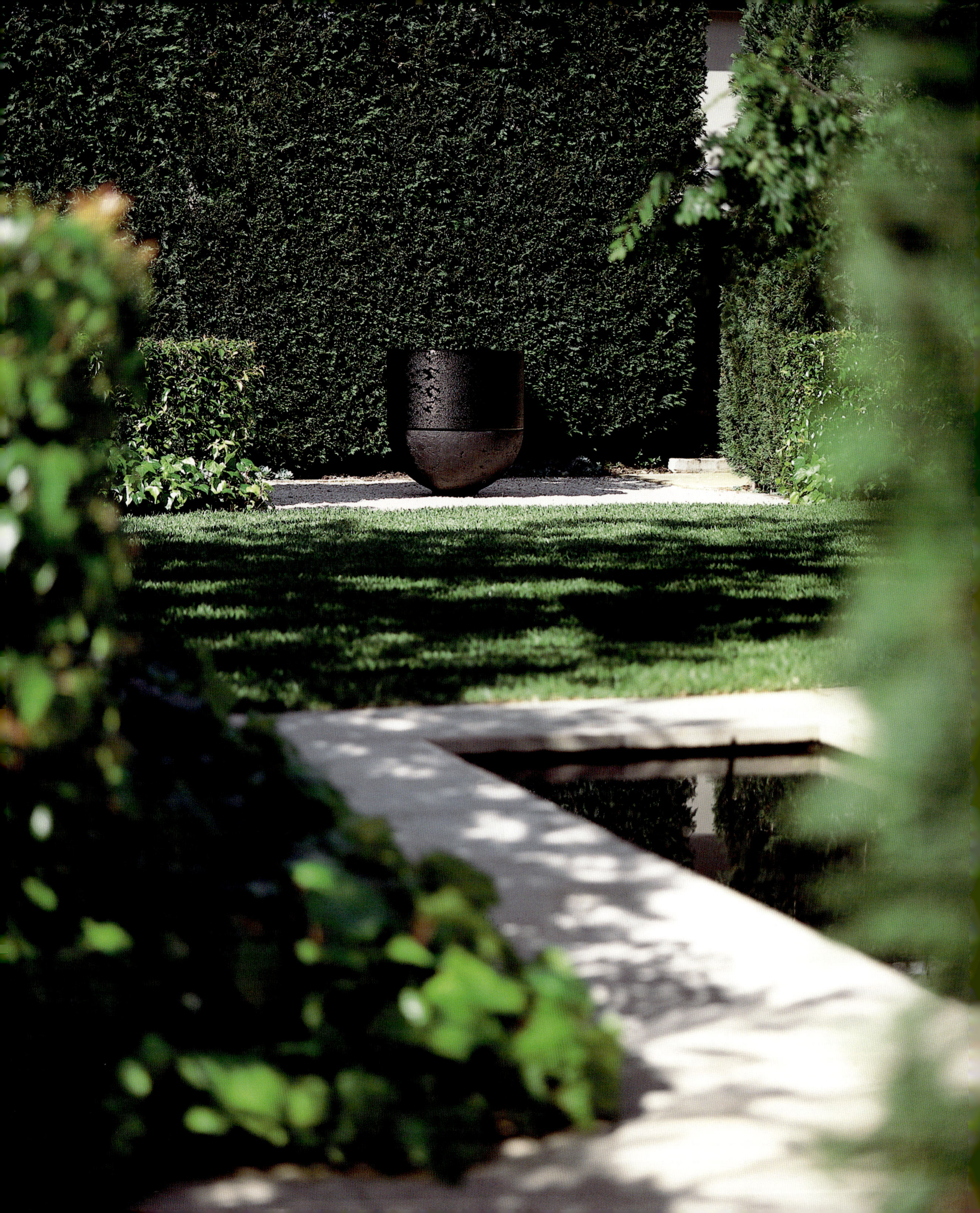

There have been some discussions recently in the media by people who think *Buxus* is being overused in modern garden design. There are gardens where I would agree with this viewpoint, but there is a place for everything and when *Buxus* is used in the right place there is no better plant. It has a gutsy, green form and complements hard construction beautifully.

Juniperus virginiana will grow in dry places and is hardy. There are many varieties of this juniper, from shrubs to tall trees. 'Spartan' has a good conical shape, and will grow to about 6 metres tall in ideal conditions. It is reasonably fast-growing and I love to use it for its colour and texture.

The main focus of the new garden design was, however, the back garden. The intention from the beginning was that the design would be kept simple and the transition between house and garden would be as smooth as possible. To achieve this, the moderately sloping back garden was made level. Against the boundary I planted x *Cupressocyparis leylandii* 'Leighton Green', which was to become a 3 metre high hedge and the 'wall' of the backyard garden room. In front of the x *Cupressocyparis* hedge is a wide bed, in which was planted a 1 metre high *Xylosma congestum* hedge, while inside that is a metre-wide large leaf ivy border, *Hedera canariensis*. I selected these plants because their habit would suit the function required and the play of contrast between the plants' heights, textures and foliages worked well.

Xylosma congestum is a shrub or small tree from Asia that responds well to pruning. I like to use it a lot, as it has wonderful bright green glossy leaves, makes an excellent perimeter hedge, tolerates all soils as well as full sun and deep shade, is fast-growing, thickens up beautifully and looks great as a backdrop plant.

On the back boundary the 'Leighton Green' hedge turns back to the house within 3 metres of each side boundary to allow for a garden shed on the left-hand side and a vegetable patch on the right. In between these screened elements, a square gravel bed houses a dramatic black water feature, highlighted by the lush green of the 'Leighton Green' hedge behind it. When viewed from the house

OPPOSITE My preference is that the focal points are subtle – this can add to the intrigue of a garden. ABOVE LEFT Large leaf ivy creates a stunning border to the paving. ABOVE RIGHT An Anduze urn fountain is an impressive addition in the courtyard.

ABOVE Phormium 'dwarf burgundy' makes a great show in this charcoal pot. *OPPOSITE* Urban elegance at its best; the permanent bench seating makes this area more versatile – and along with the stylish table, chairs and barbecue, this garden can now be used to entertain small and large groups of people.

the fountain set in amongst the 'Leighton Green' foliage takes on a modern Japanese feel, owing to the style of the fountain and the simple textures and contrasts of the green and the gravel. It also looks like another room in the garden and thus makes the whole back garden area seem bigger.

In front of the fountain a medium-sized area of traditional lawn was incorporated into the garden, while adjoining the house a large paved area was created for serious outdoor entertaining. To make this area more appealing and relaxed I created a pond that would reflect its surroundings on one side and on the other a built-in barbecue with a timber slat bench attached. In the centre of the paving, a large Chinese elm, *Ulmus parvifolia*, was planted to create shade for this north-facing garden, with massed ivy underneath the tree. I wanted a tree with a relaxed semi-weeping habit to counterbalance the perimeter planting. Three years on, the limbs of the elm have already grown and reflect in the pond, as was intended.

Chinese elms can grow to about 15 metres in ideal situations, but this one will not reach that height in the garden. It is a deciduous tree, but in warm climates will hold onto its leaves well until winter, or even until the new growth appears in spring. Its mature shape is attractive, being a rounded canopy, while the trunk is interesting, as the bark is mottled, showing green, grey and orange colours that look like jigsaw puzzle pieces separated by red–orange lines which are the inner bark.

There is an access path alongside the house – on the opposite side from the courtyard – leading from garage to laundry and on into the garden. It is made of reconstituted pavers with dwarf mondo grass, *Ophiopogon japonicus*, in between them, while star jasmine, *Trachelospermum jasminoides*, is planted along the boundary fence so that it will clamber up it and perfume the air in late spring and early summer.

THE RESULT
Three garden rooms now envelop the house, linked through repetition of plant species. The result is streamlined elegance, fulfilling the clients' brief and enhancing lifestyle. Even with its formal layout this garden is elegantly casual and inviting, with enough mystery to hold interest.

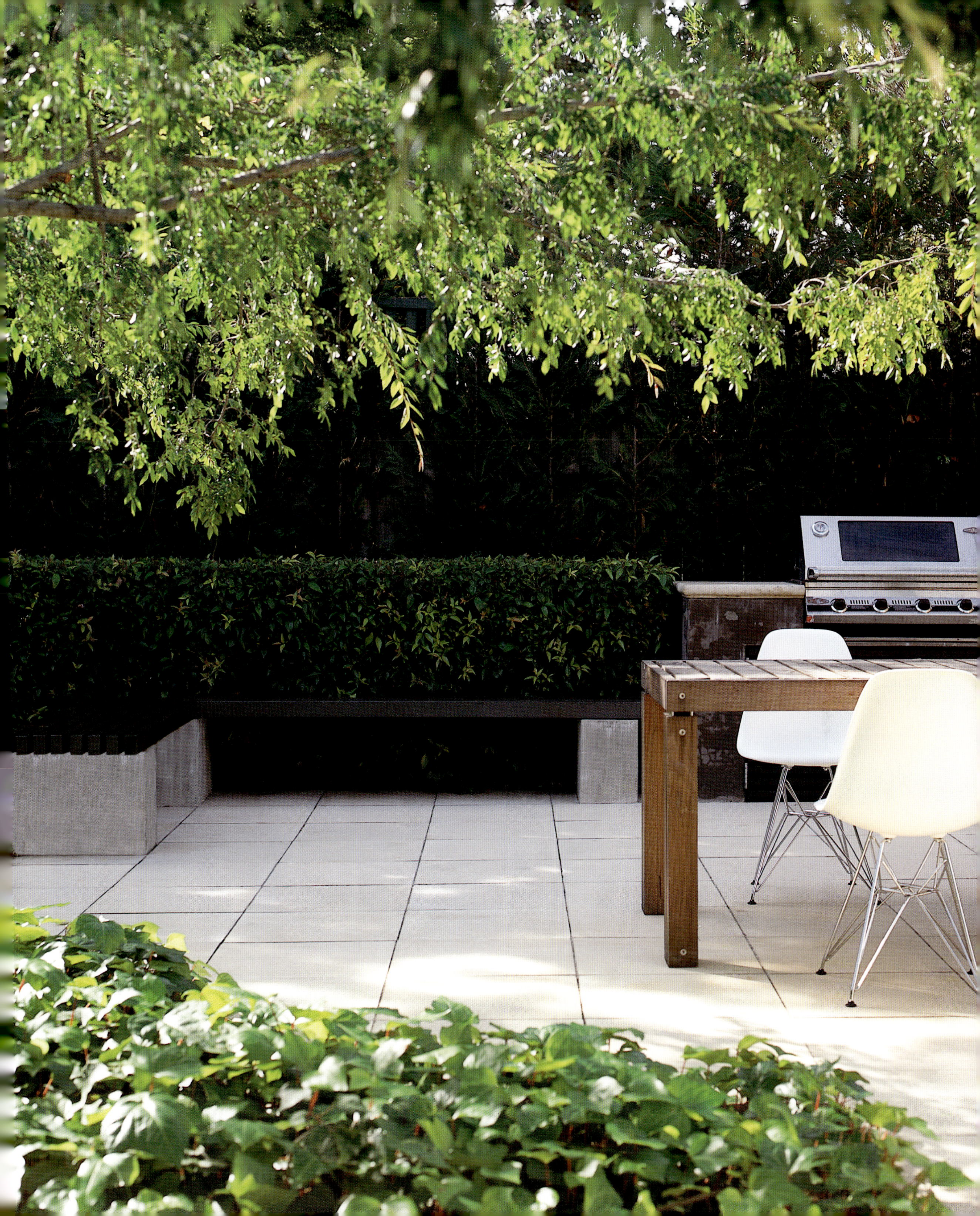

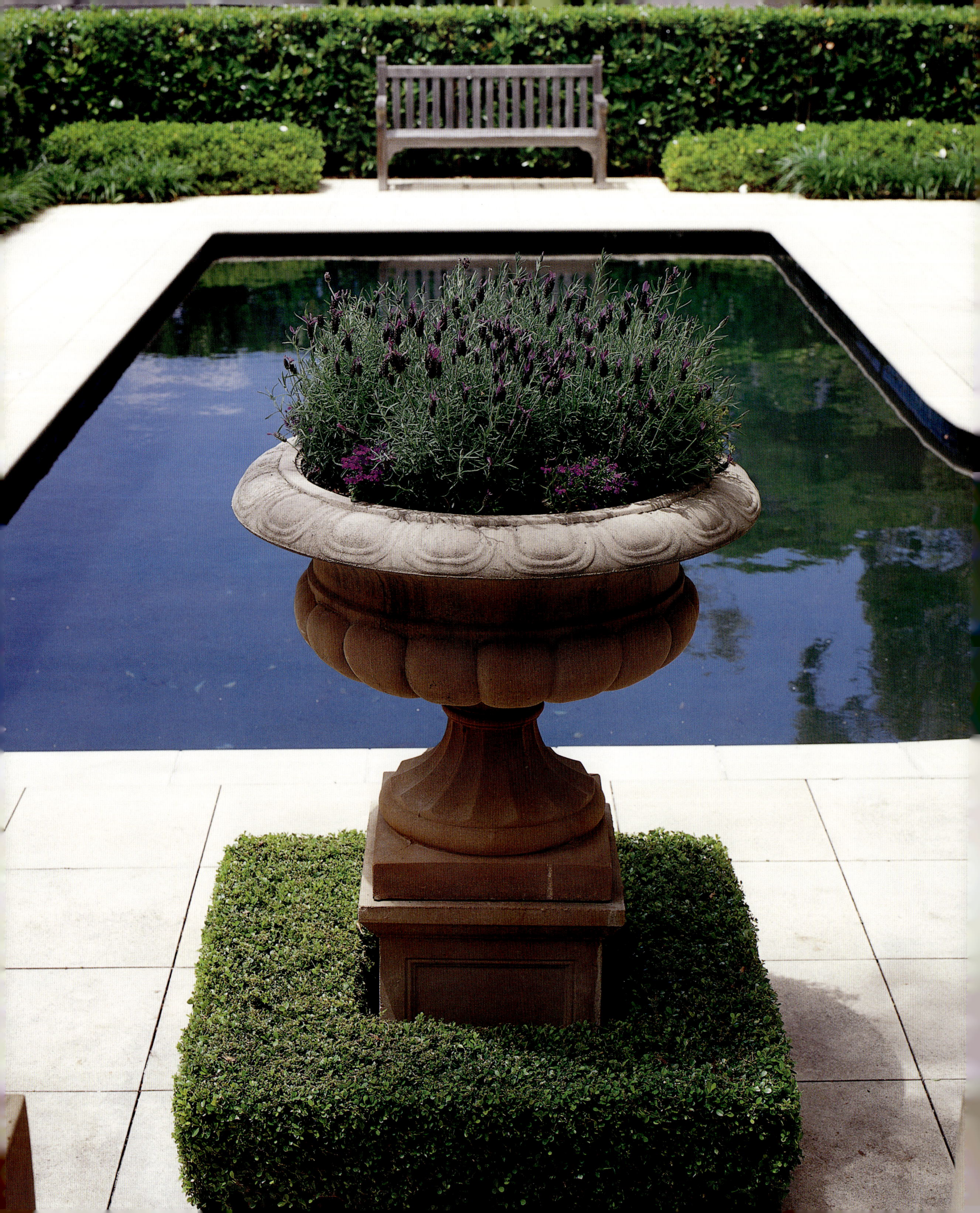

STONE AND GREENERY

THE SETTING
The setting was magnificent: a classic mansion overlooking Sydney Harbour with stunning views of the Harbour Bridge. There was an existing large swimming pool in the garden, but apart from that it could be described as a building site. My first impressions were that I would like to fill the garden with stone and greenery and soften the house, which seemed quite imposing as it sat elevated on the site.

THE BRIEF
The brief to me was very open. The feel should be fun, and the client wanted the garden to have a water feature. The approach to the front door had to be simplified. The only stipulation was that an existing *Camellia sasanqua* should be retained – I could see why, as it had a beautifully balanced shape, so I'd somehow have to work it into the design.

THE DESIGN
This garden brought up an issue which many garden designers face – how to design a garden that has a spectacular vista, a garden that must not detract from its surroundings. Although this was the paramount issue for me as the designer, one of the main issues for the client was that the new garden design should direct guests to the stairs that led to the front door! In the existing layout, people were naturally drawn to the wrong entrance.

The way I handled these two issues was to create a wide central paved path from the street entrance leading to the front stairs. The path was signalled as important by placing at its centre a bell urn in which a small

OPPOSITE The inclusion of ornamentation around the pool area makes it look more inviting.

ABOVE LEFT A stone sphere accentuates the front staircase leading to the house. ABOVE RIGHT A box of Buxus microphylla japonica *highlights the circular bell-shaped fountain, with* Liriope 'Evergreen Giant' *in the background. OPPOSITE Children, especially, are drawn instantly to the stepping stones in this shallow pond.*

fountain played, which was intended to entice people to the main entry stairs, bypassing the entry to the main lawn – which previously had been the natural inclination for people to use. I made the pathway as wide as possible so that I could accommodate access around the focal point, the fountain urn. All the pavers used in the garden were cream reconstituted stone, and these both unify the various areas and blend in with the sandstone foundations of the house.

In order to direct people from the fountain to the stairs that led to the front door, two stone spheres were placed beside the bottom of the flight. These really accented the stairs, further defining their purpose.

On either side of the path the planting scheme is purposely very directional and streamlined, to emphasise directional movement. There is *Liriope muscari* 'Evergreen Giant', with its strappy uniform foliage, and behind that a *Viburnum odoratissimum*, sweet viburnum, hedge. Underneath the bell urn, a geometrical square of *Buxus microphylla* var. *japonica*, was planted, the tight neat foliage of this small-leaved box contrasting beautifully with the more free-flowing *Liriope*.

Liriope is a hardy, evergreen perennial requiring minimal maintenance that grows well in sun or partial shade. It can be propagated by division of the large rhizomes or by seed. In autumn this *Liriope* carries spikes of purple or lavender flowers, hidden amongst the leaves.

Sweet viburnum can reach 6 metres in height and be grown as a small tree, but responds well to hedging. Tiny white, waxy flowers appear in large clusters in spring and have a heady, attractive perfume. It grows in both full sun and light shade. *Viburnum odoratissimum* originally came from Asia and is semi-tropical.

The main front garden is a large expanse situated about 3 metres below the front verandah, from which stunning Harbour views can be enjoyed. Because of its position the design and planting scheme here needed to be both simple and dramatic. As it is mostly viewed from above, I enclosed the entire front garden with a *Viburnum odoratissimum* hedge forming a 2 metre high wall, so that when you are standing in the garden you still feel enclosed and part of the garden. When viewed from the terrace, however, the height of this hedge in no way interferes with the view. The viburnum hedge was returned about three-quarters of the way along the garden, almost dividing the main area in two.

On one side of the lawn and planted in it, within the sweet viburnum hedge, is an avenue of lilly pillys, *Syzygium australe* – also known as *S. paniculatum* and *Eugenia australis*. I used 'Elite Form' shaped into dramatic cones 2 metres high, the same height as the hedge behind them. These create a sense of fun and their bold, simple forms are uncomplicated and do not compete with the vista.

Syzygium australe is frost-tender and prefers moist and well-drained soil in full sun. In summer it bears fluffy white flowers which are followed by purple–red fruits.

Further along, in the smaller, separate 'room' produced by the hedge return, was the *Camellia sasanqua* tree that the clients wished to be retained. It was a medium-sized tree, approximately 6–7 metres tall. Its single blooms are strong pink – it was identified as 'Plantation Pink'.

As my balanced design began to take shape, I found myself wondering how I would include the tree. Then, halfway through the job, the client approached me with a request to include a large bird aviary in the garden. Suddenly the camellia had a purpose. I incorporated a huge, black, Victorian-style steel aviary under the canopy of the *Camellia sasanqua*.

By doing this, on entering the garden the main focal point is the aviary, though the viewer feels it is further away than it really is due to the placement of the hedge. The lilly pilly cones help to accentuate the perspective, making the garden feel longer than it is in reality. The aviary is framed by the lilly pilly cones and is complemented by the *Camellia sasanqua*'s arching canopy. This prevented the large aviary from looking too conspicuous – it now looked like it had been part of the garden for ever.

Camellias grow slowly, only about 30 centimetres a year, but are extremely long-lived. The camellia that was prized by the clients might therefore have been growing in the garden for decades. Sasanqua camellias flower profusely in autumn and early winter, as opposed to the more widely grown *Camellia japonica*, whose blossoms herald spring; the sasanqua flowers are generally smaller than japonicas, but the prolific number of them create a wonderful show, and the fallen petals under the shrub or tree can appear to be a carpet of colour in a dull time of year.

At the end of the garden opposite to the aviary the simple form of a stone slab bench was placed centrally to the lilly pilly cones; this reinforces the balance within this design and enables the garden to be viewed in a relaxed way from this level. Three-quarters along the lawn I returned the viburnum hedge towards the centre, so that from the slab the view of the aviary was framed. From both ground level and from the house level this gave the garden more interest and the illusion of more space, due to the fact the garden couldn't be seen entirely in one glance.

Near the bird aviary a raised pond was constructed, with stepping stones forming a geometrical grid pattern that seem to float on top of the water. The cream-coloured pavers used throughout the garden produce a wonderful contrast with the black pond. A second stone slab bench, echoing the one at the other end of the garden, forms part of the coping to this pond, while a simple flat concrete bowl is home to the fountain in the middle. Massed *Trachelospermum asiaticum*, dwarf star jasmine, sits neatly around the pond, forming a beautiful low dark green mat. It has light yellow flowers with a spicy fragrance, and tolerates deep shade.

The pool garden is to one side of the house, at the southern end, and needed an update. So we squared off the paving around the pool, to bring the house lines into the garden. Black Quartzon – a cement and quartz aggregate that incorporates flecks which make the water seem to glitter and sparkle in sunlight – was used for the pool lining, creating a gorgeous surface that reflected the established trees in the garden. At one end of the pool a large urn on a pedestal forms the focal point, planted with massed Italian lavender, *Lavandula stoechas*, while traditional blue lobelia edges the rim.

The entire area is softened and unified with layered planting bands of autumn crocus, *Zephyranthes candida*, *Gardenia augusta* 'Florida', *Murraya paniculata* hedged to 1 metre and the *Viburnum odoratissimum* hedge behind.

The plants chosen to surround the pool will ensure this area is fragrant. The viburnum blossom has a heady scent and the flowers of *Gardenia augusta*, known as common gardenia or Cape jasmine, are piercingly sweet. The plant is slow-growing but may reach 1.5 metres; 'Florida' is a variety with large double white flowers. *Murraya paniculata*, orange jessamine, is a semi-tropical evergreen shrub with sweet-scented white flowers that may appear throughout the year, but are in greatest bloom in summer. It cannot tolerate temperatures that fall much below 10° Celsius.

The swimming pool garden continues around the back of the house to a courtyard simply consisting of a small square pond with a concrete sphere as a fountain. A low *Buxus microphylla* var. *japonica* hedge flanks the pond and the *Viburnum odoratissimum* hedge continues to form a dramatic backdrop to this very simple scene. Both these are echoes of those in the front path planting, once again bringing unity to the disparate parts of the garden.

BELOW The plants that surround the pool, such as orange jessamine and common gardenia, provide a constant, sweet aroma. OVERLEAF Holding interest in a garden can be more about shapes and form, rather than different planting details.

THE RESULT

This very elegant Sydney sandstone house is now surrounded by a series of garden rooms that seem to have been there as long as the house has. The glorious view of Sydney Harbour is uncompromised, and any confusion about where the front door is located has been resolved.

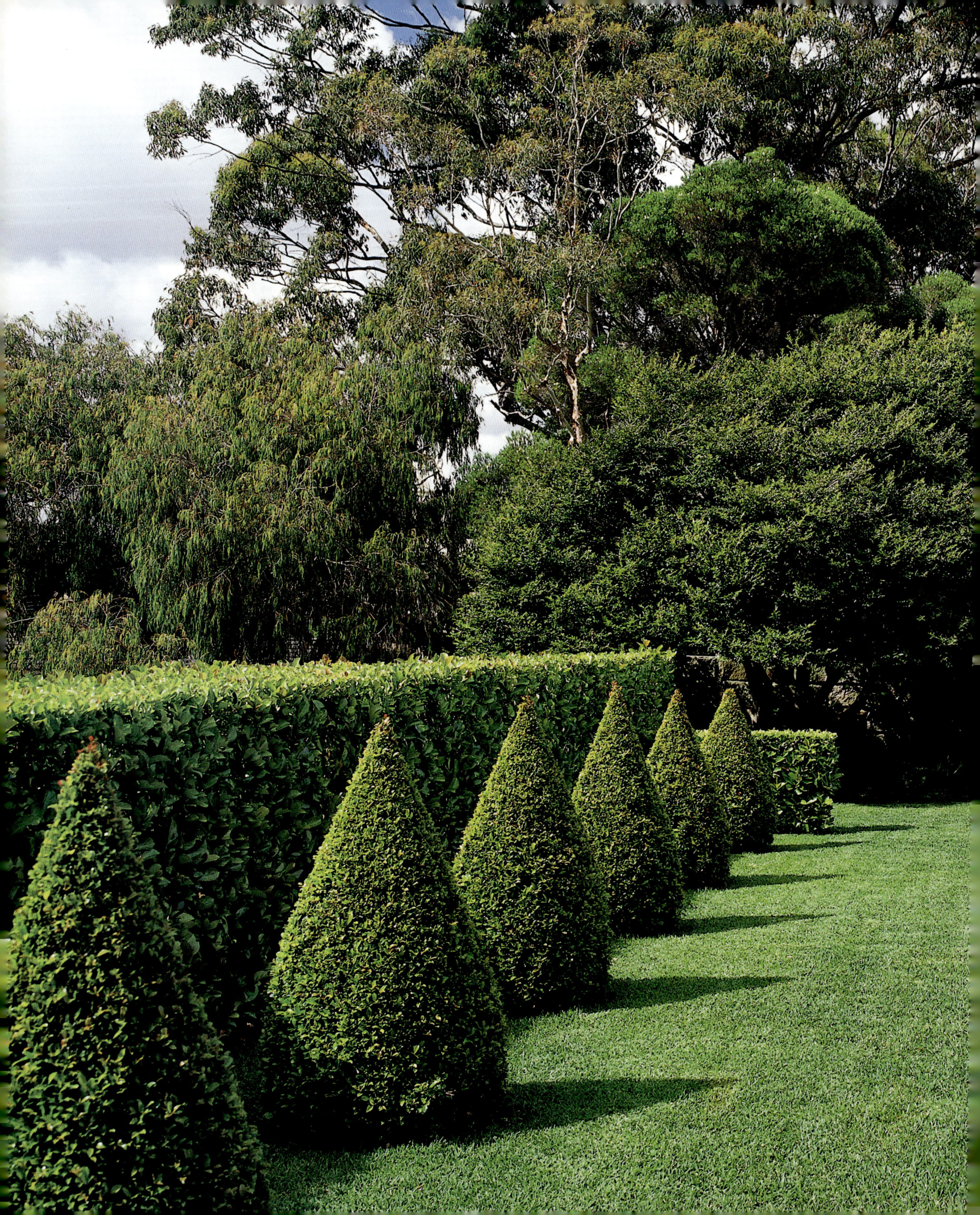

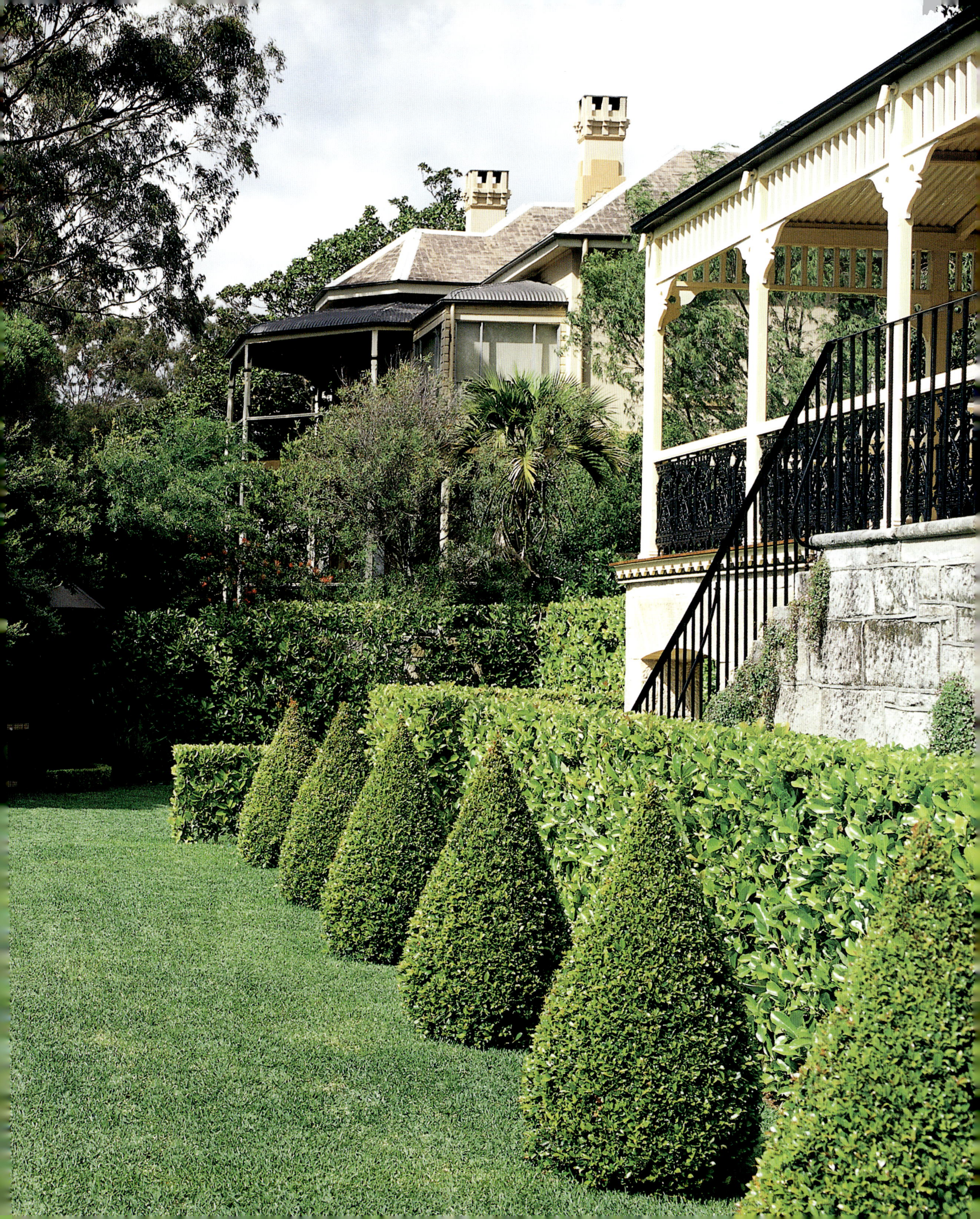

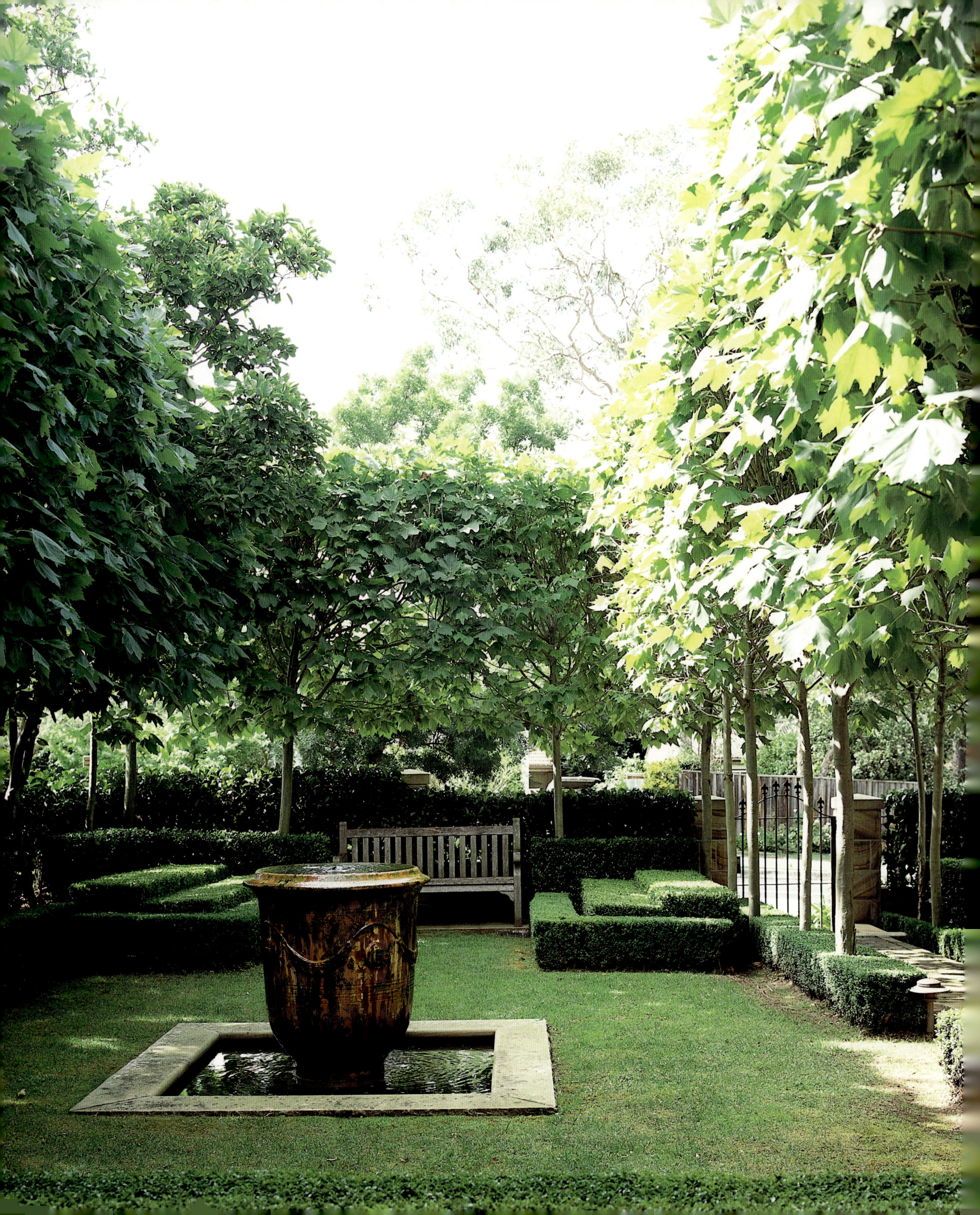

PLANE SAILING

THE SETTING
The house was newly built, in the quiet, residential Sydney North Shore suburb of Killara.

THE BRIEF
I was asked to create a garden that would have high visual impact from the street and enhance the house. Really, I had an open brief on how to do that! As the house had just been built there were no existing plantings that I had to take into consideration or include.

THE DESIGN
The entire garden area was not huge, probably only 12 metres by 15 metres in the front, the rest being driveway and boundary walls, while the back garden was a little larger.

At the front we decided to use a classic approach, with the path going directly to the front door. This was because the house, although new, was very formal and balanced. I deliberately used second-hand common bricks for the front path to give this house an 'aged' look. However, to produce a more unusual, interesting feel I designed sandstone 'inserts' within the path at equal intervals. These pick up the block sandstone that was used for the foundations of the house, helping tie the garden and house together. The paving theme is repeated throughout the entire garden.

OPPOSITE This green oasis is a world away from the busy road beyond.

The front path was lined with an English box, *Buxus sempervirens*, hedge, with a slightly taller, Japanese box, *Buxus microphylla* var. *japonica*, hedge behind it. A 1 metre high orange jessamine, *Murraya paniculata*, hedge separates the drive from the front path, while the front garden balances the driveway on the other side. Also lining the path – and growing through the English box – is an avenue of *Platanus* x *hybrida*, syn. *P.* x *acerifolia*, London plane trees.

The avenue of plane trees continues and surrounds the small lawn area on three sides. London plane is a well-known tree, used in city and street plantings the world over. It can grow to over 20 metres and is a vigorous species. There might have been some alarm at using such a tree in a small garden such as this, but these are designed not to grow into large specimens, instead being pruned back to form a pleached avenue – almost an elevated hedge. The branches intertwine and grow thickly together. In my experience I have found that by constantly pruning the trees to form and maintain such an elevated hedge you more or less stunt their growth and therefore their roots are non-invasive.

This dramatic pleached hedge creates the most cooling green environment beneath it, where dappled shade plays on the lawn. Even in winter, when the leaves will have dropped from the plane trees, the effect of the bare intertwined branches is interesting. At one end of the lawn a teak bench sits, firmly bordered by architectural layers of clipped English and Japanese box and *Murraya*.

LEFT Second-hand bricks were intentionally selected for the front path to give the house an 'aged' look. OPPOSITE Plane trees help create the feeling of a secret garden within.

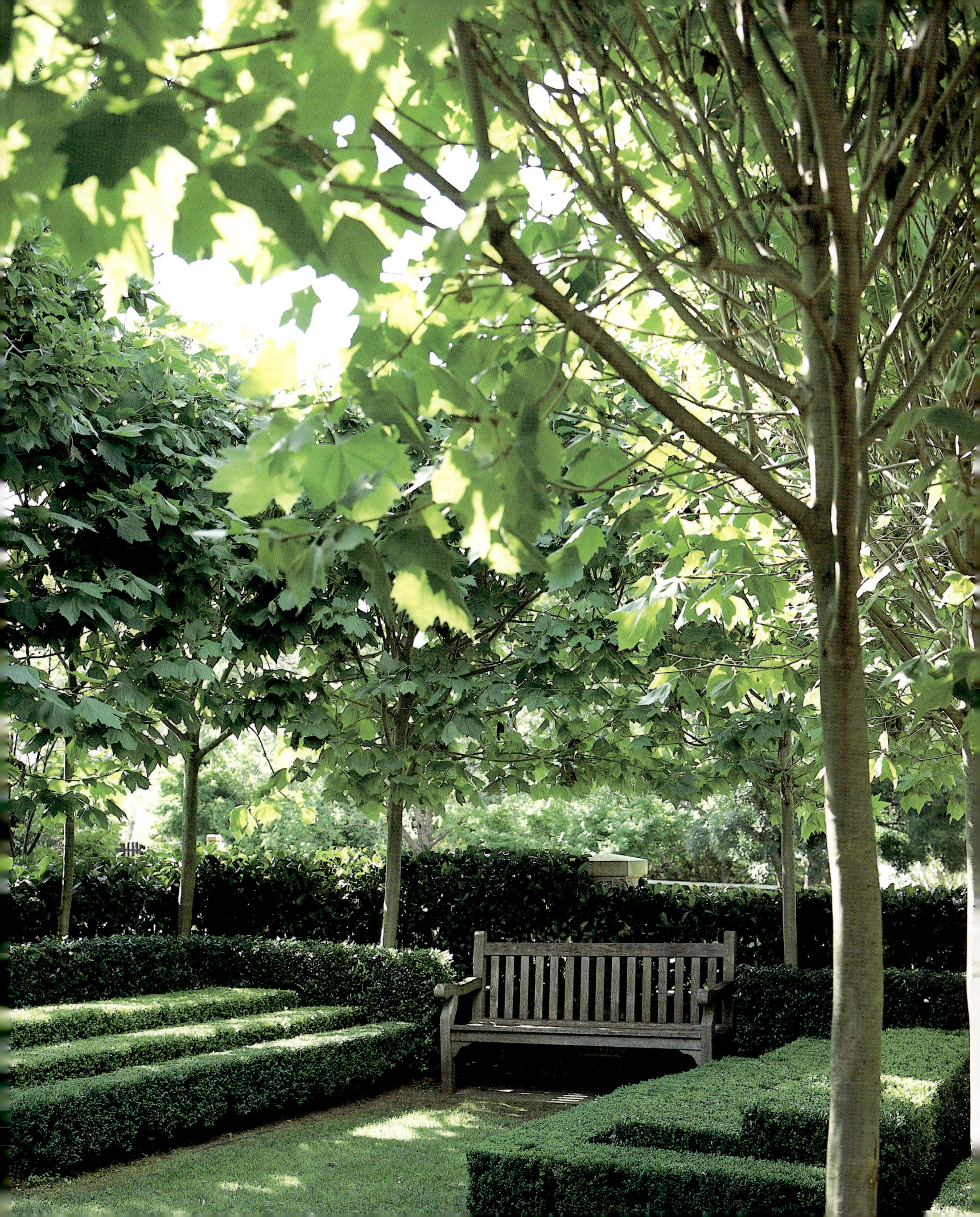

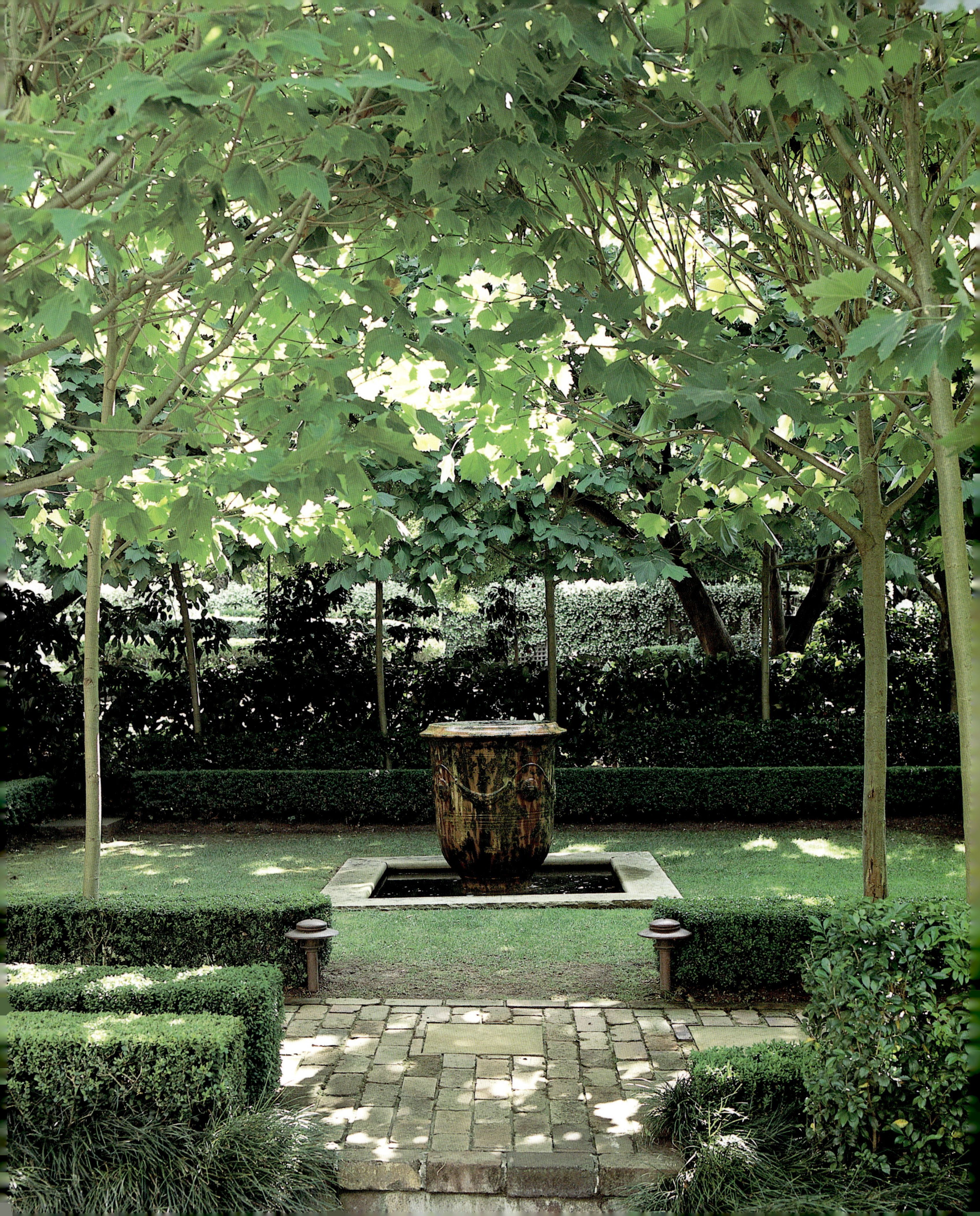

Towards the opposite end of the lawn there is a water feature: a large, decorated French provincial Anduze urn forms a fountain within a square pond, bordered by sandstone pavers. The pond sits flush with the moss and grass lawn area.

The overall effect is classically elegant, calming, green and rich. The front garden is a truly beautiful and peaceful space which is closely tied to the house.

The back garden includes some paving, a lawn area, and another teak bench but this time with diagonal latticework, which is flanked by a broad, yet low, *Buxus microphylla* var. *japonica* hedge. A sweet viburnum, *Viburnum odoratissimum* hedge, forms a backdrop to the layered planting and the bench, and its glossy green leaves produce a striking contrast with the cream wall behind.

On either side of the bench, a row of closely planted, pleached Manchurian pears, *Pyrus calleryana*, provides scale to the high wall and a cool canopy over the bench.

THE RESULT
A dramatic entry that forms a bold green axis to the front door. The planting also creates a perimeter around a cool, green, secret garden.

OPPOSITE AND ABOVE This French-inspired garden is completed by the inclusion of a stunning Anduze urn.

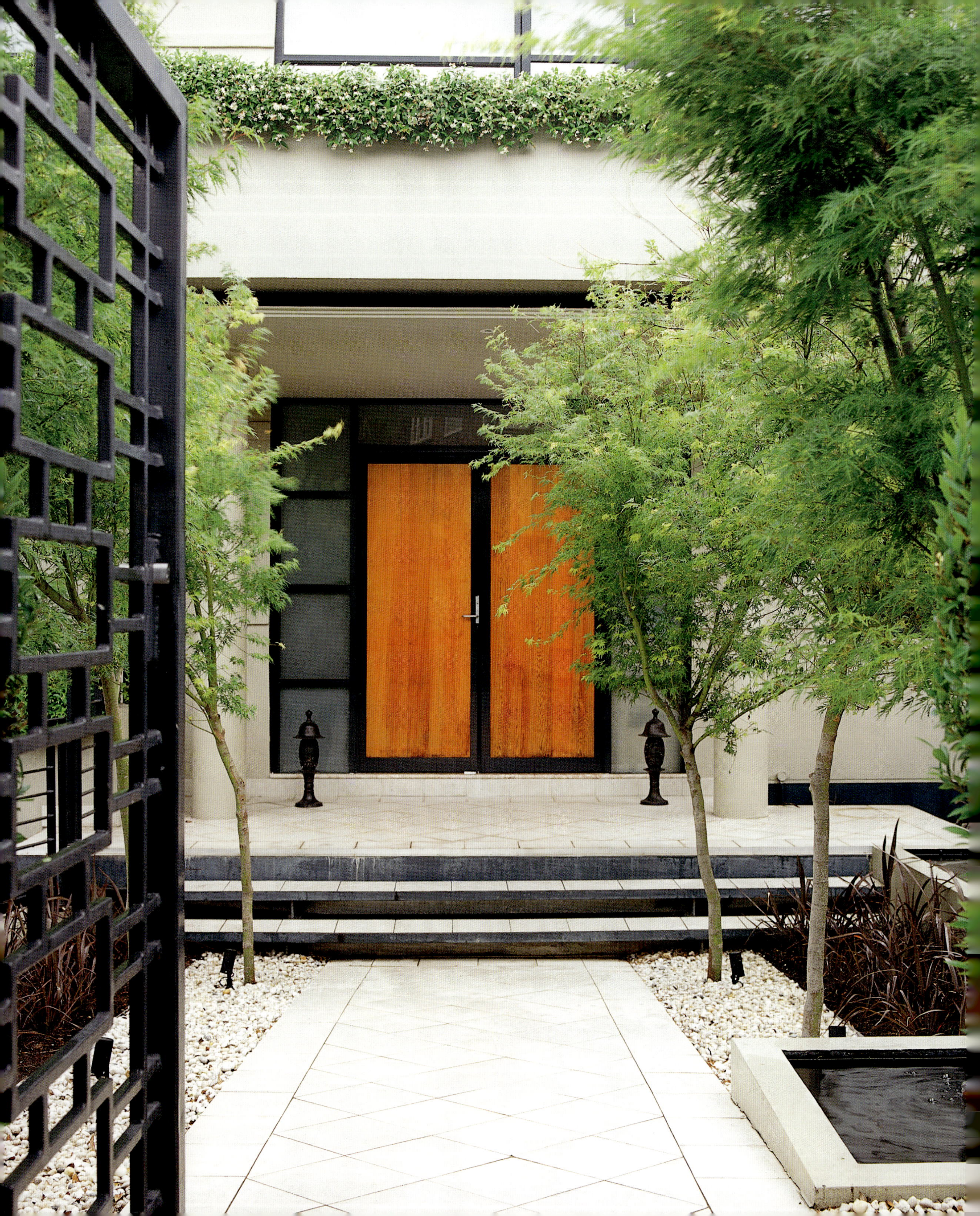

VISUAL ENLIGHTENMENT

THE SETTING
This was a modern, contemporary house in Northbridge, a Sydney suburb near Middle Harbour. The site was secluded, protected by walls.

THE BRIEF
To make the small open area around the front entrance look interesting from the house, and play with the proportions, so as to deceive the eye and make it seem larger than it really was.

THE DESIGN
The success of this modern garden lies in the design of the water feature. The narrow L-shaped pond stretches from the patio outside the front door to the front path – linking house and garden. Copper spouts below the surface give the water a rippling effect.

The pond was built to match the height of the cantilevered patio at the entrance and therefore is elevated at the house end, then runs the length of the boundary and returns towards the sloping path, with which it is now level. I did this to create a strong connection between the entry at the front gate and the front door.

The simple, clean lines of the garden also complement the modern architecture of the house. An avenue of Japanese maple trees, *Acer palmatum dissectum 'Seiryu'*, lines the stone-paved footpath to create a small–medium-size canopy over the pathway and to soften the strong lines of the house. These trees are planted within a border of large white pebbles that are a contrast in texture with the creamy paving.

Acer palmatum look delicate but are hardy trees. There is a large range of cultivars, from dwarf and weeping varieties to trees that will grow to about 6 metres. Some varieties will even grow in pots. They are deciduous and can be pruned in winter, to accentuate

OPPOSITE The influence that architecture has over garden design should never be underestimated; Japanese maple trees at the entrance relax the bold lines of the house. ABOVE The delicate shape of the Japanese maple leaf.

the branches' graceful shapes. The foliage turns brilliant shades of red, orange and yellow in autumn – some cultivars even becoming bright scarlet.

The garden's strong architectural form is reinforced by the use of New Zealand flax, *Phormium*, massed either side of the path and in front of the pond. I used the variety 'Dwarf Burgundy' for its brilliant colour and form. Some *Phormium* cultivars will grow to over a metre high, but this dwarf variety will not exceed about 75 centimetres. Its foliage is a deep, deep burgundy, and its bold sword-shaped leaves are extremely effective when used in a massed display.

A *Syzygium australe* hedge forms an evergreen screen around the garden's perimeter. This plant's common name is lilly pilly and it has glossy leaves that have a coppery tinge when young which will complement the red of the *Phormium*. It bears white flowers in summer that look fluffy owing to the large number of stamens protruding from the petals, which are followed by small ruby or purple edible fruits.

The overall effect on entering the garden is that the water forms a channel that disappears through the sword-shaped leaves of the flax and reappears at the front door. When viewed from the front door, at its slightly elevated position, the garden can be enjoyed in its entirety.

LEFT The bold and brilliant colour of the New Zealand flax is striking as a massed display. OPPOSITE Water is a powerful way to unify any space.

THE RESULT

The area as a whole now has a Japanese feel to it: the Japanese maple trees, the water feature and the stones all contribute to this. By keeping the number of elements in the small area to a minimum, I have enhanced the sense of space. The unusual elevation and shape of the water feature ensure that the eye returns to it. Now the unique architectural style of the house owns a garden to match.

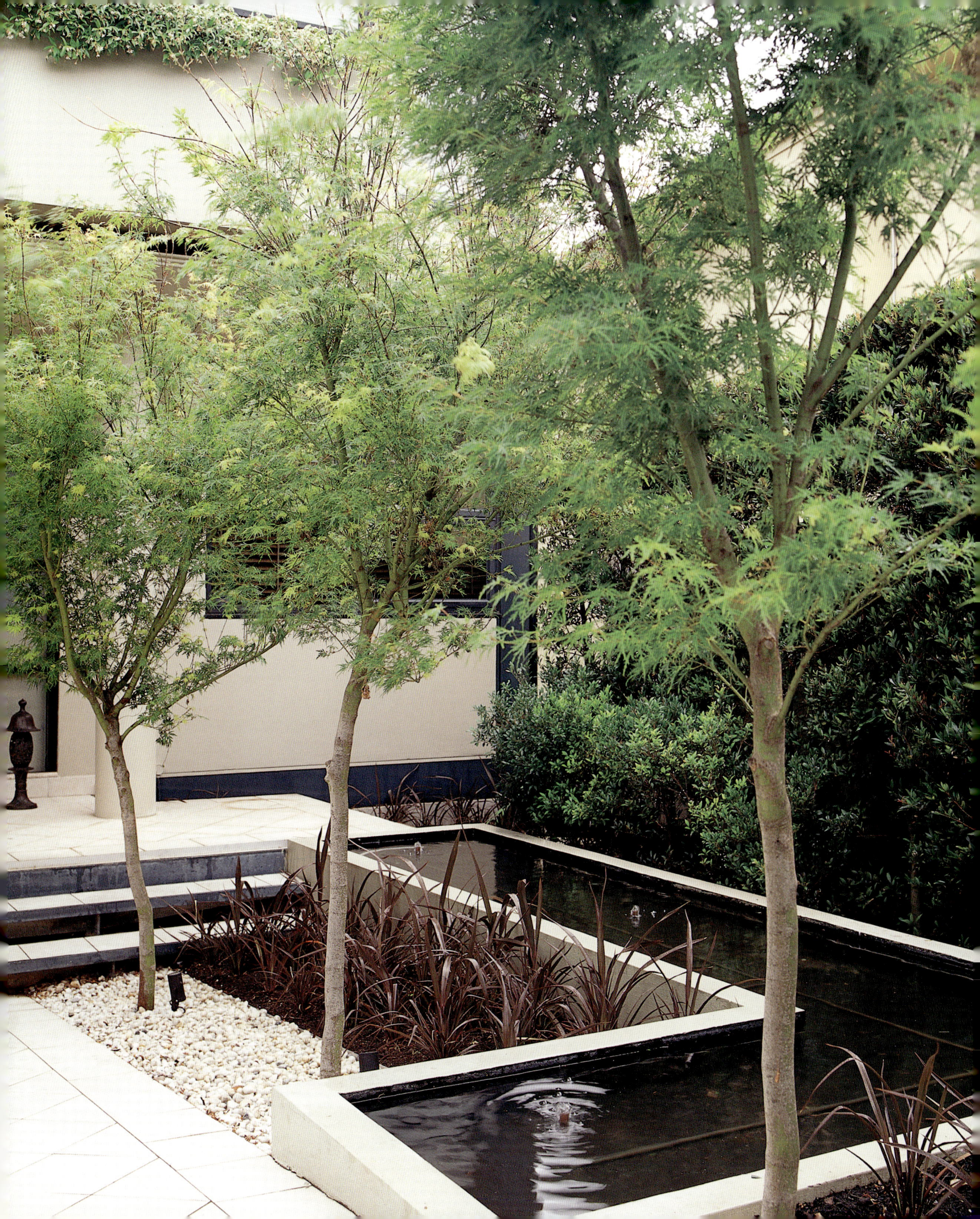

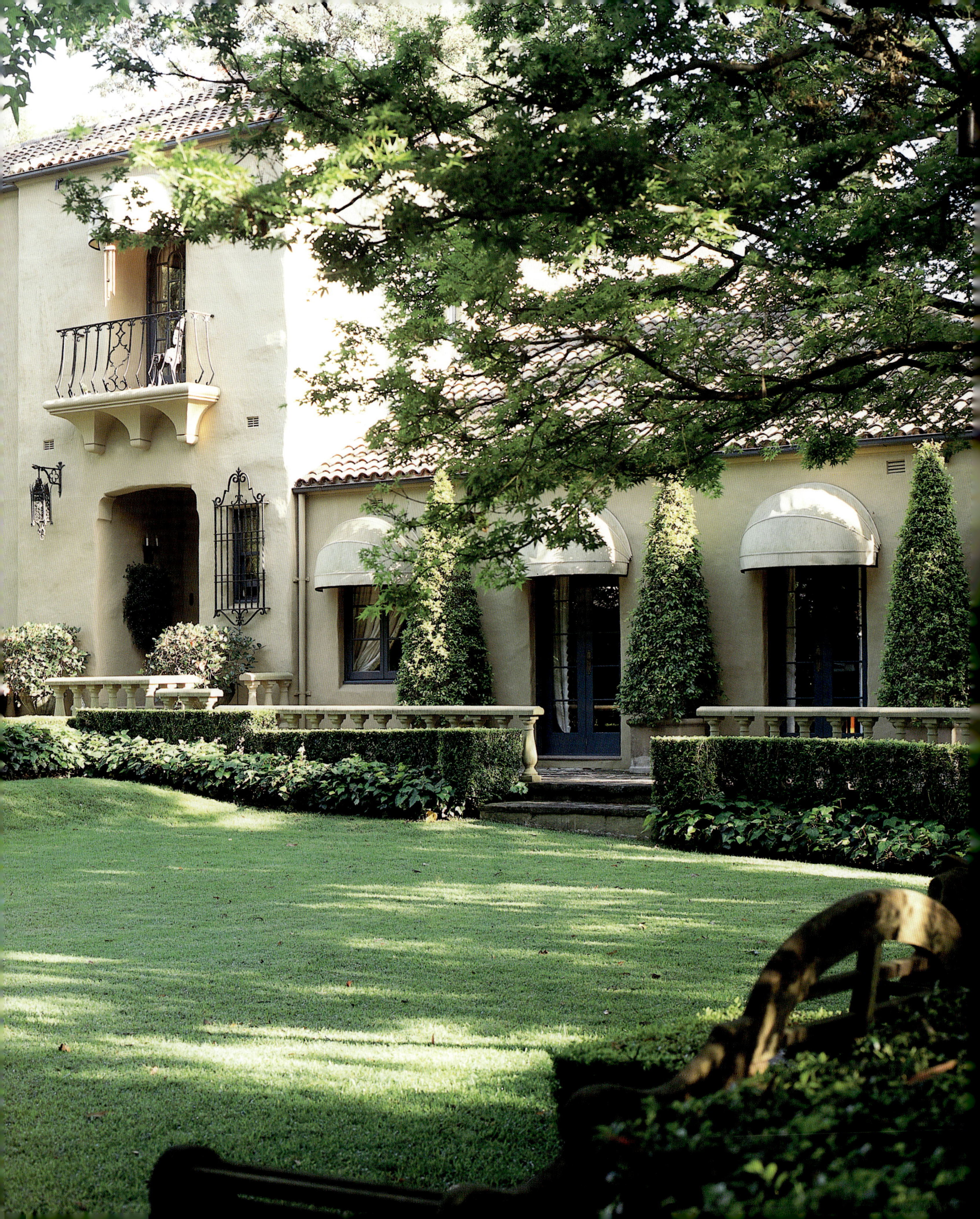

GARDEN OF EDEN

THE SETTING
This was a garden about 0.4 hectares in size – the old-fashioned one acre. It is situated in Wahroonga, on the Upper North Shore of Sydney.

THE BRIEF
Develop a garden! It was to be tackled in different stages over a period of time.

THE DESIGN
This house sits smack in the centre of a beautiful acre of land and there were remnants of indigenous vegetation throughout the site – gums and red turpentines. The whole property was mainly lawn, although a camellia walk was in existence, and around the garden were some mature trees planted by previous owners, such as a large *Magnolia grandiflora*. All of these we worked with so as to retain an established look in this garden.

The house's architecture and interiors were classically formal so I decided to design formal spaces immediately outside the house to create an easy transition between the house and garden. Because sandstone flagging was already extensively used throughout the existing garden, cream stone was used to pave the new transition areas.

The clients did not want to over-capitalise as they anticipated that they would be moving sooner rather than later, so I took this into account in my design. The emphasis was put on maximum visual impact rather than grand construction schemes. Hard construction work that was undertaken was only the bare necessities, and instead this garden relies on bold, stimulating plants in layers to create rooms and axes of view.

For example, I lined the existing drive with an avenue of pleached London plane trees, *Platanus* x *hybrida*, underplanted with a band of

OPPOSITE   Large lilly pilly cones in square pots provide the house with scale and balance. ABOVE   A large plane tree planted in the centre of the turning circle is a majestic sight on entering the property.

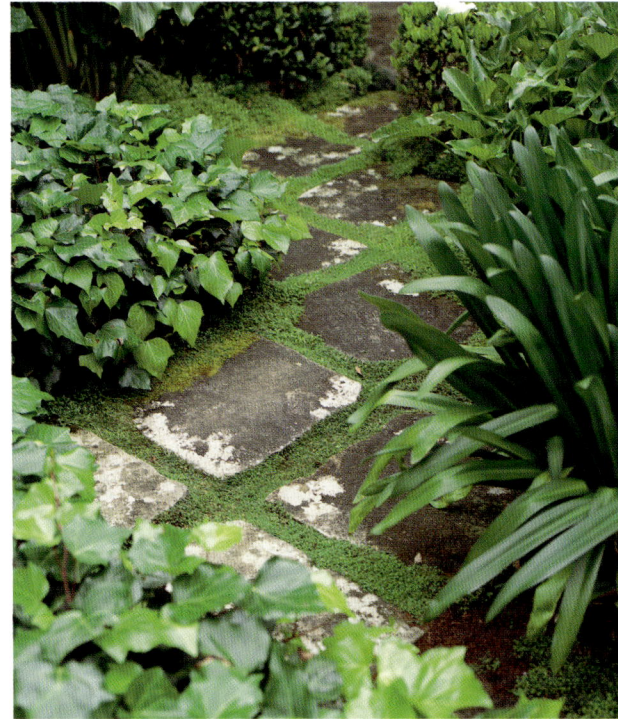

blue agapanthus, *Agapanthus orientalis*. In the centre of the drive I massed mondo grass, *Ophiopogon japonicus* 'Nana', a dwarf variety, therefore making the drive seem longer than it was, with the layers of vegetation playing off each other to create an attractive green tunnel.

Pleaching is a technique to weave together tree branches so they form a lattice or tunnel. It is known to have been practised by the Romans and is still popular today. Trees with flexible branches are most suitable for this technique, and fruit trees such as apple and pear and hawthorn, are all traditionally used for pleaching. In its most intricate form, pleaching involves making small cuts on suitable branches and grafting the tips of other trees' branches onto them, thus making the foliage one intergrowing entity; a simpler way of pleaching is to plant trees reasonably close together, then prune the branches to encourage lateral growth and in a few years the foliage will have become thickly intertwined.

Proceeding down the straight, pleached drive from the entrance, the garden opens up forming a circular bed. In there I decided to plant a mature London plane tree, left to form its natural habit, which will also provide shade and give the house scale. This also picks up the theme of the plane trees which were used in the drive. Under this central plane tree I planted descending circular beds of hedged *Murraya* and agapanthus again, to repeat the scheme elsewhere – so the disparate parts of this very large garden remain connected.

Plane trees are fast-growing and can reach up to 20 metres in height. I did not want to wait for the impact of this tree to make itself felt, however, so I planted a 5 metre tall specimen that came in a 400 litre pot! Planes' canopy is spreading and they are useful as shade trees. In addition, the bark on their trunks flakes attractively, leaving visually appealing patterns in brown, grey and silver.

The front garden was not used much by the clients, so I kept it really simple: mostly lawn, with *Camellia japonica* 'Nuccio's Gem' around the outside. The camellias would grow higher, but these are being pruned to about 2 metres. 'Nuccio's Gem' has medium-large, white, formal blooms, double rather than single, the petals being arranged in a spiral pattern – it's a stunner, in fact. 'Nuccio's Gem' likes shelter from sun and wind but apart from that is easy to grow. Its glossy evergreen foliage forms a constant perimeter around the extensive boundary of the front garden, and in spring the beautiful formal white flowers are a delight to the eye. In front of the camellias, forming a border around the entire lawn, we planted a band of *Hedera canariensis* – large-leaf ivy, which is sometimes

OPPOSITE The Lutyens bench is positioned centrally on the eastern boundary between two stone sphinxes and offers captivating views of the expansive front garden.

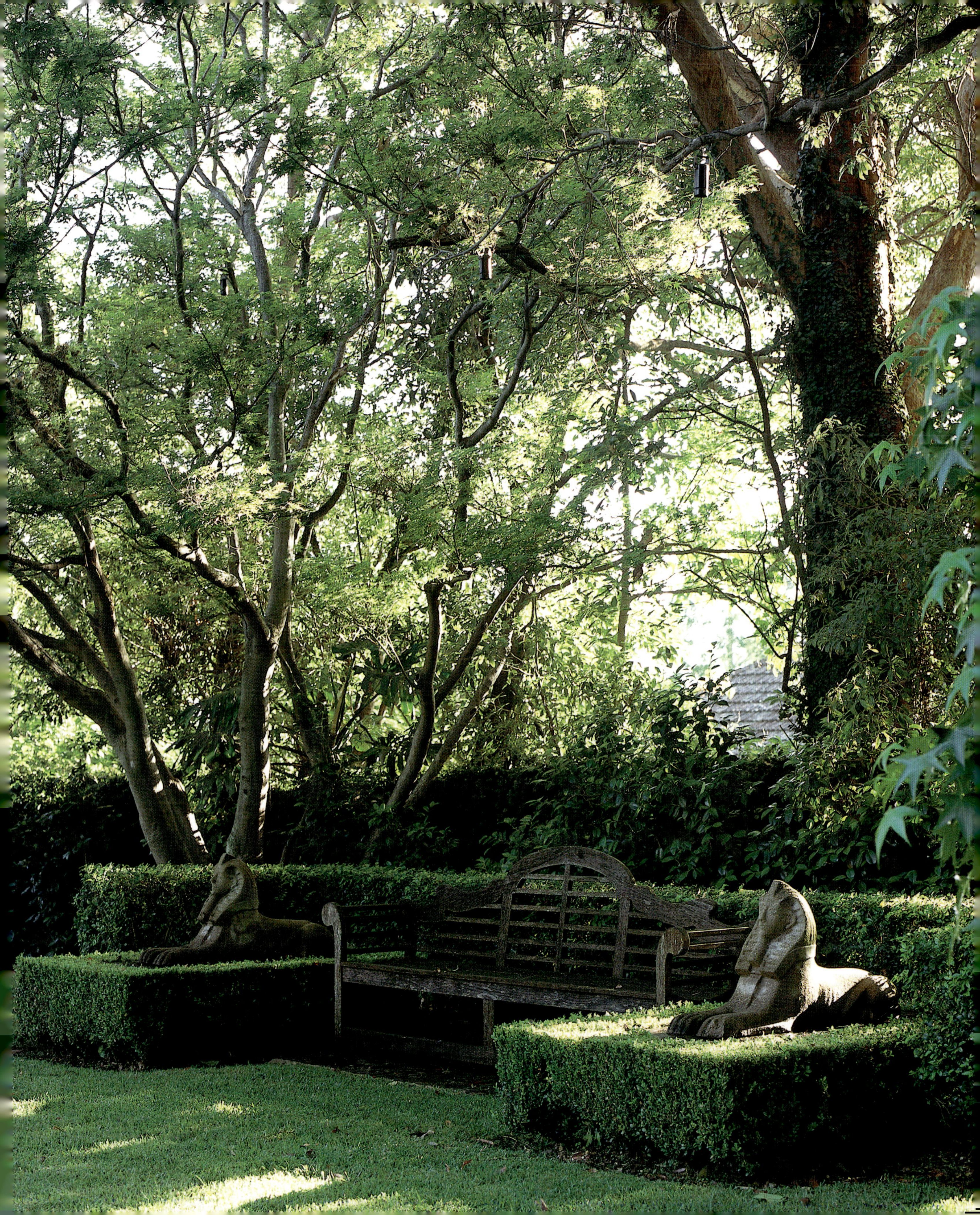

ABOVE Buxus cones in stone pots give the terrace a greater level of intimacy and some separation from the vast back garden. *OPPOSITE* The canopy of existing Camellia japonicas has been lifted to encourage them to form a living green colonnade over the path.

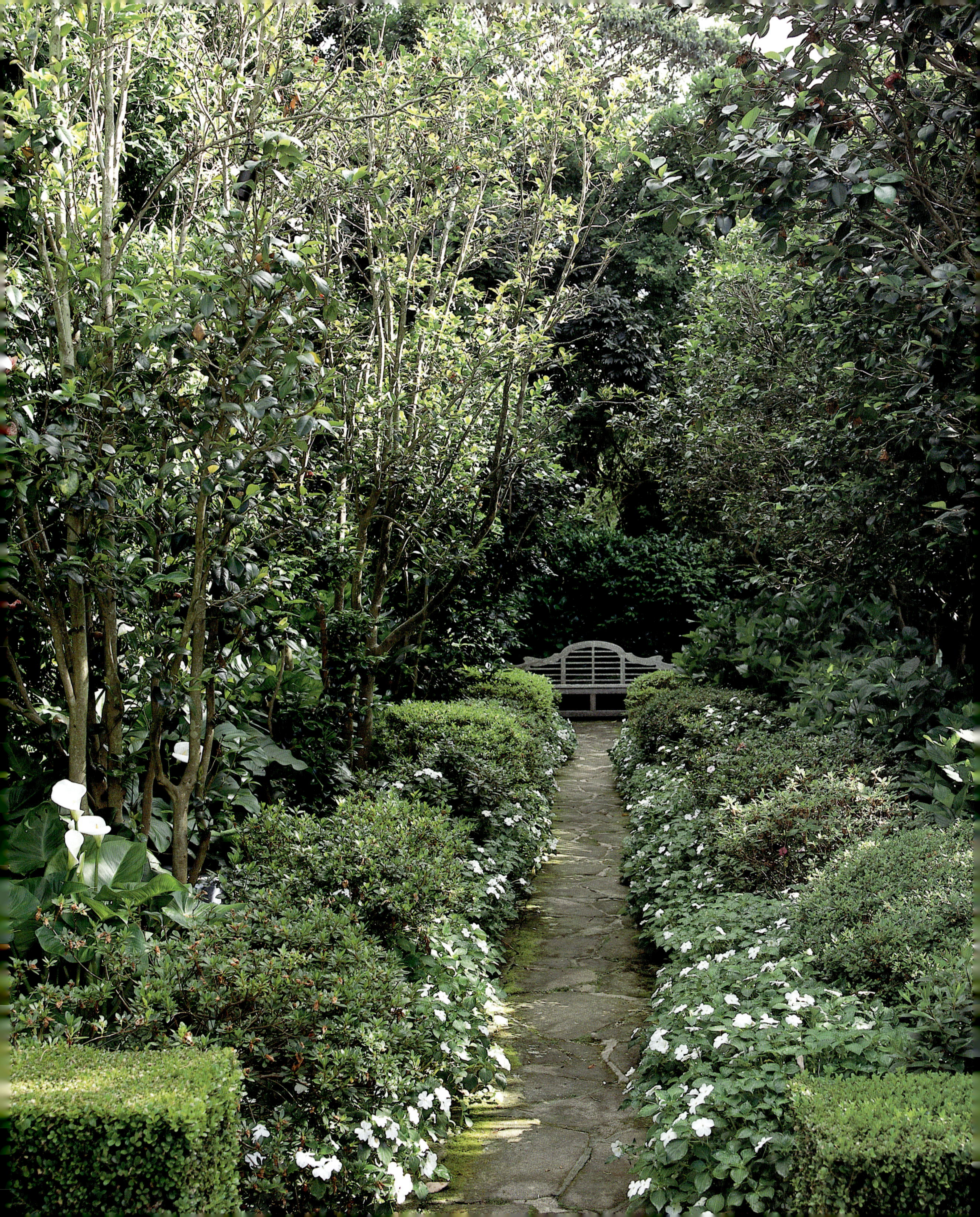

known as Canary ivy, or Algerian ivy. The effect of rolling green lawns running into large-leaf ivy, one of my favourite groundcovers, with the camellias as a backdrop, is sumptuously lush and green.

There are some beds close to the front of the house behind the expanse of lawn. These are bordered by agapanthus and arum lilies, *Zantedeschia aethiopica*, with a *Murraya* hedge forming a green foundation behind them, against the wall of the house.

A stone path lined up with agapanthus and arums once again leads to the front door. Opposite the front door a centrally located Victorian urn with a square of clipped *Buxus microphylla* var. *japonica*, a small-leaved box, at the base breaks up the paving and creates directional certainty for the visitor about the location of the front door.

At one end of the massive lawn area two stone sphinxes sit at either side of a Lutyens teak bench, all enveloped by *Buxus microphylla* var. *japonica*, forming green block work. A *Murraya* hedge is the backdrop to the bench. This type of bench has been perennially popular since it was designed by the renowned British architect Sir Edwin Lutyens for his friend, the garden designer and prolific author Gertrude Jekyll. They worked together on many English gardens in the early twentieth century – Lutyens was often the buildings' architect in these shared projects – and their designs were very influential; Jekyll brought the English country garden into prominence, while Lutyens' garden furniture combined elements of the Arts and Crafts movement with classic simplicity.

I had originally intended a 'canal' garden at the front, but this idea had been shelved as it would have required an excessive amount of construction. However, I was still able to work with water, incorporating two features in the garden. The back garden had an existing pond with a fountain that sat 'floating visually' at the rear of the house. I therefore extended the paving from the house, creating a terrace for welcoming wicker furniture. On the terrace I placed plain concrete pots planted with *Buxus microphylla* var. *japonica*, clipped into dramatic rounded cones. These cones give an element of formality to the terrace without intimidating – their shapes create visual interest and are a talking point. The terrace is now a place from which the occupants of the house can view the garden in comfort and yet feel part of it, while drinking a coffee or cocktail.

The existing fountain, which is located centrally to this aspect of the house, sits below the terrace; we connected the two with a network of stone-paved paths. Four corner beds surround the fountain, and in each of these we massed a formal parterre consisting of *Buxus microphylla* var. *japonica* hedge containing blocks of dark green *Buxus sempervirens*, which grows taller than the *B. microphylla*. A mop top robinia – unpruned – sits in the centre of each of those four beds while a stone path, lined up with the fountain, forms an axis from the house to the back boundary. I bordered this path with white balsam, *Impatiens balsamina*, whose flowers edge prettily along the stone paving, then existing azalea bushes and, behind these, existing *Camellia japonicas* form the green walls of this colonnade. The path led to another Lutyens bench surrounded by *Buxus microphylla* var. *japonica* in pots – clipped into balls here – and with formal squares of box around them.

Mop top robinias are relatively recent introductions to the garden, but have quickly become very popular. They are made by grafting a dwarf *Robinia pseudoacacia* 'Umbraculifera' top to a more vigorous *Robinia* stem. The result is a round ball of foliage which retains its shape without requiring constant attention. *Robinia* is deciduous, with attractive jade green foliage that turns yellow in autumn. There are drawbacks in planting this tree, however, as *Robinia pseudoacacia*, also known as black locust or false acacia, is prone to suckering; its roots throw up suckers wherever they meet an

OPPOSITE This ornate fountain, with a flower and leaf pattern, was moulded from a unique terracotta tile that I purchased in France on holiday.
ABOVE The formal planting is instantly made more casual with the inclusion of the birch groves.

obstacle in the soil. This will not be a problem in a garden of this size, but can be a nuisance in a small suburban block. If the soil is undisturbed around robinias' roots they are less likely to sucker.

To the left of the camellia walk a large expanse of lawn grows under the remnant native red turpentines, *Syncarpia glomulifera*, and blue gums, *Eucalyptus saligna*, forming a woodland that is a pleasing contrast to the formality that surrounds the house.

To the right of the camellia walk another lawn area was created to form a birch garden room. The lawn is surrounded by a *Murraya* hedge, with a band of gardenias in front of it and then autumn crocus, *Zephyranthes candida*. Once again the layered look was implemented, giving consistency across the different areas of this large garden. We planted groves of silver birch, *Betula pendula*, throughout this lawn to form a different style of woodland, complementing the native gums.

Between the birch woodland lawn and the boundary I designed a Mediterranean garden. A tiled feature wall sits on the boundary; this lines up with the fountain in the parterre along a visual axis that crosses three garden rooms. I had purchased an antique terracotta tile with a leaf and flower pattern in France one holiday and I had this moulded and copied in reconstituted stone. These new tiles were placed within the niche of the feature wall, making a rectangle approximately 2.5 metres high by 1.6 metres wide, and the whole was turned into a water wall. That is, water flows over the tiles into a narrow pond, playing over the patterned tiles as it does so. In front of the feature wall stone square pavers surrounded by mondo grass form a chequerboard floor covering, while an Anduze urn sits central to this area. Garden areas to either side of this water feature are massed with blocks and layers of *Buxus microphylla* var. *japonica*, *Murraya* and *Viburnum odoratissimum*, sweet viburnum.

Anduze urns are very large, hand-thrown earthenware pots traditionally made in the town of Anduze in Languedoc, southern France. Their shape is based on Greek and Roman amphora and they are decorated with garlands and seals whose inspiration comes from eighteenth-century motifs. Anduze urns have always been made as outdoor, planter pots. They are unmistakably French, and therefore the urn was ideal for the Mediterranean theme of this garden room.

Because the Mediterranean garden is viewed from the house at the same time as the birch woodland, I also extended the birch planting into it. The elegant, pendulous branches of the trees soften the feature wall, giving scale as well as a mysterious air.

One further, smaller garden room was created on one side of the house. Here a large colonial urn was the focal point. It was planted with *Liriope muscari* 'Evergreen Giant' and had a frame of clipped box underneath, all under the canopy of the large *Magnolia grandiflora*.

THE RESULT

It is sometimes difficult to work with existing structure in a garden, but in this case I managed to tie the bones of what was already in the garden together with the new look, and to link it all in with the architecture of the house, creating a harmonious whole. In fact, the overall look of the garden now is one of luxuriousness, with a hint of mystery in places.

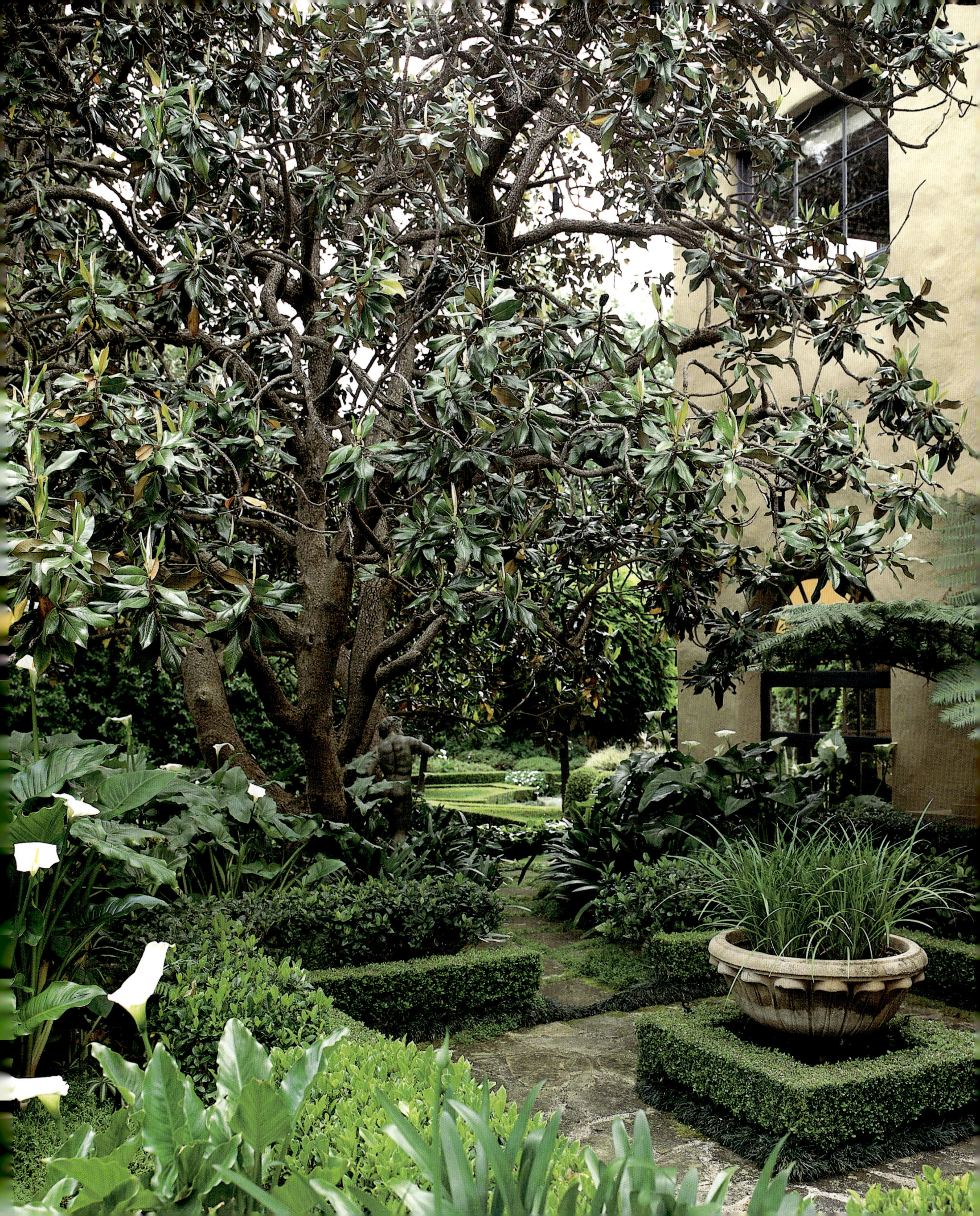

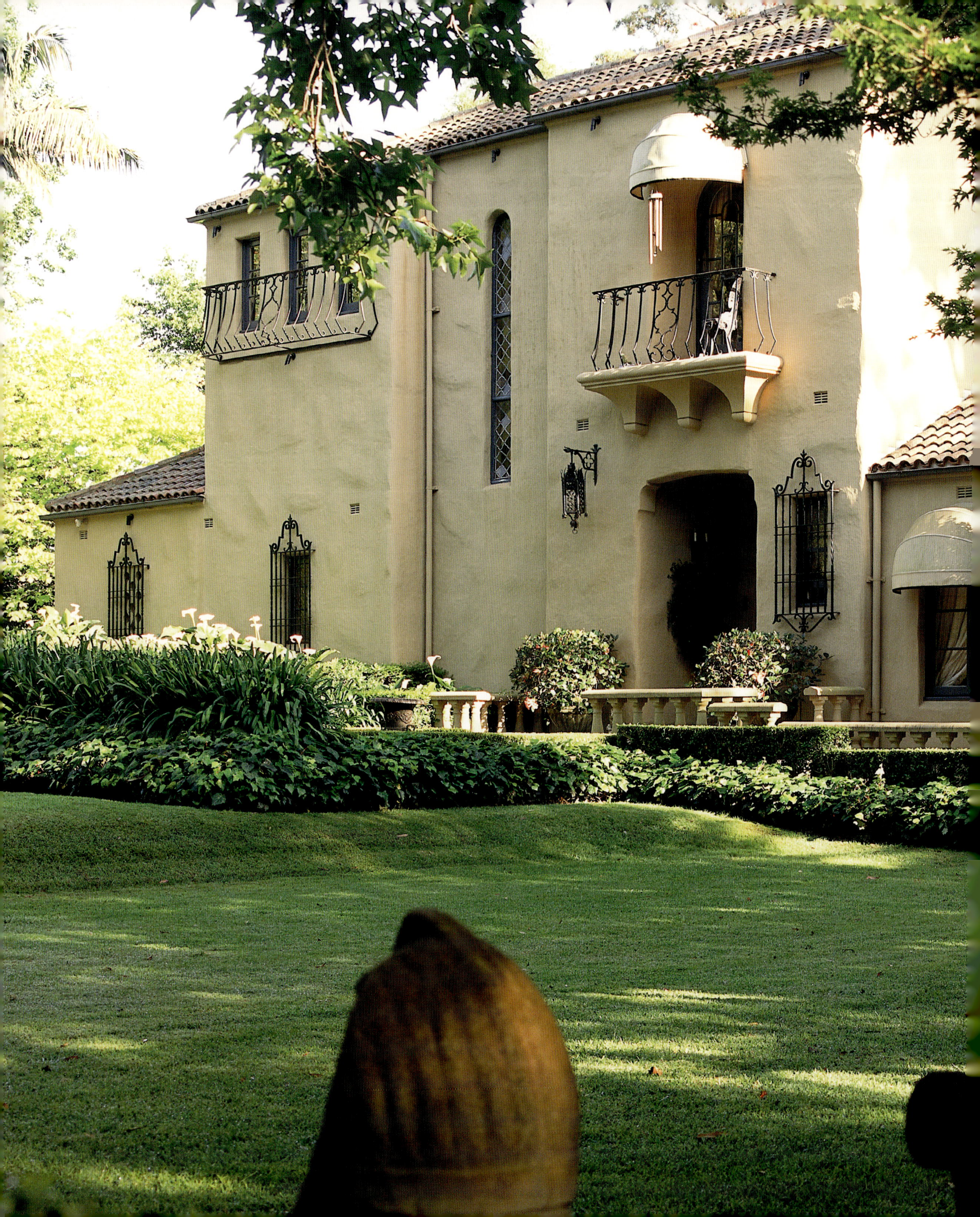

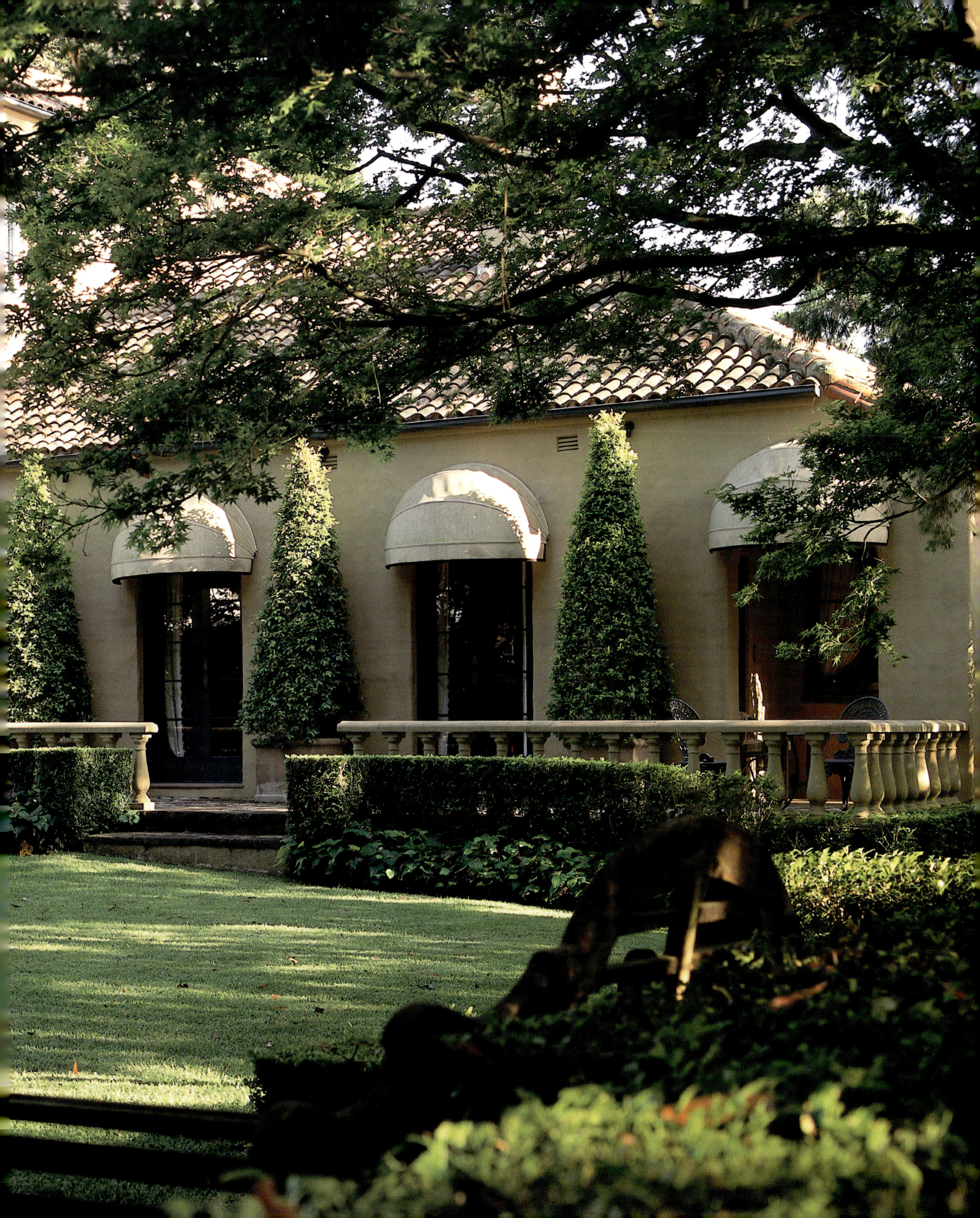

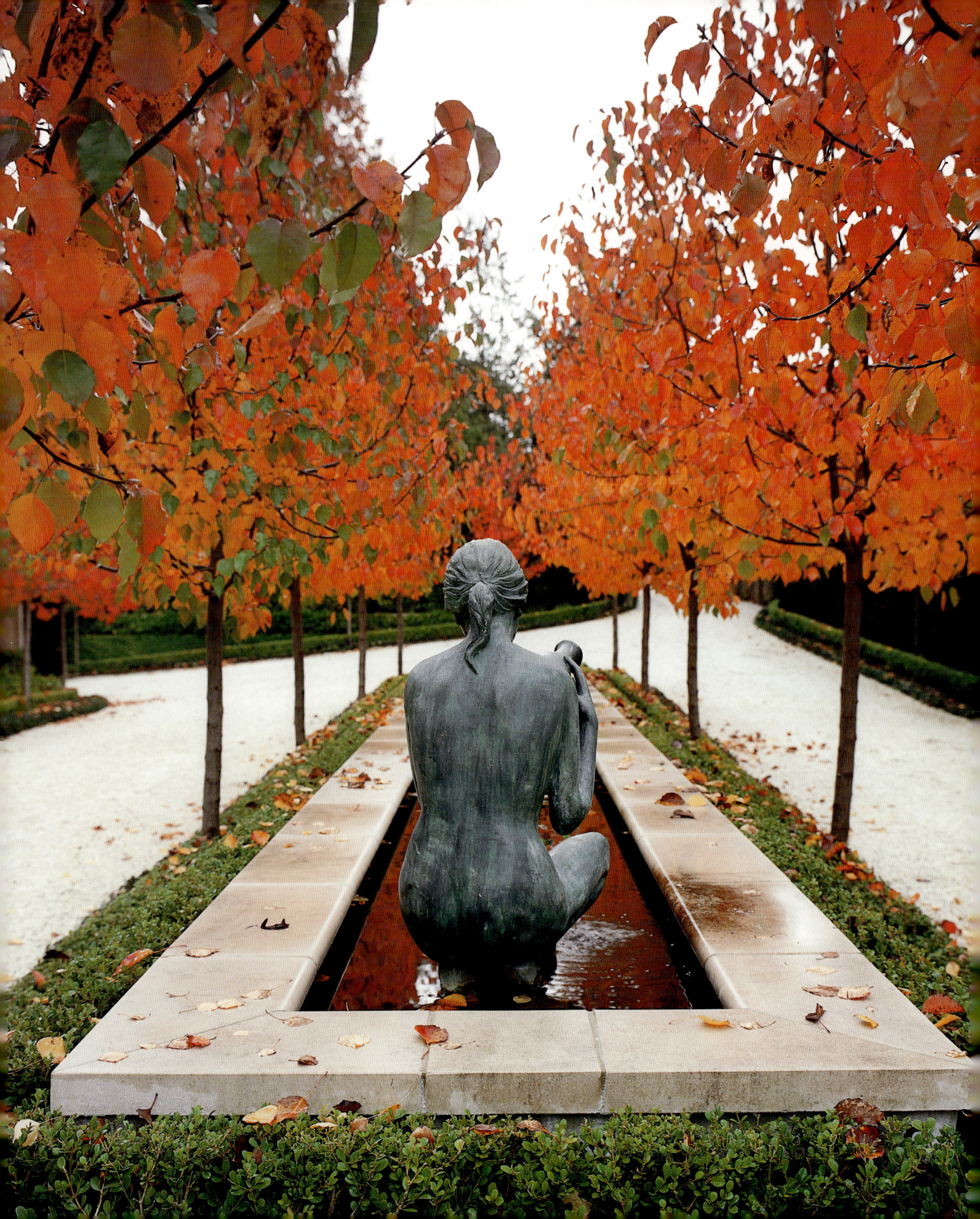

MANCHURIAN DRIVE

THE SETTING
A new front garden was required. The existing garden had a long, battleaxe-shaped drive leading to the imposing portico entrance of the house. The house itself is in French chateau style, and is situated on the Upper North Shore in Sydney.

THE BRIEF
This was an awkward space to design and beautify. The long driveway led to a large area directly in front of the house. The client was keen to create a classic turning circle so cars could easily enter and leave the property. The style and grand scale of the house dictated a formal, classical design of generous proportions.

THE DESIGN
For this design to work the area would need to be level, so the first job was to construct medium-sized walls that created terraces, instantly separating the new circular drive garden from the rest of the garden.

Once the driveway and the area around it was level I then enclosed the space with tall narrow hedges of *Juniperus chinensis* 'Keteleerii', a dense juniper that grows to 5 metres and can be hedged easily, and *Murraya paniculata*, orange jessamine, hedges where height was not required. To separate the drive area and the house a 1 metre high *Murraya paniculata* hedge was planted between the two. In front of the *Murraya* and *Juniperus* hedges, lower *Buxus microphylla* var. *japonica* hedges defined the elongated drive shape.

In the centre of the turning circle at the top of the drive I designed a bed with a centrepiece of a 12 metre long by 60 centimetre wide raised pond. The pond is centrally positioned outside the front door and portico, across the circle. At one end of the pond a simple bronze lady fountain lines up directly square with the living-room windows. To soften the impact of the raised pond and to provide

OPPOSITE The autumn foliage of the pear trees is always a stunning surprise for visitors arriving at the house.

OPPOSITE *The bronze lady fountain was chosen for her simple yet true-to-human scale and form.*

a more seamless result, double *Buxus microphylla* var. *japonica* hedges were planted to envelop the pond, supporting its elevated position but at the same time connecting it visually to the ground.

On entering this garden from the long battleaxe-shaped drive, an important axis has been created, looking down the length of the pond. To emphasise the pond's length and to create a 'wow' factor, I planted an avenue of *Pyrus calleryana*, Manchurian pear, either side of this dramatic feature. I then repeated another row of these pears in the bed against the house, either side of the portico, thus connecting this garden to the house.

When we were installing the garden I made a point of asking the client to test the space intended as a turning circle to make sure it was practical, as I wanted to minimise the dominant drive as much as possible. A thin layer of cream gravel was used as the surface for the driveway, to make the area seem less severe.

On either side of the drive's narrow battleaxe 'handle', from the pond to the gate, I continued the Manuchurian pear avenue, planting the trees straight into the gravel – a very dramatic look. All the pear trees are pruned to retain their natural shape, but also to keep them small.

Beside this part of the driveway there were painted paling fences, up which *Trachelospermum jasminoides*, star jasmine, was trained. The jasmine has now covered the fences and been pruned into a tight, narrow hedge, forming a wonderful backdrop to the Manchurian pears.

THE RESULT

I was really happy with the result as my fear was the entire front garden would need to be given over to the drive, leaving no garden at all. The pear trees provide scale and soften the classical lines of the house and driveway. They also give a majestic sweep of colour – both from the house and coming down the drive – and changing seasonal interest.

The pond, which breaks the drive's expanse, provides balanced views from most rooms within the house. The scheme is bold, simple and practical.

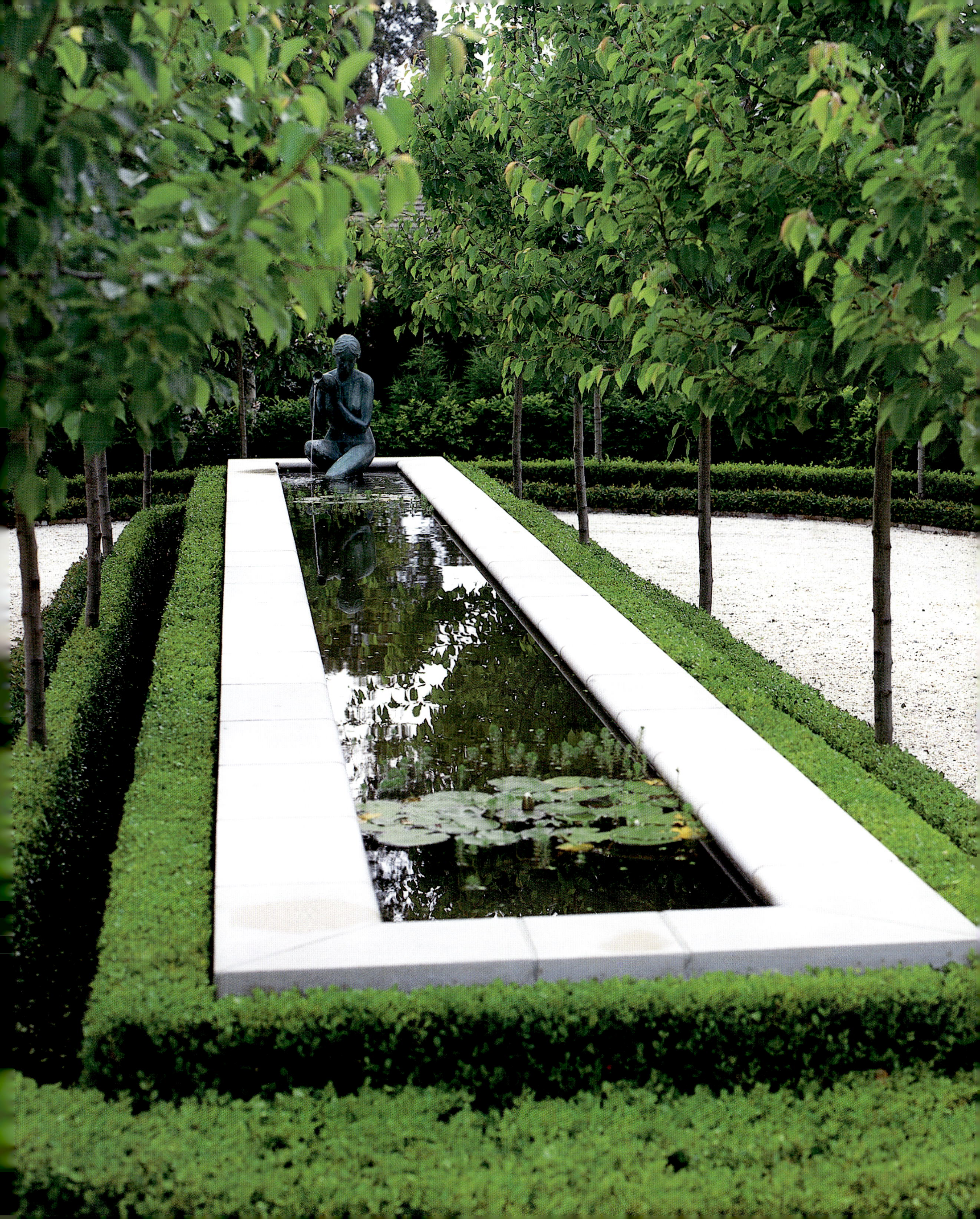

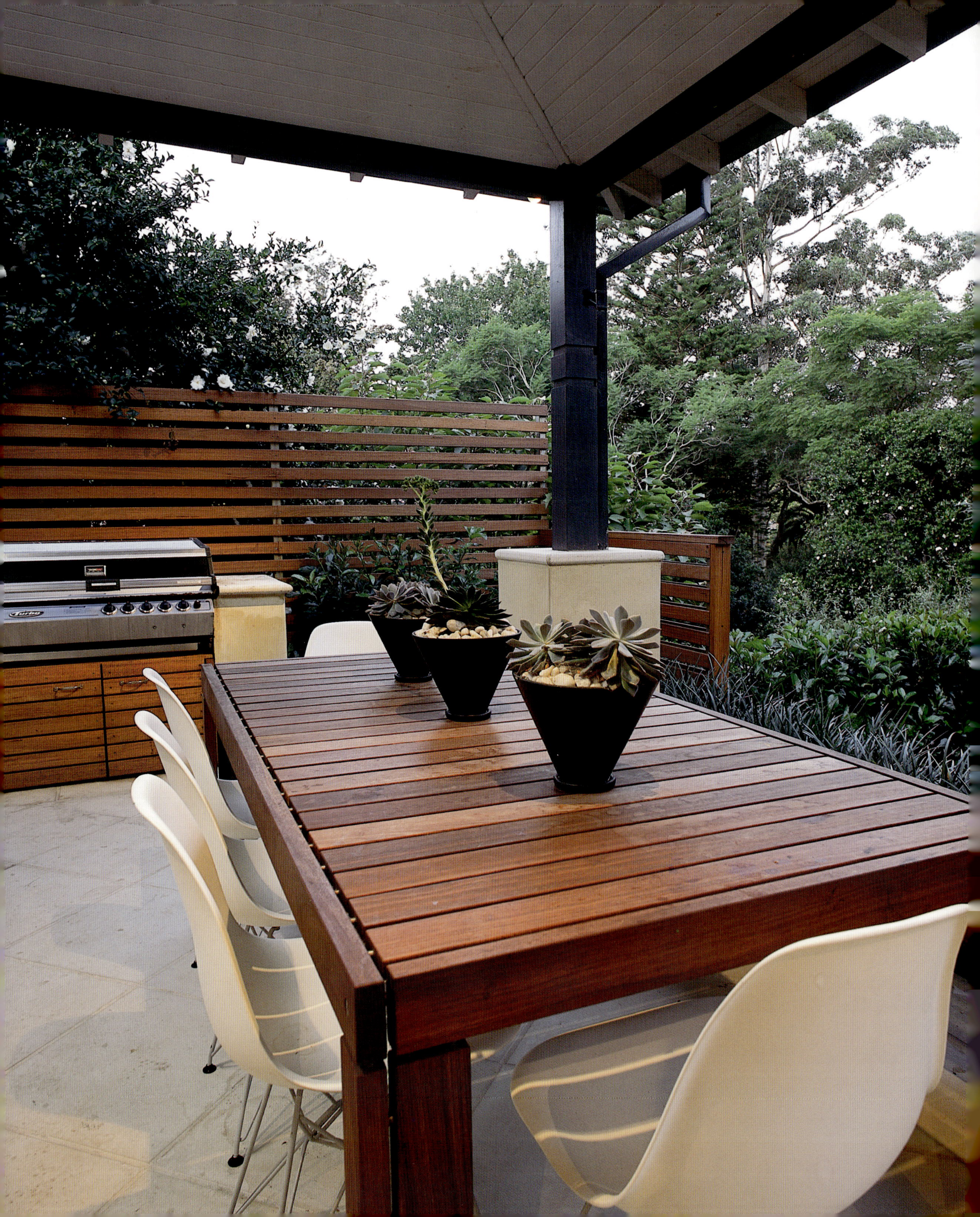
Turbo

INTEGRATED LIVING

THE SETTING
This was a large Sydney North Shore garden in Lindfield. It surrounded a Federation house set on a large block owned by a family with young children.

The new owners of the home had modernised it internally, especially the living spaces leading out to the back garden, but the house's Federation façade had been maintained.

THE BRIEF
The owners' brief was a welcome challenge. They wanted a garden that related to the traditional shell of the house and yet with a style that exhibited a more contemporary edge, which fitted in with their contemporary interior taste.

THE DESIGN
I love houses such as this one that exhibit a contrast in style – when you expect the Federation style of the exterior to continue internally, and then you are surprised with a modern twist.

In the end my strategy for the garden was quite simple. I decided to create a series of garden rooms flowing from the house that were balanced and complementary to the classic style of the building. However, instead of using some of the obvious, traditional plants that I feel help make a classic garden whole, I decided to suggest to the clients that we complement the proposed garden bones with a more contemporary palette of plants. They were open to this and after some toing and froing we had a list of plants that would soften the structure, create a visual 'wow' factor and require relatively little maintenance.

First, I decided to excavate half of the front garden in order to construct a sunken garden, one that was in fact level with the carport that was situated on one side of the front garden. Opposite

OPPOSITE Mixing up seating with conventional chairs and permanent benches instantly relaxes your entertaining space. ABOVE Mass Pennisetum aloepecuriodes *is at home against the sandstone wall of the verandah, and contrasts with the layered hedging of* Michelia coco *in the foreground and the* Viburnum odoratissimum *behind.*

the front door in this sunken space a square paved area with a central pond and fountain was created. I also lined up the front gate and pedestrian entry to the garden with the front door, which produced a powerful axis. The paved area was more than just visually important to me as it also had a practical role. In any garden the area directly outside the front door needs to be generous, otherwise people leaving the property feel rushed as they do so. In other words, 'transition zones' need to be large enough to feel welcoming (even though people may be leaving!).

So instead of using a formal planting scheme to define the garden structure I selected a more contemporary selection. However, in order to complement the classic garden lines, I planted in formal bands. Surrounding the paving a 60 centimetre wide band of striking, dark-leaved *Ajuga reptans* 'Jungle Giant' softens the stone; traditionally I would have used box hedging. Behind the *Ajuga* is a band of *Lomandra longifolia* 'Tanika', which forms a beautiful bright-green contrast. Its habit is like a perfectly rounded spinifex form approximately 60 centimetres in diameter, with very fine strap-like leaves; the species is a native Australian rush, whose leaves were used for weaving baskets and eel traps by Aboriginal people. Traditionally, instead of the *Lomandra* I would have planted a band of *Gardenia augusta* 'Florida' or a *Hebe* species.

The next layer that defines the perimeter of the sunken garden is *Michelia figo* 'Coco', a dwarf port wine magnolia. With its superbly scented flowers and less vigorous habit than standard *Michelia*, this dwarf version forms a neat hedge both against the house and the walls that separate the sunken garden from the raised garden above. In each corner of the paving and highlighting the central axis I planted four *Pyrus nivalis*, snow pears, which grow naturally over the paving to form a beautiful canopy and shade the sunken garden.

A central axis from the pond draws the eye to the bench and garden above. This higher garden consists of a rectangular lawn bordered by bands of a New Zealand rush, *Isolepis nodosa*, and a spectacular avenue of the pink-stemmed Japanese maple, *Acer palmatum* 'Sango Kaku'. It is sometimes called the coral-barked maple and its bright pink trunk and branches can be a stunning eye-catcher in winter when the foliage has fallen.

Along the side path a row of *Viburnum odoratissimum* 'Emerald Lustre' forms the perimeter hedging and a 1 metre high *Michelia coco* in front of it produces a double hedge to the side stone path. To break up and complement the sandstone foundations of the house and sandstone paving I selected the beautiful *Pennisetum alopecuriodes*, fountain grass, forming a really dramatic contrast with the clipped hedging on the other side of the path. *Pennisetum alopecuriodes* is an Australian native, a clumping grass that is found naturally from Queensland to Tasmania. It bears pinky–purple feathery flowerheads on long stems held above the arching leaves.

ABOVE LEFT *The entry courtyard provides glimpses of the garden beyond.*
ABOVE RIGHT *A steady flow of water bubbles from the fountain.*
OPPOSITE *The tall fountain in lower garden room lines up with the bench in the above garden.*

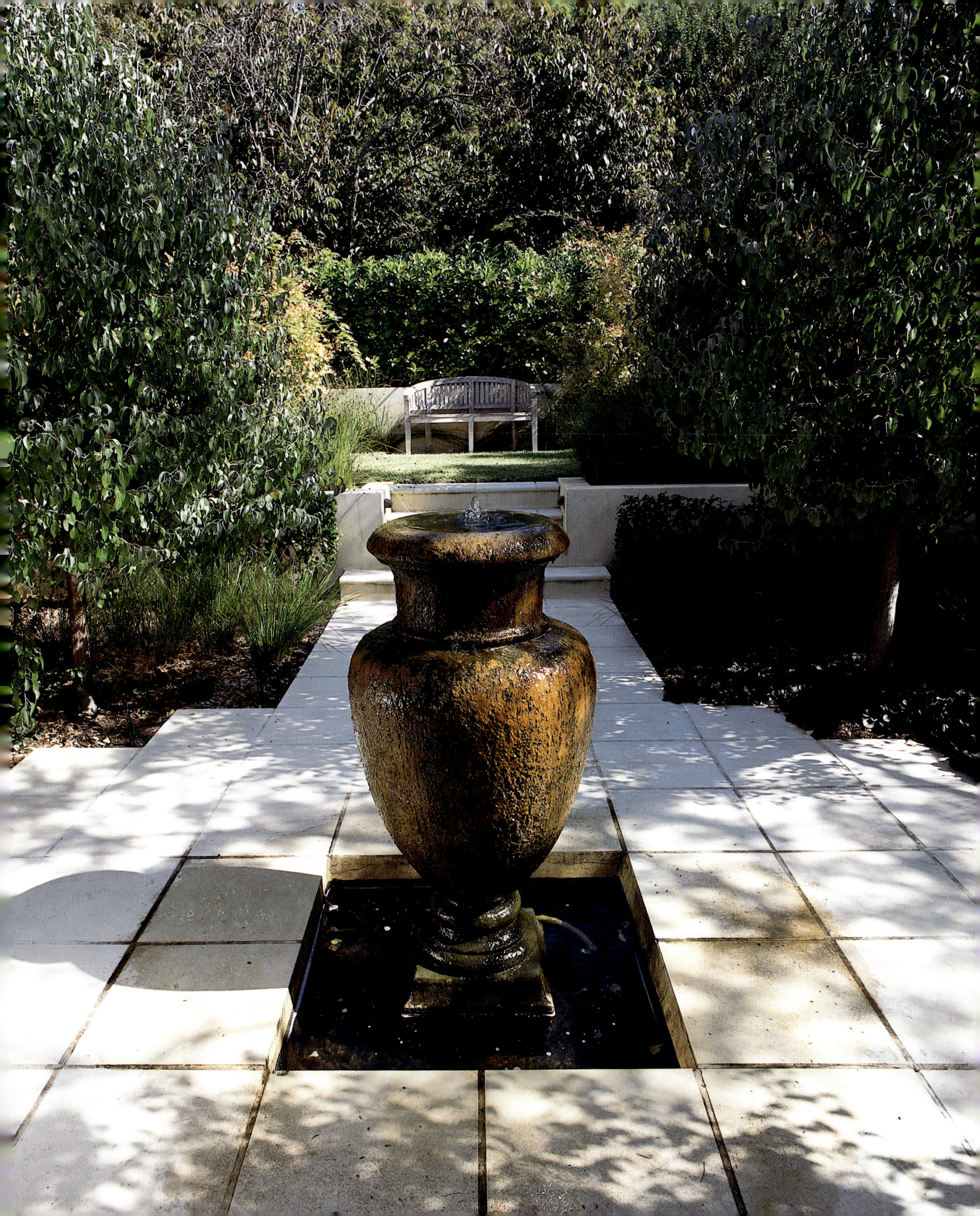

as the house's back elevation was not flat but had a recess, the entertainment terrace lent itself to being divided into two zones. The main entertaining area – for serious wining and dining – was located directly outside the French doors. To give this area a sense of casualness, I designed two slatted timber benches between four pillars, which help to declutter the entertaining space as the outdoor dining table can be moved against them when it is not in use. At one end of the terrace and not too far from the table I designed a built-in barbecue with a slatted screen behind it to provide more intimacy for this area. The use of timber slatting also brings continuity. Large 50 centimetre square pavers were used here, matching those in the front paved area.

In the semi-recessed space, on the same level as the parents' entertaining area, I designed a timber and steel day bed/bench which the kids could sit at, play on or lie on. In this area I broke up the paving with three individual garden beds where I planted Magnolia 'Little Gem' (a dwarf variety of *Magnolia grandiflora*, with the beautifully fragrant white flowers of its parent), which form 3 metre high cylindrical cones. This was my attempt to give this very tall house a bit of scale.

The second level was two steps lower than the entertaining level and to one side of the property. I designed a pool here that lines up with the dining room windows and sits directly below the children's entertaining area, giving them easy access to it. As the pool is dramatic, being long, narrow and black, it also becomes an attractive water feature when viewed from the dining room. The simple lines of this rectangular pool are balanced by a planter box along the perimeter wall so that it sits more comfortably in its elevated position above the lawn to its rear. The planter box supports a continuation of the *Viburnum odoratissimum* 'Emerald Lustre' screen that is carried through from the front garden, with massed *Liriope muscari* 'Evergreen Giant' planted in front of the viburnum. Its dark foliage tones in well with the pool's colour and forms a strong contrast to the viburnum.

The third terrace level was a level lawn that could be accessed from both the main terrace and the pool. The steps leading to the lawn from the main terrace line up with the French doors at the back of the house. Four bowls planted with striking *Agave attenuata* and mulched with black pebbles sit on specially designed pedestals either side of both flights of steps.

In the big back garden I had a lot of scope to play with, and the clients' brief was quite open – they wanted a large entertaining area consisting of two zones, one for parents and one for children. They also wanted a swimming pool, a level lawn area and an area where the children could run wild and have all their necessary play equipment. Because this large block had a significant slope on it I thought the best way to design it would be to really familiarise myself with the house's rooms that adjoined the back garden. Having done this I decided to create four different levels within the back garden, each with a different function.

The first level adjoining the house I made into a large, paved entertaining area that spanned the width of the property. And

OPPOSITE Placing the pool close to the house is a good utilisation of space in the garden.

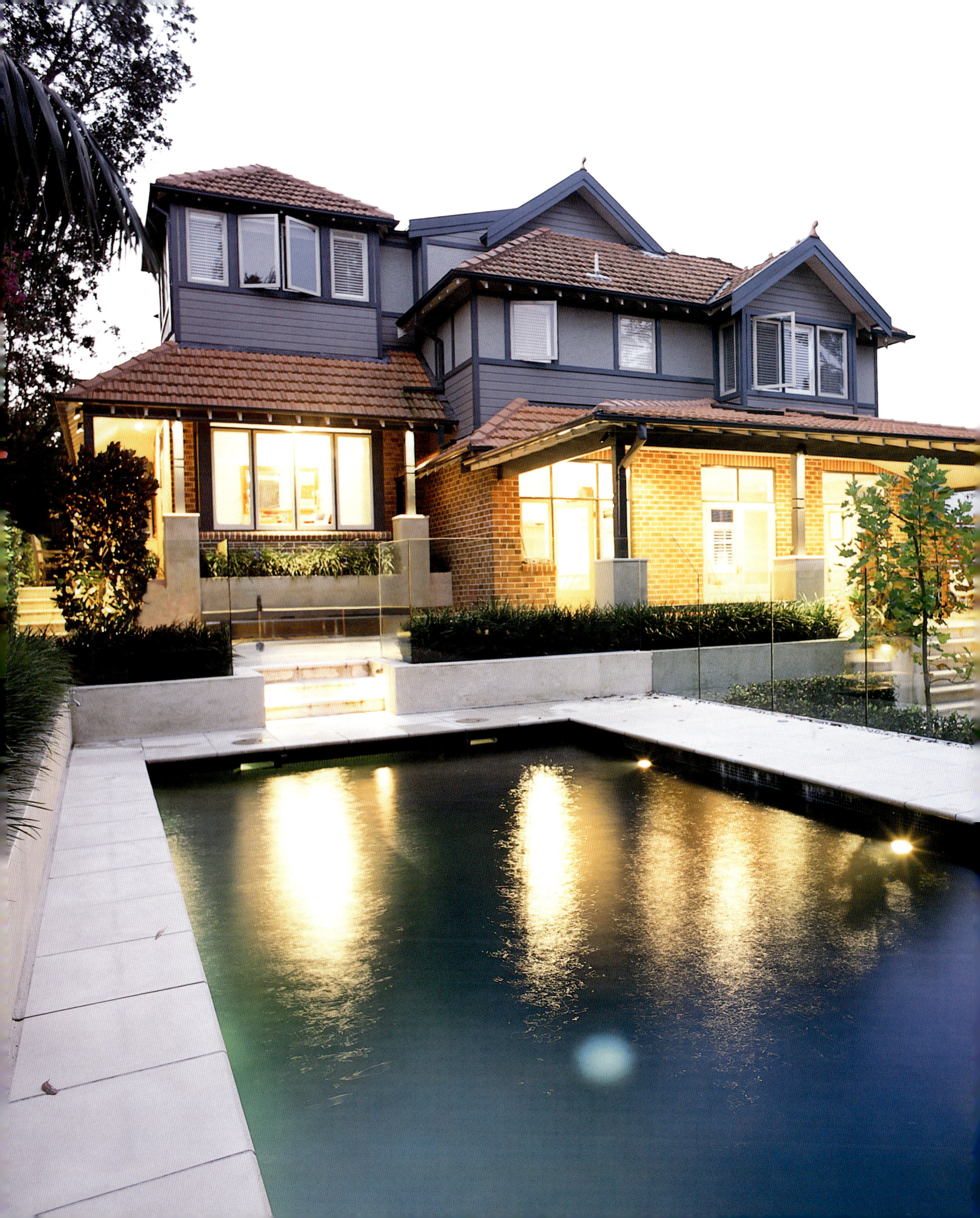

Since this lawn terrace is clearly visible from the house we decided to create a bold statement with it. This was achieved by installing a gravel path through this garden to a woodland garden beyond. A double avenue of tulip trees, *Liriodendron tulipifera*, was planted either side of the gravel path, visually connecting both sets of stairs. For me the contrast of the gravel with the vertical shapes of the trees makes a bold but simple statement. This is sometimes much easier on the eye than busy garden beds, not to mention the benefits that are brought about by distorting the perspective of a viewer, by making the garden appear larger than it really is.

ABOVE LEFT Pleached tulip trees line the path.   ABOVE RIGHT The broad green leaves of the Agave attenuata. OPPOSITE Terracing a large garden will create interest as well as indicate the different functions of each area.

At the far end of the garden is the children's zone; this area already had a beautiful stand of native turpentine trees, *Syncarpia glomulifera*. For me this formed a wonderful transition to a more natural style of garden – and a perfect children's playground – so we just planted a lilly pilly hedge, *Syzygium australe* syn. *paniculatum*, around the perimeter and nothing else.

THE RESULT

Due to the clients' openness to using different plants the garden still displays the characteristics of a balanced classic style to match the Federation feel of the front of the house, though with a more casual air. Their contemporary taste and the way that they live is evident in the selection of plants and the way the outdoor spaces have been designed, thinking of both the growing family and the adults' own space.

I really enjoyed playing around with varied planting schemes in this garden, combining species that look so different in colour and texture, and feel the result of this innovative planting is visually rewarding.

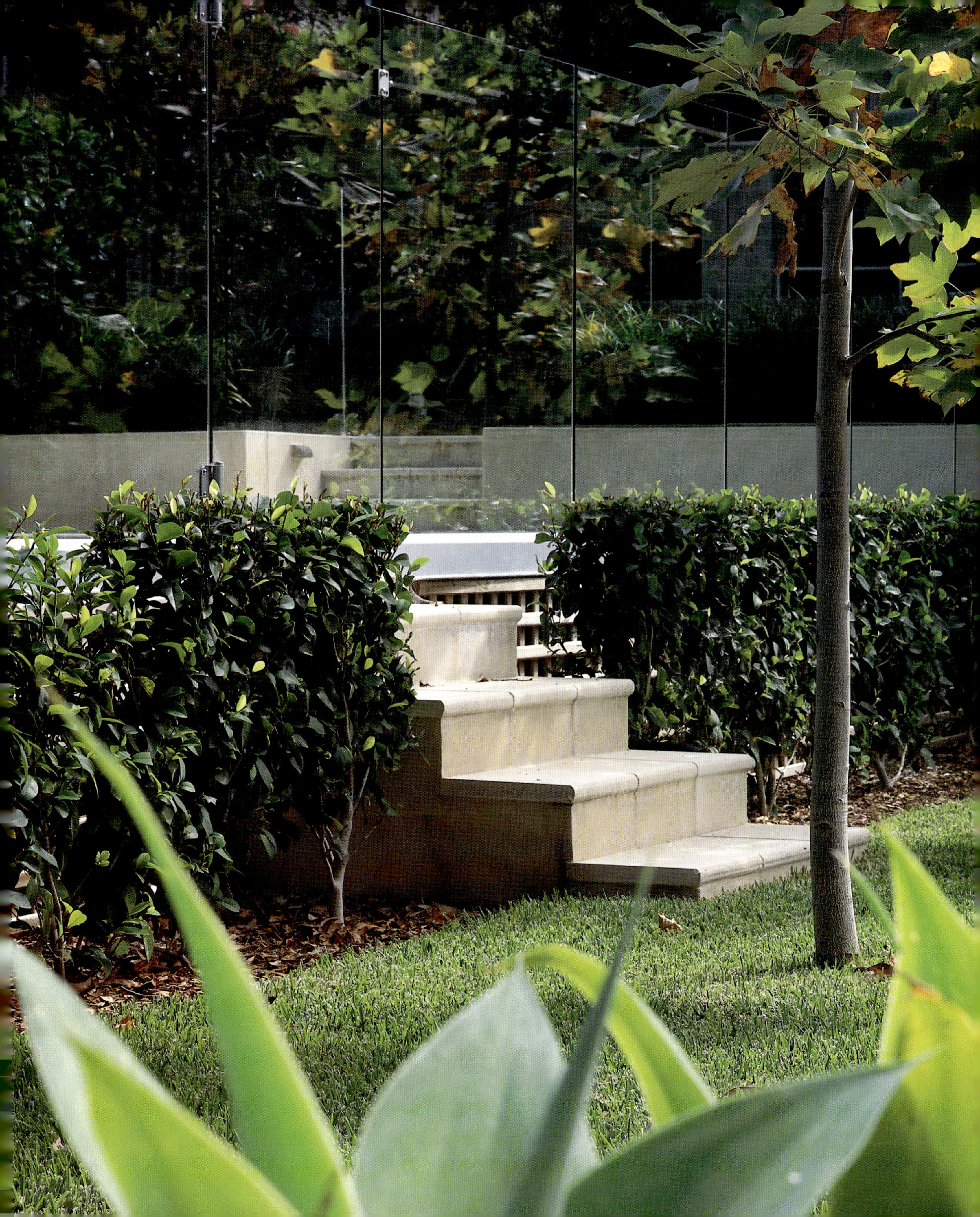

COURTYARD gardens

Extending the design of the interior into small exterior spaces ensures visual harmony.

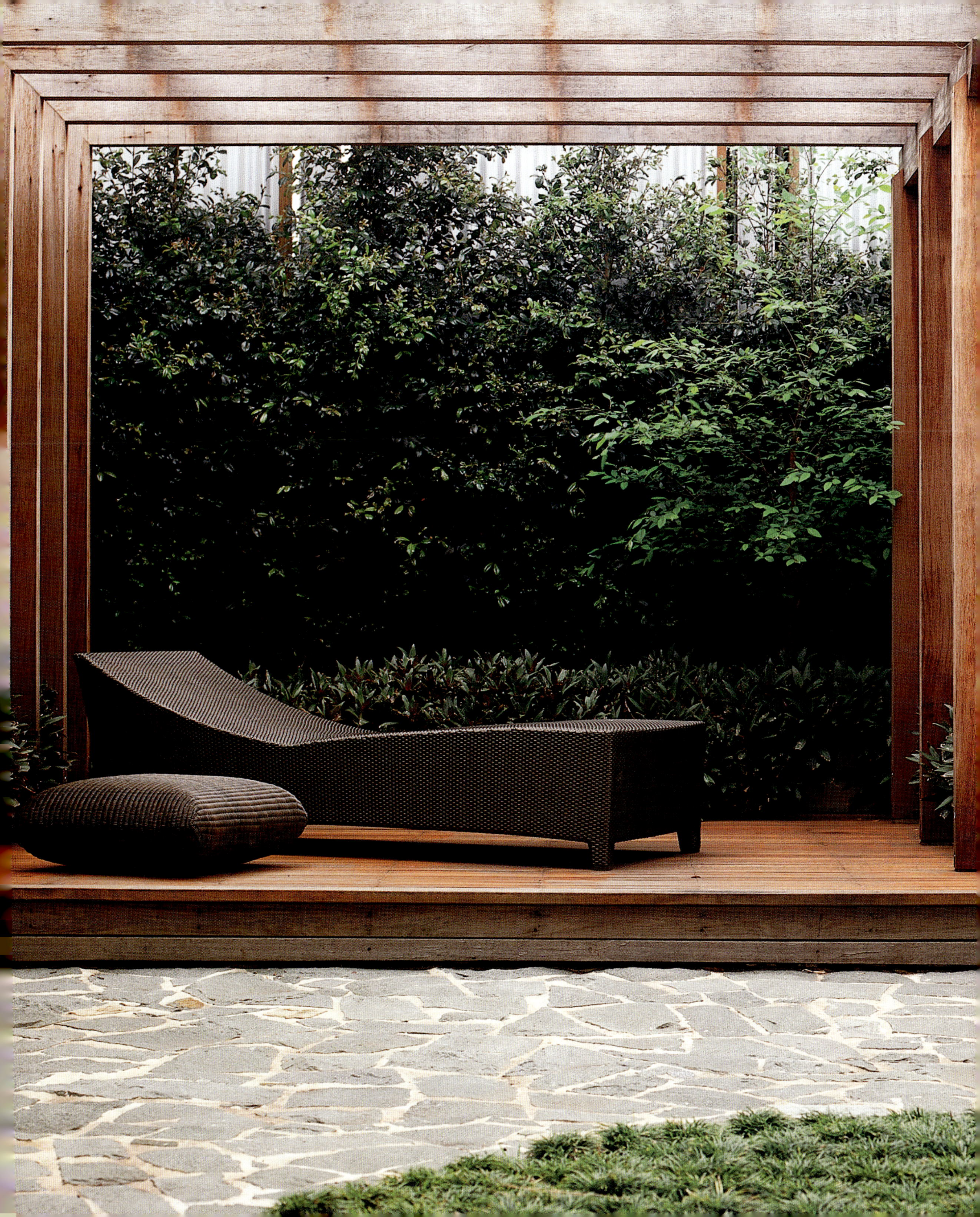

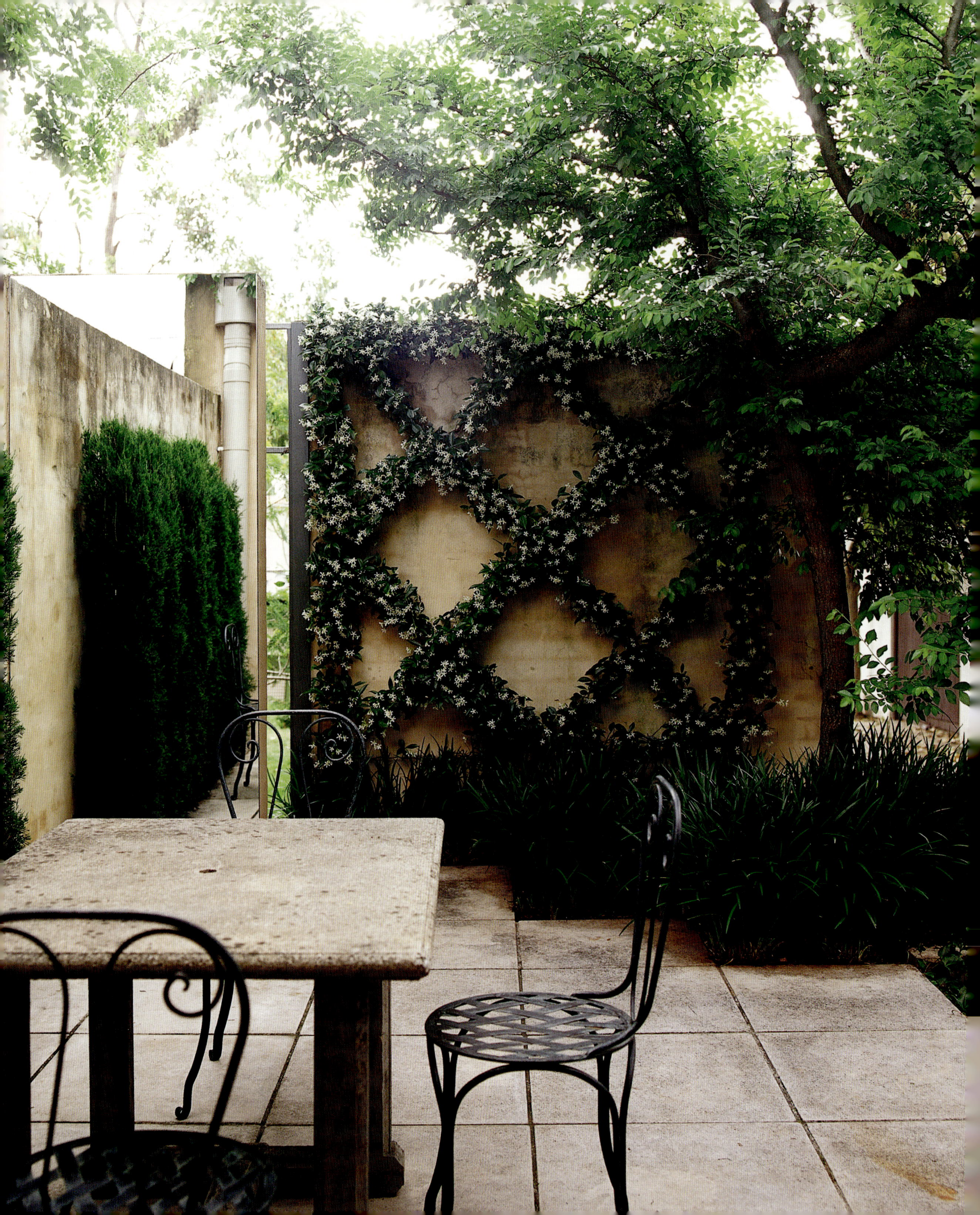

ECHOES OF LIGHT

THE SETTING
The area to be transformed was a small courtyard in an inner suburb of Sydney. It was not exposed to the elements and was bathed in plentiful natural light for much of the day.

THE BRIEF
To create an outdoor entertaining area with a sense of space and shade.

THE DESIGN
I think the greater the challenge and the more limitations you are faced with, often the better is the resulting design. Small spaces are so critical to get right, as there are so many practical elements to be considered and yet the garden still needs to be attractive.

With this garden I thought at first that the client was joking when he requested that the courtyard, which was only about 5 x 6 metres, had to contain a space for a car, a shade tree and an outdoor entertaining area. However, street parking is scarce in this inner city district, so it was a priority for the client. The car parking space was cut into one end of the site, making it about 30 centimetres lower than the house; this lowering slightly removed its impact, helping the car to 'disappear'.

On the high level, outside sliding doors from the rear of the house, I designed a small outdoor entertaining area. The floor was covered with 60 centimetre square stone pavers, which were also used in the parking area, so that when the car was not there the courtyard feel would continue. Again, the use of larger than normal pavers makes the whole area seem bigger than it really is.

On the boundary with the next-door neighbour I suggested a row of *Juniperus virginiana* 'Spartan', pencil cedars, to soften the high rendered wall. This cedar grows tall and elegantly thin, and

OPPOSITE   The canopy of the weeping elm offers protection from the western sun.

ABOVE Loosely structured plants soften the lines of the parking area.
OPPOSITE Crisscrosses of star jasmine are a bold statement in this garden oasis.

is well suited to a small space. It also happily tolerates hot and dry conditions, which it will encounter in this courtyard in summer. The leaves are aromatic so will perfume al fresco meals.

In front of the back gate I returned this boundary wall to screen the gate and placed a mirror on it, with a small square water feature in front consisting of pebbles over a grate where a trickle of water gurgles from the centre. There are very few situations in garden design where mirrors truly work and I have to say I think this is one of them. From inside the house the *Juniperus virginiana* 'Spartan' hedge looks three times as long as it is, which in turn makes the courtyard appear greener than it already is; the entertaining area is also replicated in the mirror, making it seem larger.

On the back boundary wall a diagonal star jasmine pattern was created to reinforce the paving – the paving was 60 centimetres square and the star jasmine was trained into diagonals of the same measurements. The star jasmine, *Trachelospermum asiaticum*, is a vigorous grower which can be easily trained. The result is almost as if the paving continues up the back wall, but thrown onto a diagonal – an effective and very unusual feature.

At the base of the wall a staggered bed was created, in which was planted a Chinese weeping elm, *Ulmus parvifolia*, which shades the whole area. It is being carefully monitored and limbs are removed as necessary to ensure that its shape remains dignified, that its canopy covers the courtyard with medium shade, and that it does not grow too large. Underneath are massed *Liriope* 'Evergreen Giant', a trouble-free perennial with purple or lavender flower spikes in late summer and early autumn.

The Chinese weeping elm has small, glossy, dark green leaves. Although deciduous in cold climates, it is almost evergreen in Sydney, retaining its foliage until the spring growth appears. It likes sun, will tolerate poor soil conditions, and is a hardy tree.

THE RESULT
This small courtyard is now an inner city oasis. There are a couple of illusions that make the space look bigger but, more importantly, it's an extension of the home that is easily accessible after a heavy day.

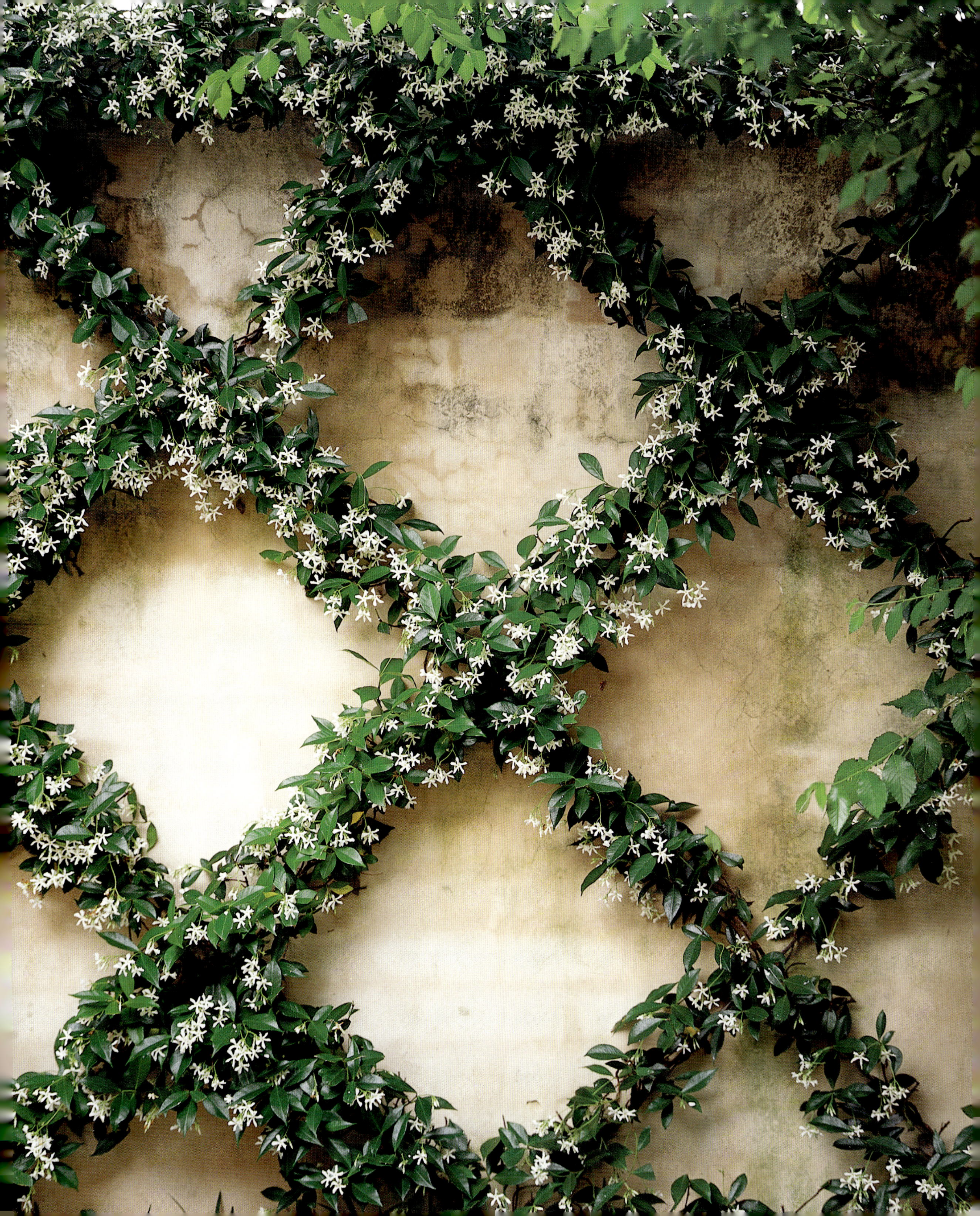

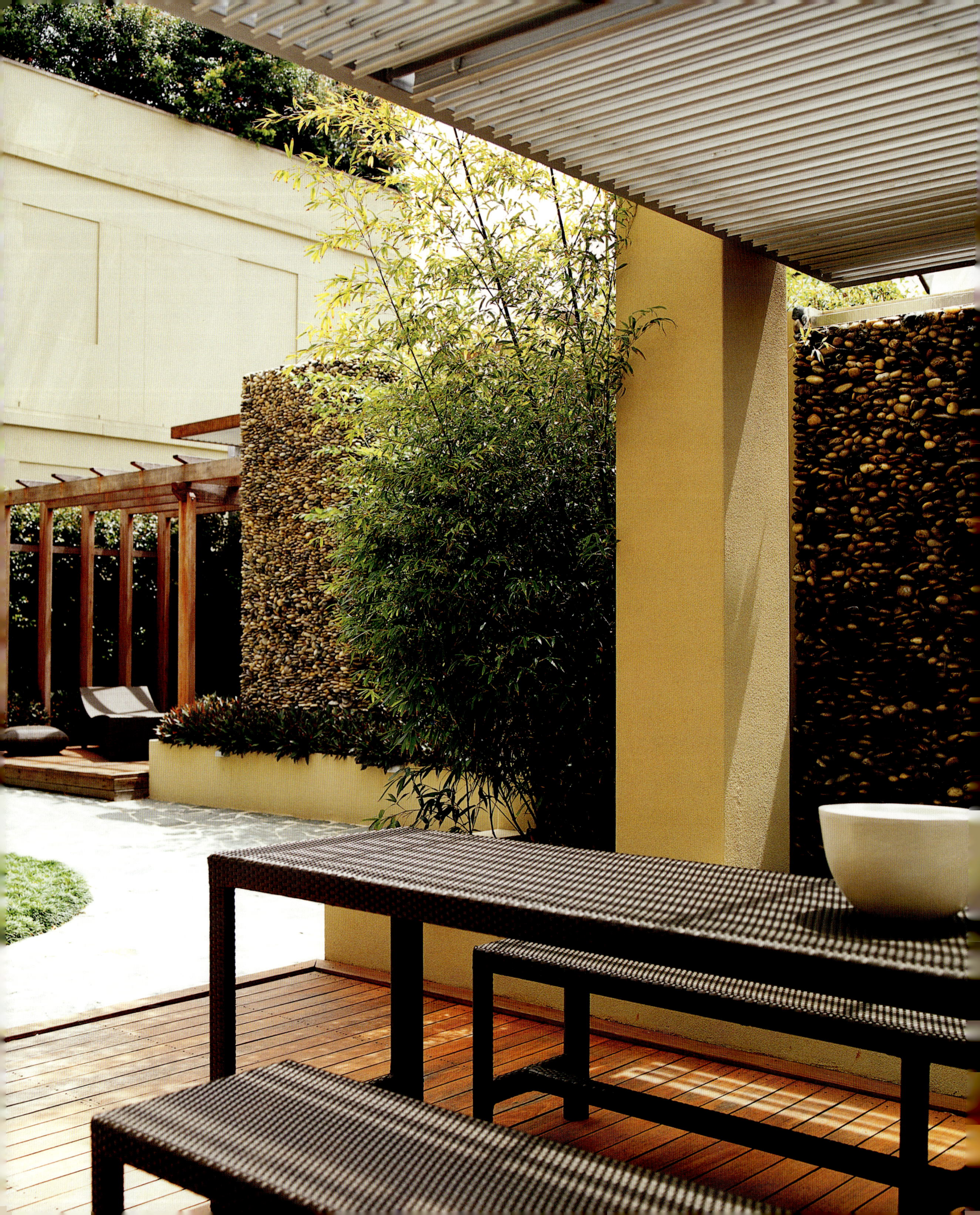

SULTRY FUSION

THE SETTING
This was a courtyard garden, starting from scratch, as the house was newly built. It was in a Sydney suburb and was secluded and sheltered from the elements.

THE BRIEF
The developer already had a garden proposed for the building, but the client wanted a more stimulating and interesting design than was on offer. Nevertheless, the builder completed the timber decking and slate paving before handing the outdoor area to me. The client wanted some massed colour in the garden.

THE DESIGN
Although a courtyard garden, it was not a tiny space. There was sufficient room to allow a number of elements.

The deck areas were already designated, and one became an al fresco eating and entertaining area, while the other was given to an unusually elegant lounger – it is constructed of hand-woven man-made fibre over an aluminium frame, and is weatherproof and will not fade in the sun. A timber pergola and adjustable screens over these areas give them a Japanese feel.

The centre of the courtyard was covered with green slate paving. Although an attractive stone, I thought the paved area was too large, so we broke it up with an oval of massed dwarf mondo grass, *Ophiopogon japonicus* 'Nana', in the middle. This acts visually as a lawn – but without needing any of the continuous attention lawns require. Dwarf mondo grass will grow to about 15 centimetres at maximum height, and forms a dense mat. It is a perennial and will grow in full or filtered sun.

To create interest and to complement the natural elements of slate and timber, I decided to incorporate two walls covered with mixed

OPPOSITE AND ABOVE Wet and dry cobblestone walls create a contrasting thread throughout the courtyard.

ABOVE *The variegated spear-like leaves of the* Phormium *'Chief' are striking.* OPPOSITE *The bamboo frames the cobblestone wet wall and rustles beautifully in the breeze.*

cobblestones that were laid on end. One of the walls is in fact a vent, but with this treatment it now became a garden element rather than an intrusion of the building. The second cobblestone wall is directly opposite the living room and forms a backdrop to the entertaining area; this one is a water feature, a wet wall. The water trickles over the cobblestones and creates wonderful light and sound, as the water is continuously recycled around and over.

On either side of this wet wall I planted Timor black bamboo, *Bambusa lako*, mulched with white gravel, which forms a relaxed association with the pebbles and water – again, giving something of a Japanese flavour to this area. The bamboo also connects the wall to the garden visually.

The remainder of this large courtyard consisted of a wide garden bed around the perimeter which I wanted to mass with lots of colour, as the clients had requested. A raised planter bed, 60 centimetres high, was constructed for the display, then the beautiful *Tradescantia discolor* was planted as a low border surrounding the planter box. We planted a band of *Duranta repens* 'Sheena's Gold'; a dwarf variety which will grow to 1 metre, but which is to be clipped to a continuous round mound 50 centimetres high. Its beautiful lime-green foliage contrast with the *Tradescantia*'s green and purple leaves.

Then came a band of *Phormium* 'Chief' – a striking plant with 80 centimetre high pinkish-red and bronze-green striped spear-like leaves, which also contrasted well with the *Duranta repens* – followed by a band of *Strelitzia reginae*, bird-of-paradise flower, whose distinctive orange and blue flowers will highlight the garden with colour over long flowering through spring and summer. Finally, we planted a lilly pilly screen, *Syzygium paniculatum* 'Elite Form', to make a backdrop. Feeling that the result might seem a little formal, two *Betula nigra* 'Tropical Birch' trees were added to the planter box, which helped to give this garden a sense of depth and to soften the architectural components within it and beyond.

Betula nigra 'Tropical Birch' is a useful tree for a small garden as its roots are non-invasive and will not harm paving or foundations. The trees grow quickly, can reach 10 metres, and thrive in a wide range of conditions. They are deciduous, but the attractive foliage is held for a long time, being present from September to June. Not all birches do well in hot conditions, but this cultivar lives up to its name and can be grown in humid, tropical areas.

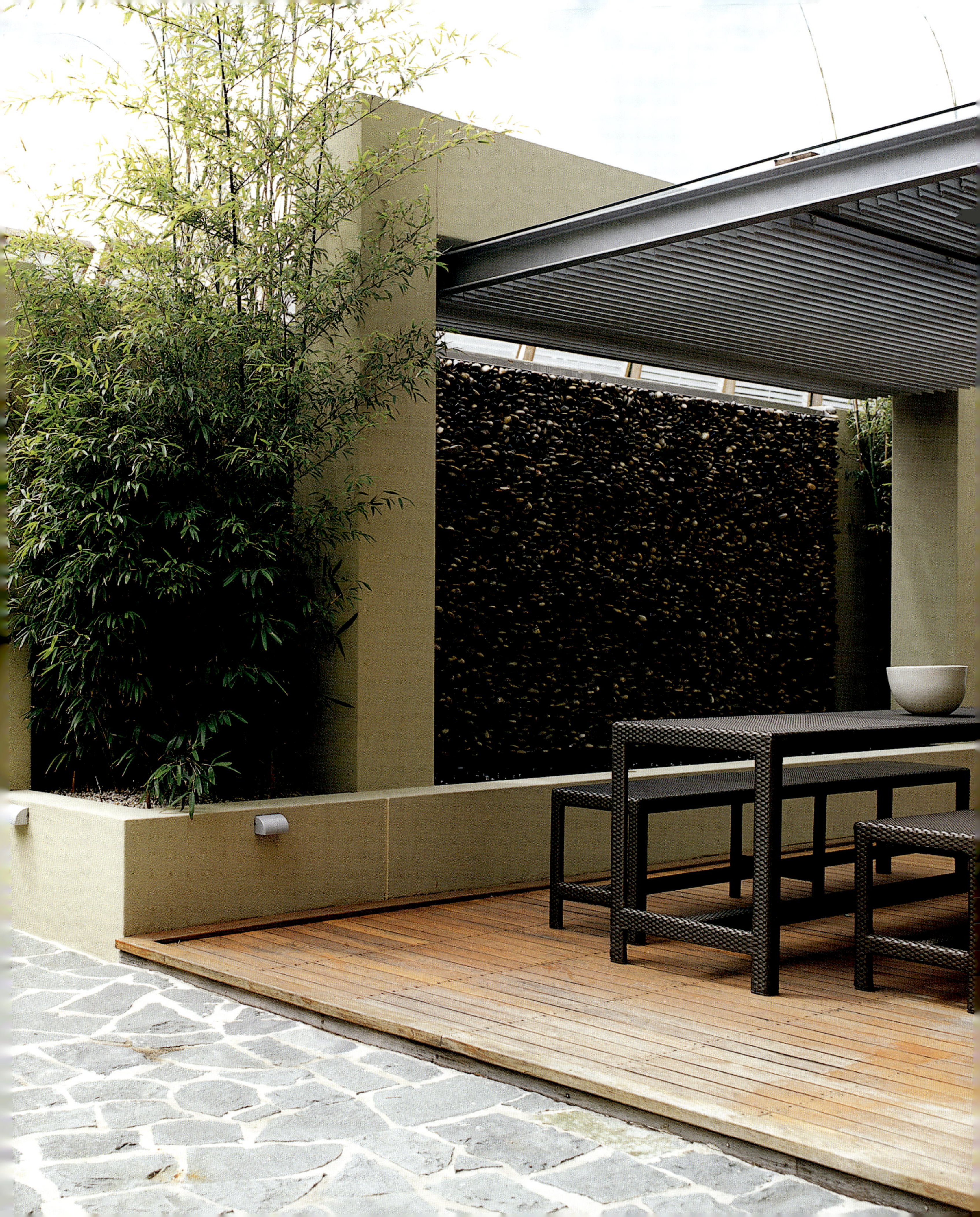

THE RESULT
The overall look is semi-tropical but still within my layered philosophy. I feel that this courtyard garden proves the point that a tropical garden does not need to be chaotic – as such gardens so often are. On the contrary, a tropical garden can be quite stylised.

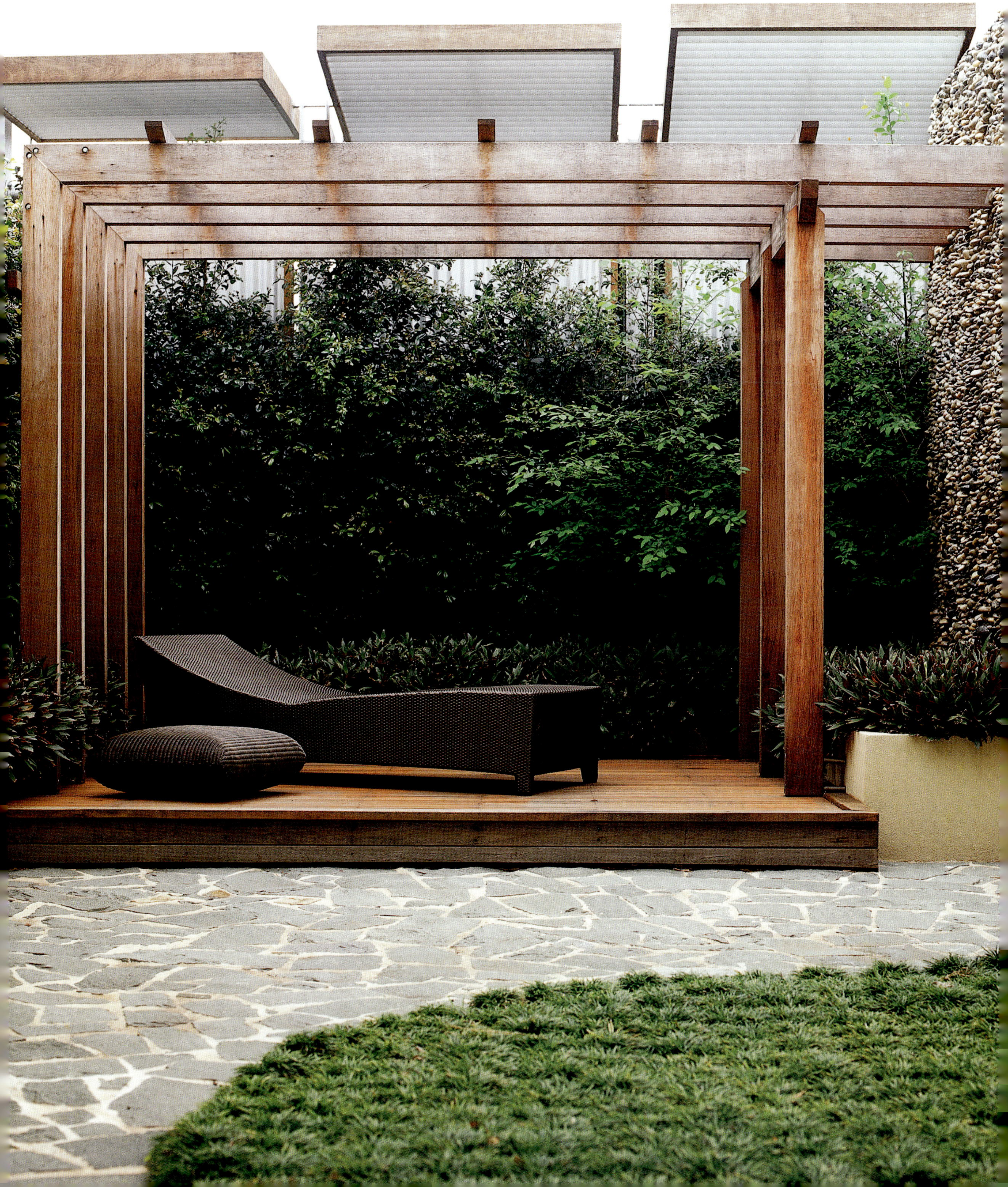

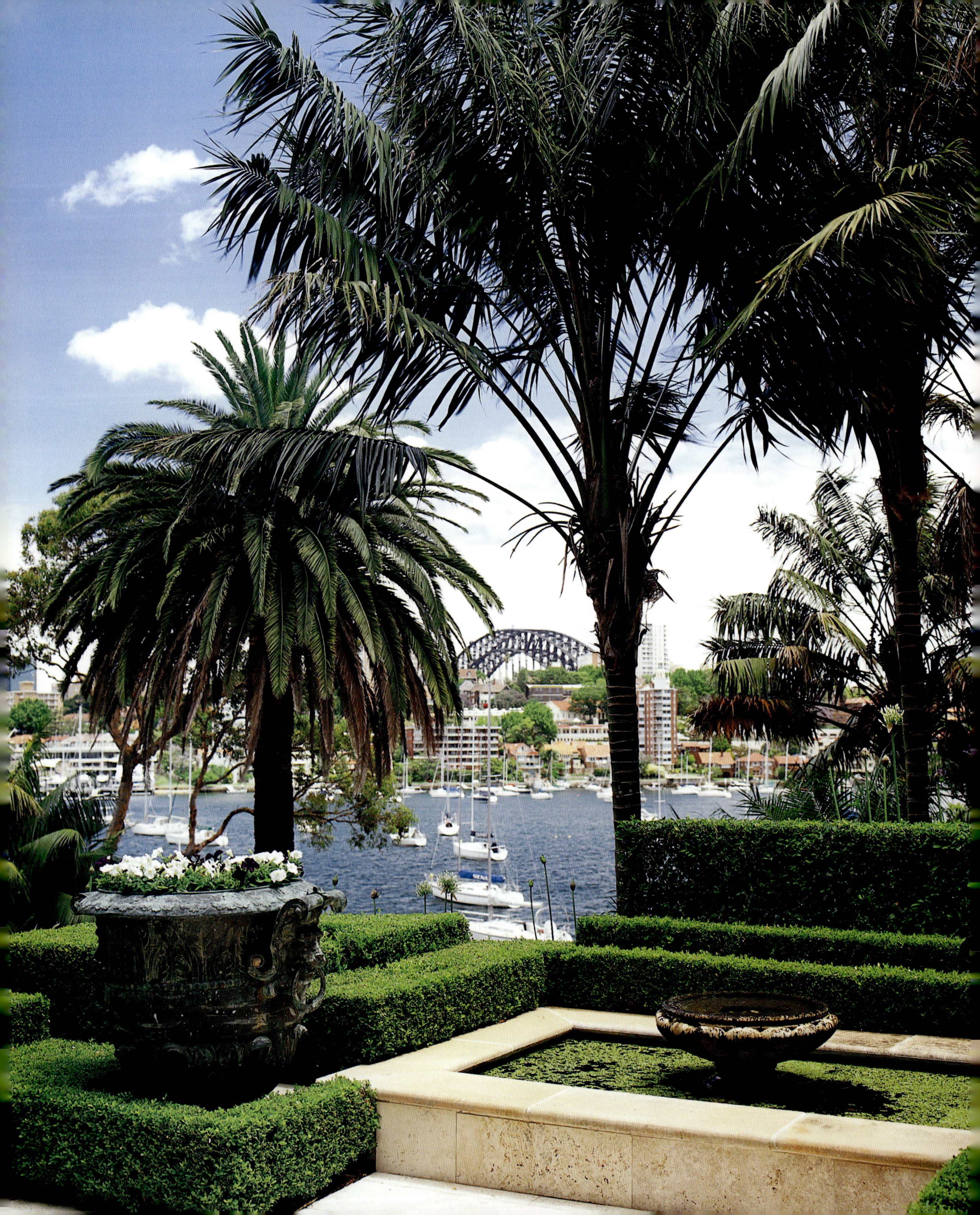

A CLASSIC REFLECTION

THE SETTING
The client had recently downsized – selling the family home and acquiring a harbourside apartment in Neutral Bay, Sydney. The 'garden' essentially consisted of three large courtyards.

THE BRIEF
The client wanted something in the three courtyards that surround the apartment that was easy to care for while being dramatic to look at. There was also a requirement to provide screening from the apartments next door.

THE DESIGN
This client's taste in interior decoration was quite classic, and I felt the garden design should reflect this. The apartment's setting was dramatic, the garden having the Harbour Bridge as a backdrop. Taking both these factors into consideration, I decided to adopt a formal layered planting style. Using hedges of small-leaved box, *Buxus microphylla* var. *japonica*, orange jessamine, *Murraya paniculata*, and star jasmine, *Trachelospermum jasminoides*, the resulting effect is simple yet complements the apartment and leads the eye onto the vista beyond.

Off the main bedroom there is a waterside courtyard. Here a raised pond has been recessed within a paved and hedged area accentuated by two massive bronze urns. The pond contains a soothing water feature where water is pumped up to a raised bowl and then spills over into the pond itself. The urns frame the view of the water feature – and of the Harbour beyond – from the bedroom.

The urns are planted with seasonal colour. Depending on the time of year, they may be filled with petunias or pansies or such like, with the client sticking to a blue, purple and white theme which forms a subtle yet cooling effect against the solid green backdrop of

OPPOSITE Simple foreground planting enhances the captivating view.

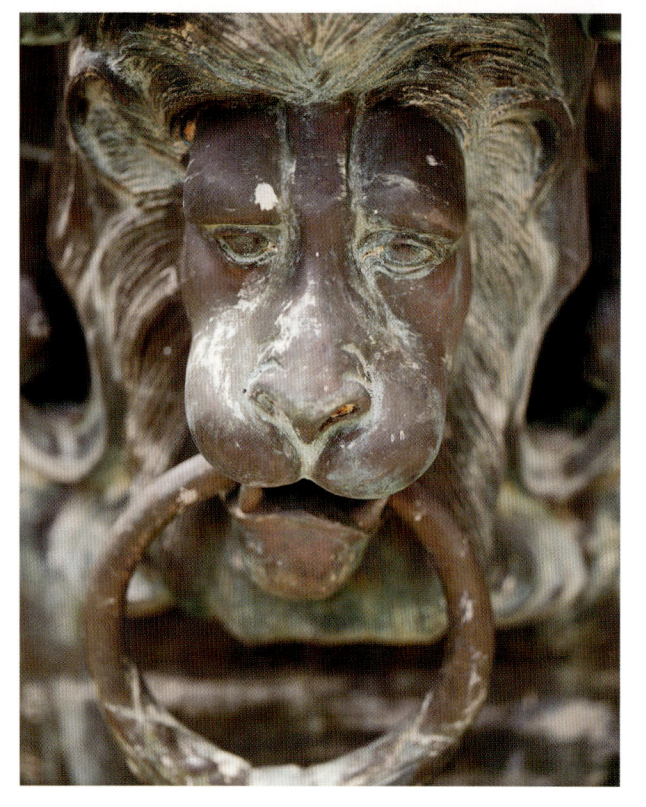

the garden. The urns themselves are of classic design; the handles – consisting of a lion's head with a ring through the mouth – have appeared on pots since Roman times. These lions are luxuriantly maned and the bronze of the urns has a delightful green patina.

The planting beyond this water courtyard, which is in the common grounds of the apartments, becomes more relaxed, with agapanthus, strelitzias and Kentia palms, *Howea forsteriana*.

At the entrance to this apartment is another small courtyard garden, with stairs leading down to the front door. Beside the stairs I have set a line of tall, reconstituted stone pots. These are planted with lilly pilly shrubs, *Syzygium australe*, pruned into conical shapes, and make the entrance a formal and dramatic space. To soften the concrete rendered walls on either side of the stairs I planted star jasmine, *Trachelospermum jasminoides*, against them, which was clipped tightly to the wall, helping to extend the feel of the garden. The jasmine will cling and climb and cover the wall with its delightful foliage and flowers. On either side of the front door itself, two formal stone pots with acanthus leaf decoration sit, planted with graceful dwarf date palms, *Phoenix roebelenii*. These are slow-growing and have a dense but delicate canopy of bright green leaflets arranged along the leaf stems; they will thrive in most soils and can be grown indoors or out.

The third courtyard, on the opposite side of the apartment to the main bedroom, continues the planting theme. It has a narrow raised planter box in which *Buxus microphylla* var. *japonica*, *paniculata*, and star jasmine, *Trachelospermum jasminoides*, are layered, thus connecting all three courtyards.

LEFT The urn has a timeless design and includes a lion's head with a ring through the mouth. OPPOSITE Contrasting casual groves of palms behind a more formal setting creates high visual impact.

THE RESULT
Three disjointed areas have now been brought together through repetition of plants. The design aimed both to create a courtyard atmosphere and to take into consideration the views beyond, as well as framing them.

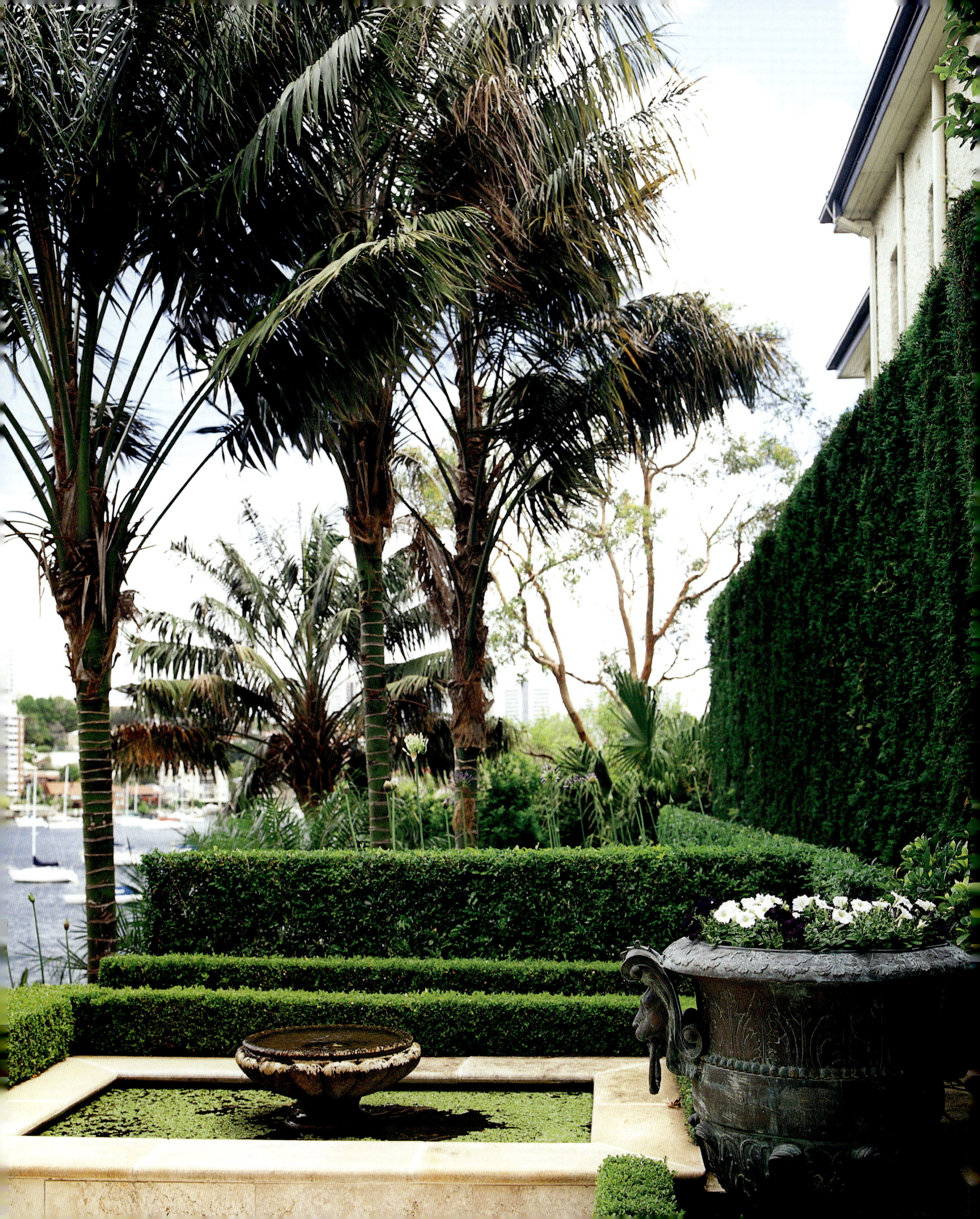

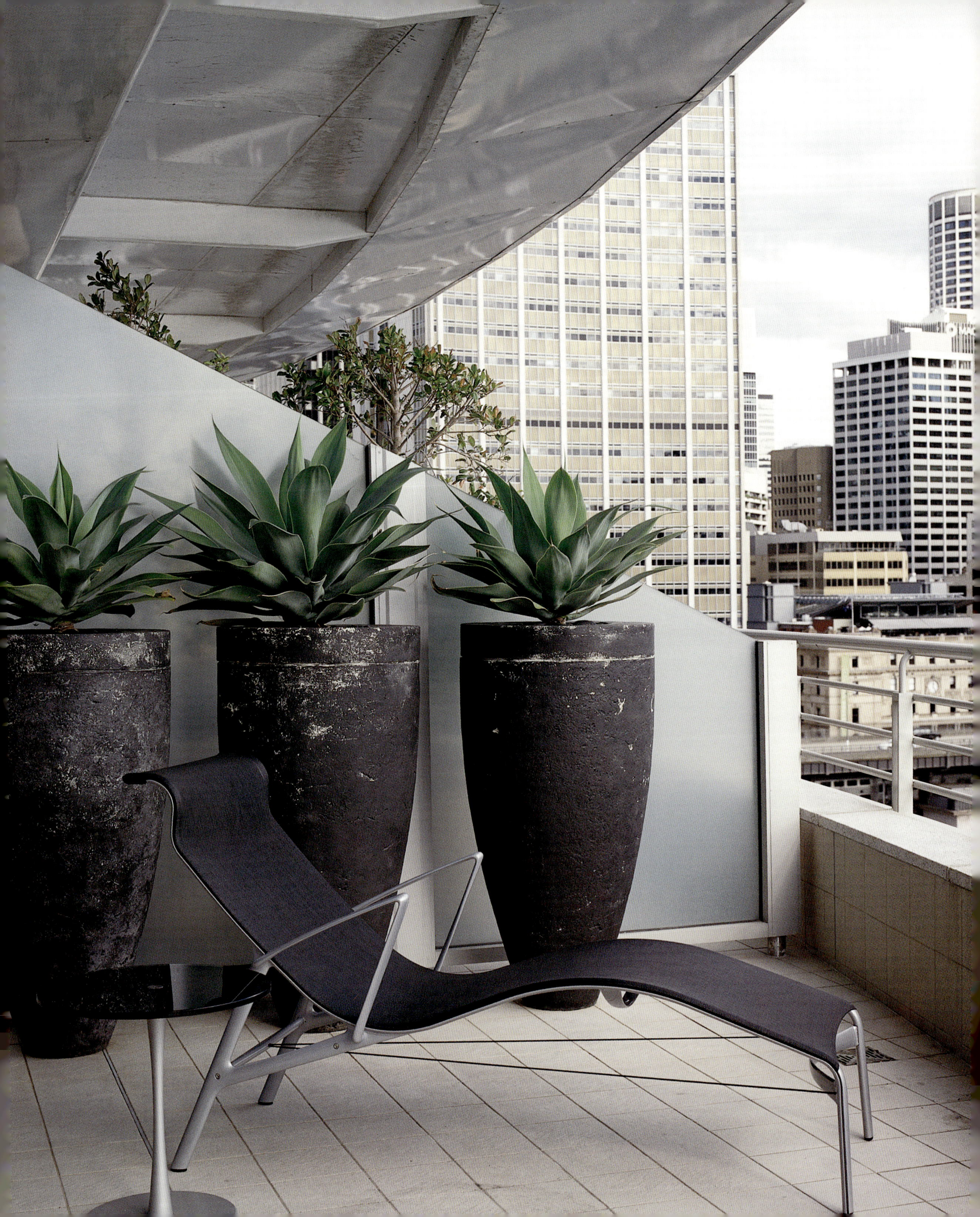

POISE AND BEAUTY

THE SETTING
A penthouse at the top of the new apartment building at East Circular Quay, Sydney, that has been dubbed 'The Toaster' by locals.

THE BRIEF
To design courtyard spaces for the penthouse's four balconies that would soften the spaces, make these areas less sterile and yet complement the stunning background vistas. The brief was open ended.

THE DESIGN
I remember this as a really, really challenging job, not due to the hardship of the site but because of the surroundings – this penthouse possessed one of the world's most magnificent views. The penthouse at East Circular Quay has four balconies, which overlook the Opera House, Sydney Harbour and the Royal Botanic Gardens, and its position could be said to capture the essence of Sydney. The pressure was on to get the design absolutely right, because of this magnificent setting.

I was aware that the client had moved from a large garden and therefore might want something that would look 'pretty', but as the design came close to completion it had become clear to me in which direction I should go. I was able to convince the client that in this situation the numerous focal points were all around us and that we should not try to compete with them. Instead the design should highlight them. Restraint was to be the key to this design. Fortunately, the client appreciated this direction.

There were technical difficulties however. Plant selection for these high-rise balcony gardens was critical – the balconies are covered by eaves so rainfall is restricted, while for half the day they receive no sun and for the other half it is blazingly hot and bright, due to the aspect.

ABOVE AND OPPOSITE The tall round shape of the pots softens the strong elements in the courtyard.

ABOVE AND OPPOSITE The use of fewer species in a small area minimises clutter.

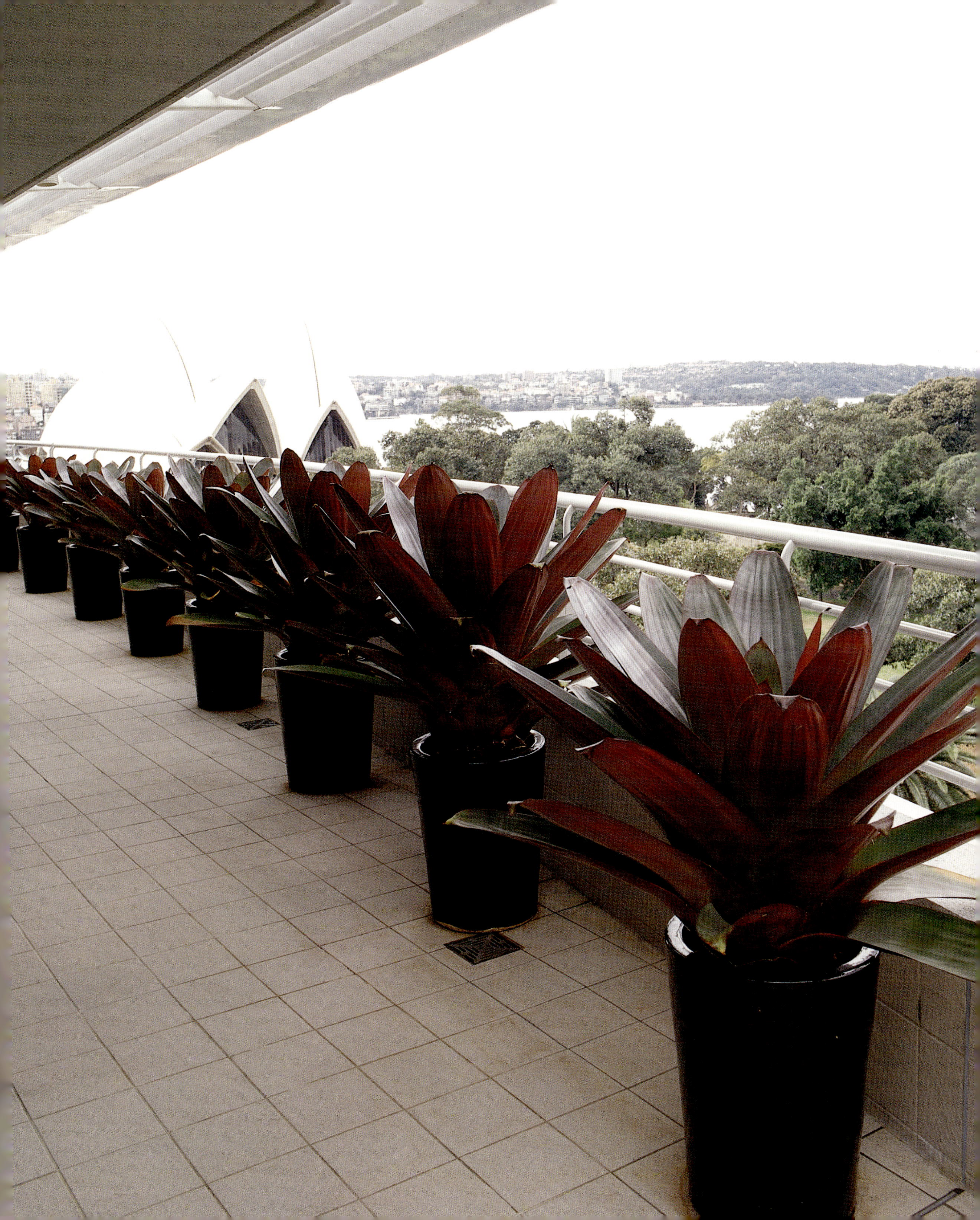

Both west-facing courtyards were lined with contemporary charcoal-coloured pots. These tall pots were planted with the stunning aqua-coloured *Agave attenuata*, picking up the colour of the Harbour and framing the postcard view. This succulent is a native of Mexico, from the mountains. Many agaves have spines, but this one does not, making it suitable as a plant for this situation. It is drought tolerant and will not mind the midday heat.

To echo the stainless steel used in the building we built a stainless steel feature wall against a frosted glass panel. This broke up the space and formed a structure on which we could affix two contemporary aqua wall fountains. On another stainless steel wall we suspended stone candle holders planted with succulents – *Kalanchoe* species. A lot of succulents aren't identified fully at nurseries, but this one has silver, oval-shaped leaves that have a trailing habit, and pretty pink flowers.

On the eastern side of the two courtyards we repeated the pots of *Agave attenuata* except this time we also used stainless steel troughs planted with *Juniperus virginiana* 'Spartan' to provide screening from the neighbours. This juniper was also chosen for its hardiness and its ability to withstand the balcony conditions.

For colour and dramatic foliage, purple-leafed bromeliads, *Vriesea imperialis*, in black pots line a narrow section of one east-facing balcony, their leaves picking up the shape of the Opera House beyond. *Vriesea imperialis* is a wonderful bromeliad species that grows to approximately 1.5 metres high. The rosettes of leaves need bright sun in order to develop the purple coloration, but there is more than enough sunlight on this balcony. After some years they should flower in summer: the inflorescence is raised high above the foliage and is spectacular and long-lasting.

Bromeliads are an unusual family of plants. Many species are epiphytes – they grow high on trees and absorb their nutrients from moisture in the air. They are also tough and will survive balcony life.

THE RESULT
This was a garden where restraint and continuity were used to frame – in fact, to emphasise – the magnificent views around this unique location. The choice of materials and plants was critical as a balance to the backdrops behind.

ABOVE The stainless steel feature wall echoes the use of stainless steel in the building, whilst the two wall fountains form a distraction from city noises.

POISE AND BEAUTY | 127

CONCEPT gardens

Concept gardens introduce to the public new products in design and current trends, such as using water-wise plants and organic materials.

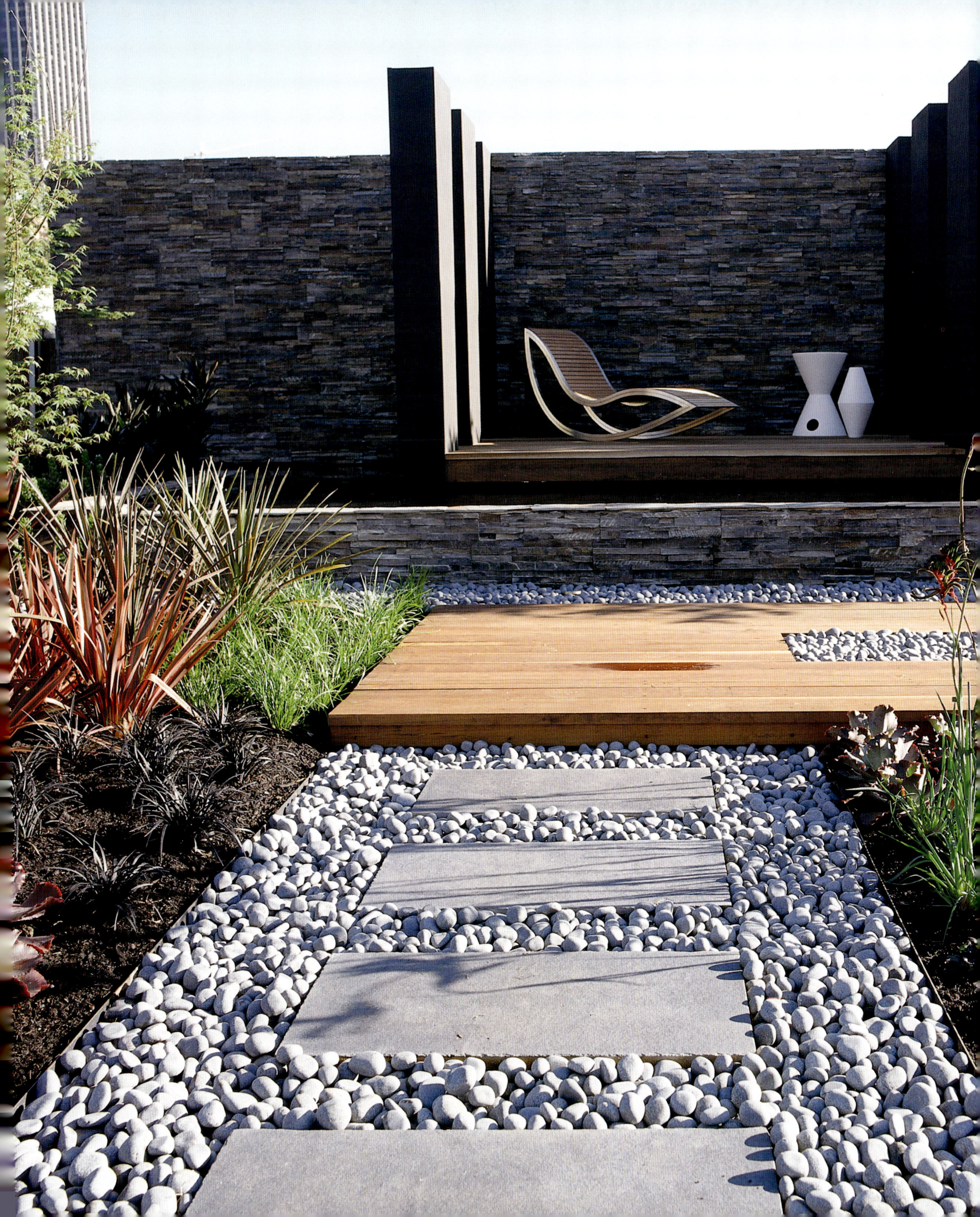

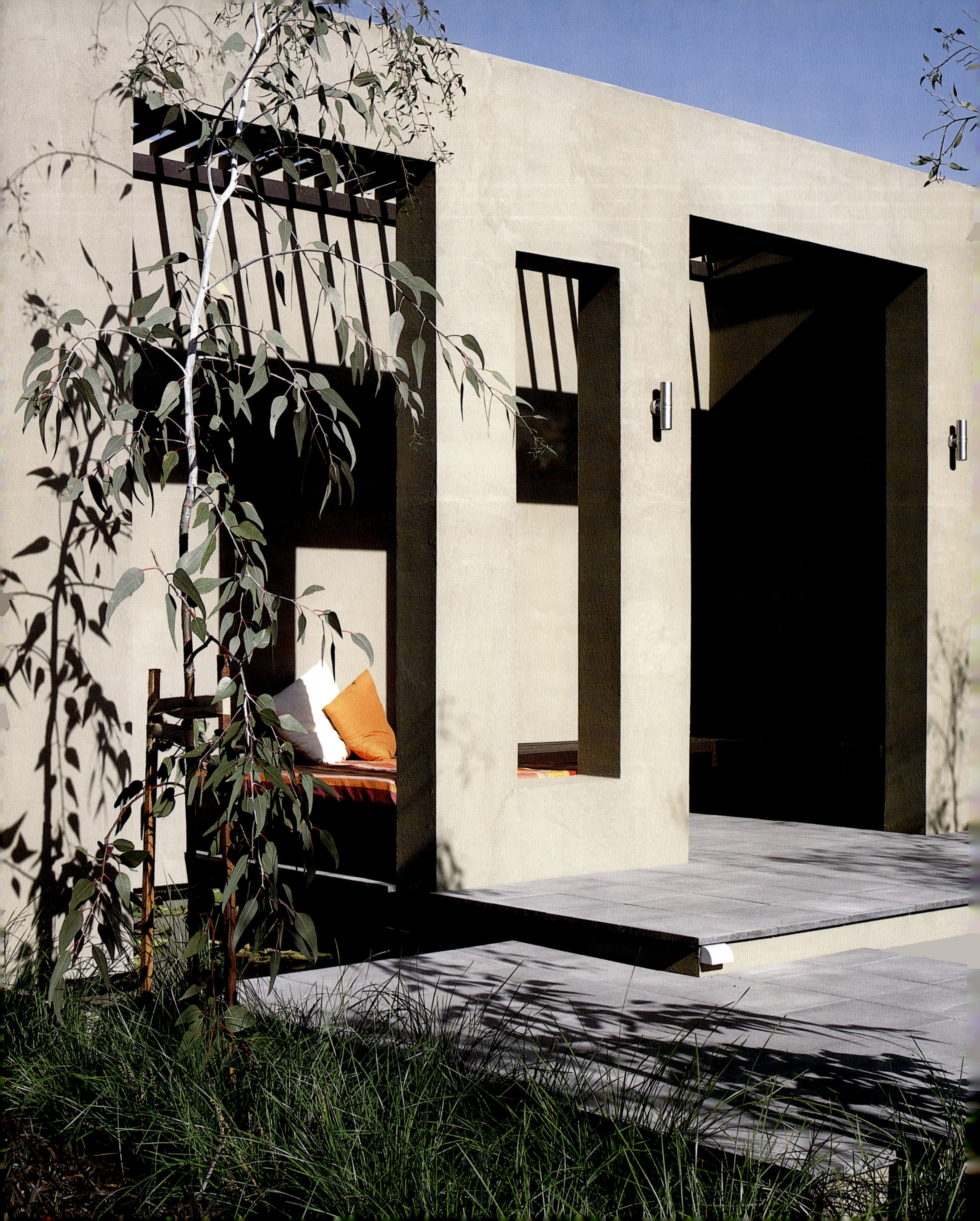

CONTEMPORARY AUSTRALIAN DESIGN IN A BUSH SETTING

THE SETTING
I was asked to design a small display garden as part of the ABC's *Gardening Australia* LIVE show, which was held at Olympic Park, in the Sydney suburb of Homebush Bay. It was to be 7 x 10 metres in area.

THE BRIEF
The brief was open, but I wanted to emphasise the issues of waterwise landscaping, and that new varieties of natives with their attractive forms and colours can be used in a stylised design to create a stunning garden. People seeing the display were likely to be searching for ideas on making an Australian garden, so I wanted to give them inspiration. I also wanted to get across ideas on how to make a small space look larger than it is, and how to get the proportions correct. I also wanted to design a display that could be anyone's inner-city back garden.

THE DESIGN
With this garden I tried to create a display that emulated what I believe is an Australian contemporary style of garden – a modern, millennial house in a native garden setting. Architectural trends have become more stylised in recent years but my philosophy is that a house and its garden should be visually linked. Natural landscape should dominate rather than the architecture. The Australian landscape is the perfect setting for such a house.

Environmental issues have become increasingly important to all Australians' lives, and this garden utilises native plants – in particular eucalypts and grass – that require little water and provide a low maintenance approach.

My first problem was the site. Because the display garden was to be built in an existing park, restrictions included being unable to dig up soil due to the many services lying just below the surface.

OPPOSITE Inspiration for the colours used in the structure, paving and timberwork came directly from the Australian landscape.

ABOVE The rich green Lomandra *'tanika'* grass presents well all year round.
OPPOSITE Paved landings entice you into the colourful oasis beyond.

I wanted to give a feel for the house in the design, not just the garden and had designed 'architecture' about 4 metres high. To build it without any foundations but with adequate support was going to be a challenge! So beneath the rendered blueboard of the 'house' lay an intricate timber framing system that, along with steel bracing, would be able to resist the gusty winds at Olympic Park.

Eucalyptus trees growing through grass are a common sight in many parts of Australia, so whilst it may be seen as an obvious choice, it was the most appropriate foil in this display. The grass will present well all year, as it was chosen for its adaptability to all types of conditions. The grass is not a fescue grass, but a perennial called *Lomandra longifolia* 'Tanika'. This is a fine-leafed, grass-like plant with a neat habit, growing to 50 centimetres in height. Its colour is a pleasing green that looks particularly good when massed.

The foliage of the trees is dramatic and will soften the strong lines of the paving. The eucalypts provide scale and structure and in time will give the garden a distinctive Australian character with their gnarled trunks. The species I used was *Eucalyptus caesia* 'Silver Princess', a grafted Western Australian species with eastern seaboard root stock, making it suited to the more humid environment on the New South Wales coast. It has stunning silver foliage and a weeping habit, growing to 4 metres. It bears red flowers followed by large, silvery gumnuts.

A screen of native conifer, *Callitris rhomboidea*, was positioned to form a backdrop to the garden. This tree occurs naturally in south-eastern Australia, growing in hills and ranges, and will reach to 9 metres. It has fine mid-green foliage with gracefully drooping shoots. In cold winters the foliage can turn a deep purple–brown. It also makes a good hedge and will, in a suburban application, afford privacy from neighbours.

Closer to the stylised 'house' I brought water into the design. Paving that led from the 'verandah' or 'patio' to the planting was surrounded by ponds planted with waterlilies, so that the paving appeared to be an asymmetric bridge across the water. The paving was a natural volcanic stone from Italy, chosen because I thought it suited the contemporary architecture and choice of colours used in the display. I also wanted to reduce glare, as this was a hot site with a good deal of reflection from the sun, so used a dark coloured stone rather than a cream one.

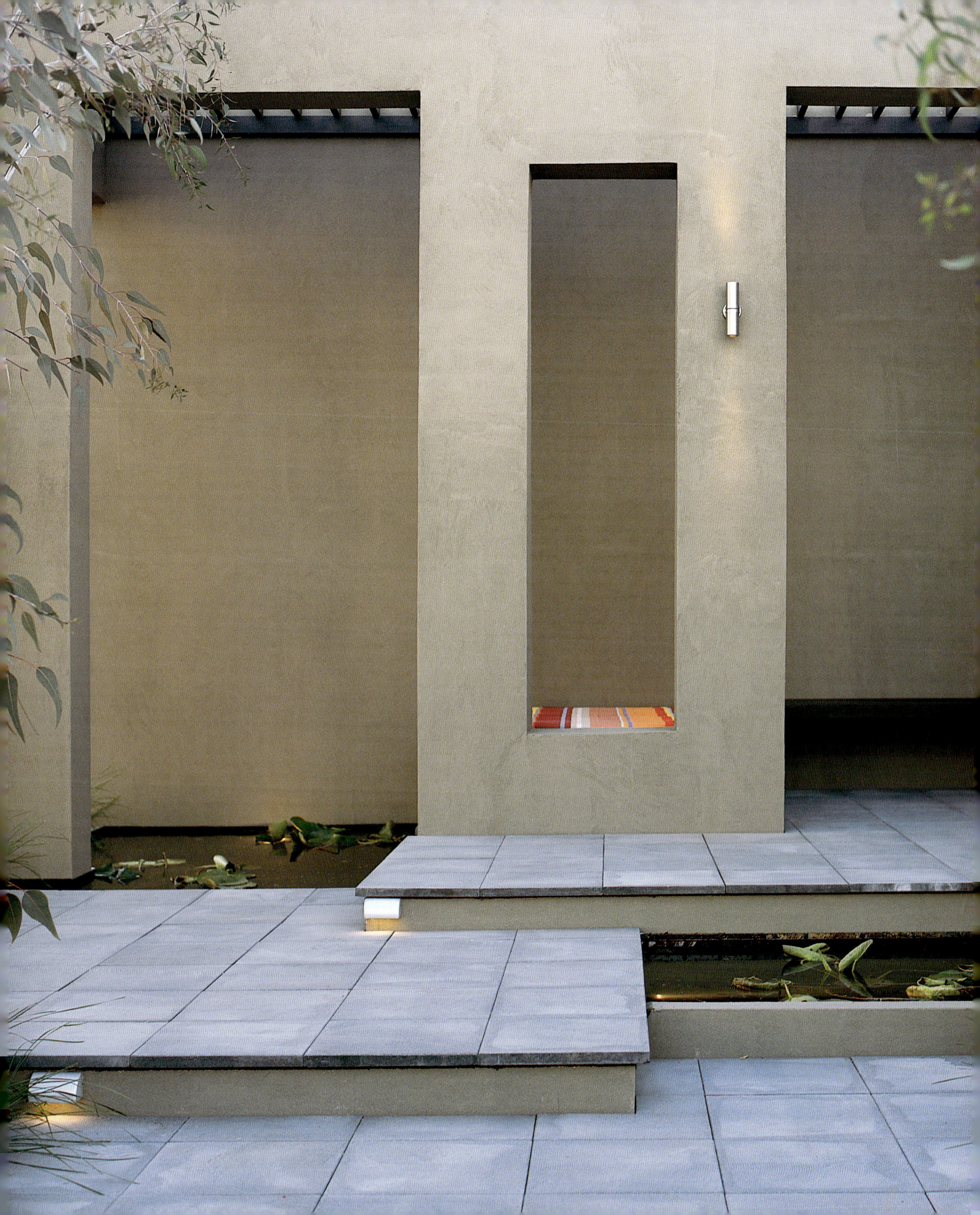

ABOVE Ponds planted with waterlilies are interspersed amongst the paving. OPPOSITE The corrugated iron wet wall gives this garden space a typically Australian edge.

The concept for this bridge and pontoons was drawn from a typical bush setting, where discoveries are made by walking over a creek via a log, or crossing exposed rocky outcrops on the way to a clearing, dwelling or viewpoint. The discovery of water at this point encourages reflection of the beauty of the Australian landscape. The eucalypts, as they grow, will be mirrored in the water.

Within the Australian landscape we need water to revitalise and soothe us. As the ponds are situated near the 'living areas', they are able to give the greatest benefits to the inhabitants, although they are visually and audibly anonymous.

Materials such as timber, stone and corrugated iron with rendered bricks sit harmoniously in our native landscape. The addition of colour to the garden, in the form of cushions and a mattress on the day bed and behind a pond on a wet wall, has been used to contrast and complement the surrounds. The wet wall was constructed of a mini-corrugated iron sheet, and water was recycled from the pond below to fall down the corrugations. To reinforce the Australian theme – and to create a more contemporary feel – the wet wall was painted a red–purple colour.

THE RESULT

This display garden won the gold medal at the ABC's *Gardening Australia* LIVE show in 2002. I hope it showed visitors that even on a suburban block in our towns and cities, a contemporary Australian design can be adapted, giving an urban garden a sense of space and an affinity with our native flora.

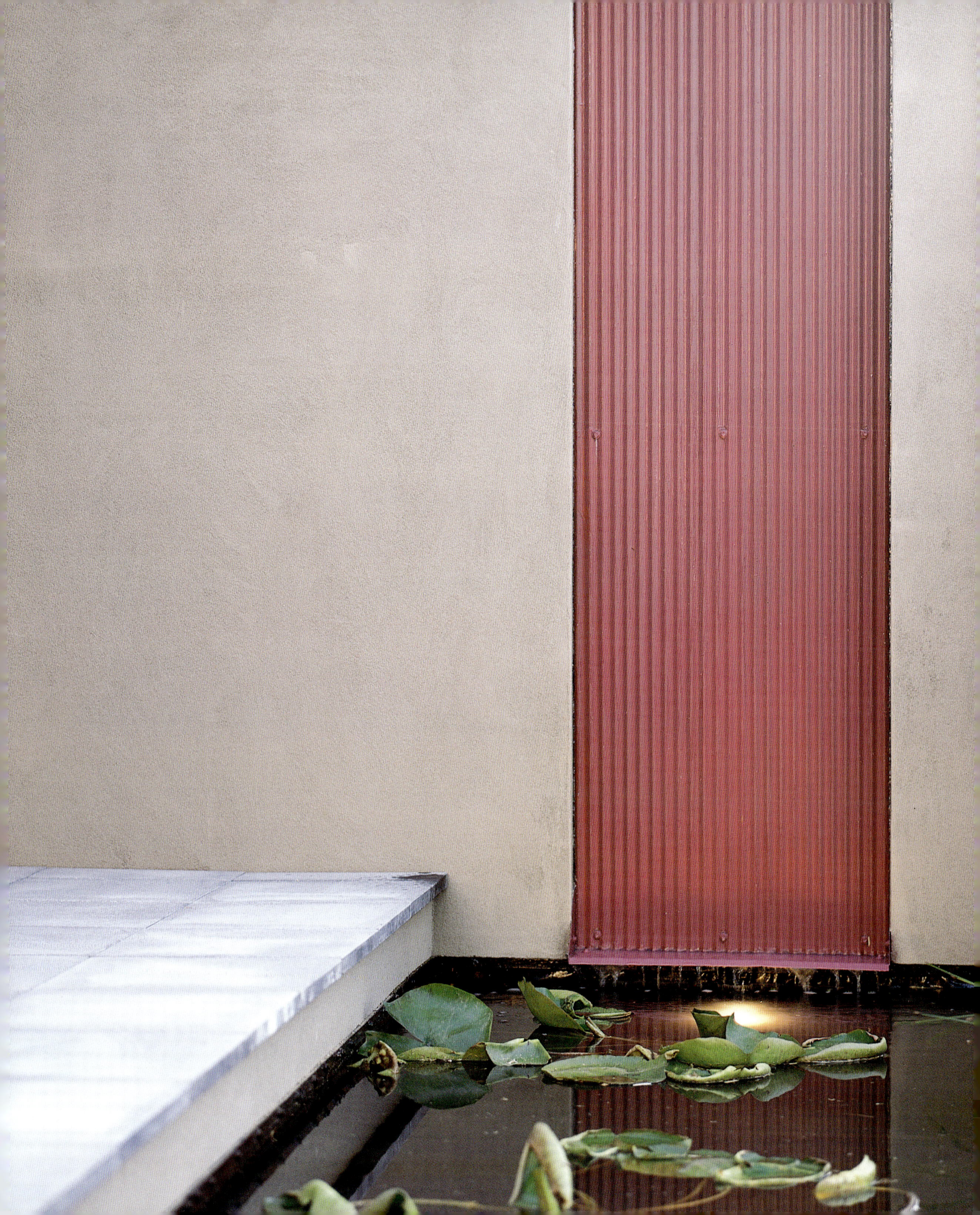

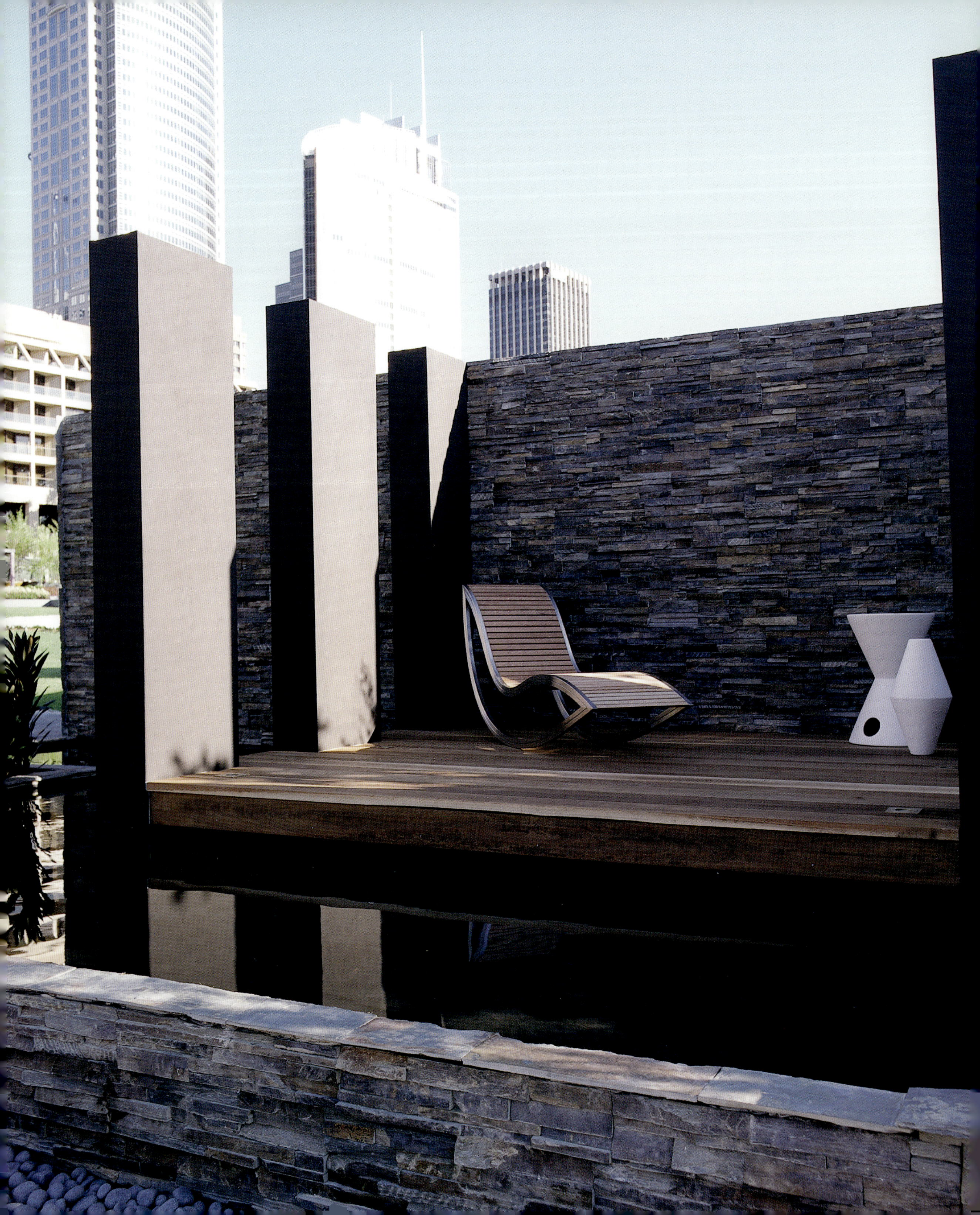

SYDNEY IN BLOOM
A DISPLAY GARDEN IN SYDNEY'S DOMAIN

THE SETTING
Sydney in Bloom was an exhibition of gardens, garden design and all matters horticultural that was held in the Domain, Sydney, in the spring of 2003.

THE BRIEF
The brief for this display was open. The site was 10 x 10 metres, and once again there were restrictions on any digging or penetration of the earth, as electrical and water services lay just below the surface. Great care had to be taken and a condition of participation in the show was that the site had to be left as we found it, so the turf had to be relaid. This was understandable, as the Sydney in Bloom exhibition was being held in one of the city's public gardens, the Domain.

THE DESIGN
With this garden, I wanted to express my thoughts on where I thought garden design was heading in 2003 and what influences were contributing to this trend. It was also an opportunity for me to showcase a more contemporary style of landscape design than I had been doing for clients over the previous five years – and perhaps introduce a style for which I wasn't known.

Wonderful new plants and products had been launched on the horticultural scene over this time, while the architecture on projects I was working on involving modern, newly-built houses had become more streamlined than ever. This was an opportunity to combine these factors into an innovative garden.

I love designing gardens in contemporary spaces as well as around classic homes. My approach to each is very different – around

OPPOSITE Kohl-coloured columns mimic the form of the city skyline and reflect calmly in the water. ABOVE The vibrant colours of the plants bring this garden to life.

ABOVE These plants, the Cordyline *'Sundance' and the* Protea *'Silver tree', were carefully chosen for their striking shapes and colours.*
OPPOSITE Bold garden furniture and pots balance the strong design of the display.

period houses my style of design is generally very symmetrical while modern architecture seems to me to call for asymmetrical garden spaces.

I decided that for this display garden I wanted to create a casual space with organic textures, therefore the design included timber, granite, black limestone and pebbles. An elevated ironbark deck was surrounded by a body of water, fed by a granite wet wall behind the deck. Water from the top pond fell over the granite pond walls into a trough flush with the garden.

Six kohl-coloured columns framed parts of the feature wall. Limestone stepping stones surrounded by anvil pebbles were staggered from the timber steps leading to the deck through the garden. The 'building' part of the display was built from scratch and therefore was constructed using a timber frame and blueboard.

I chose the plants carefully in order to frame this setting and enhance the architectural concept. They were all included for their colour, form and hardiness. I planted them in groups: New Zealand flax, *Phormium* 'Chief'; *Hebe albicans*; black mondo grass, *Ophiopogon planiscapus* 'nigrescens'; *Cordyline nigra*; and the succulent *Crassula ovata*.

The *Phormium* has strong, spear-like, red–bronze leaves, while *Hebe albicans* makes small, mounded shrubs about 30 centimetres high with dense foliage – a good contrast. The black mondo grass is unusual in its coloration, as is the *Cordyline nigra*: there are very few black plants to be found and so it is an interesting addition to this design. The *Cordyline* will grow in a clump to about 2 metres and is very striking when mature. *Crassula ovata* has a number of common names: it is sometimes known as the friendship tree, the jade tree, or the money tree. It grows very slowly and in ideal conditions has been known to reach 4 metres in height. It has a swollen stem and its thickish green leaves – which look a little like coins – are edged with red at some seasons of the year. Again, it is a very striking plant.

Finally, three graceful Japanese maples, *Acer palmatum*, form a canopy over this mixed planting and soften the granite walls.

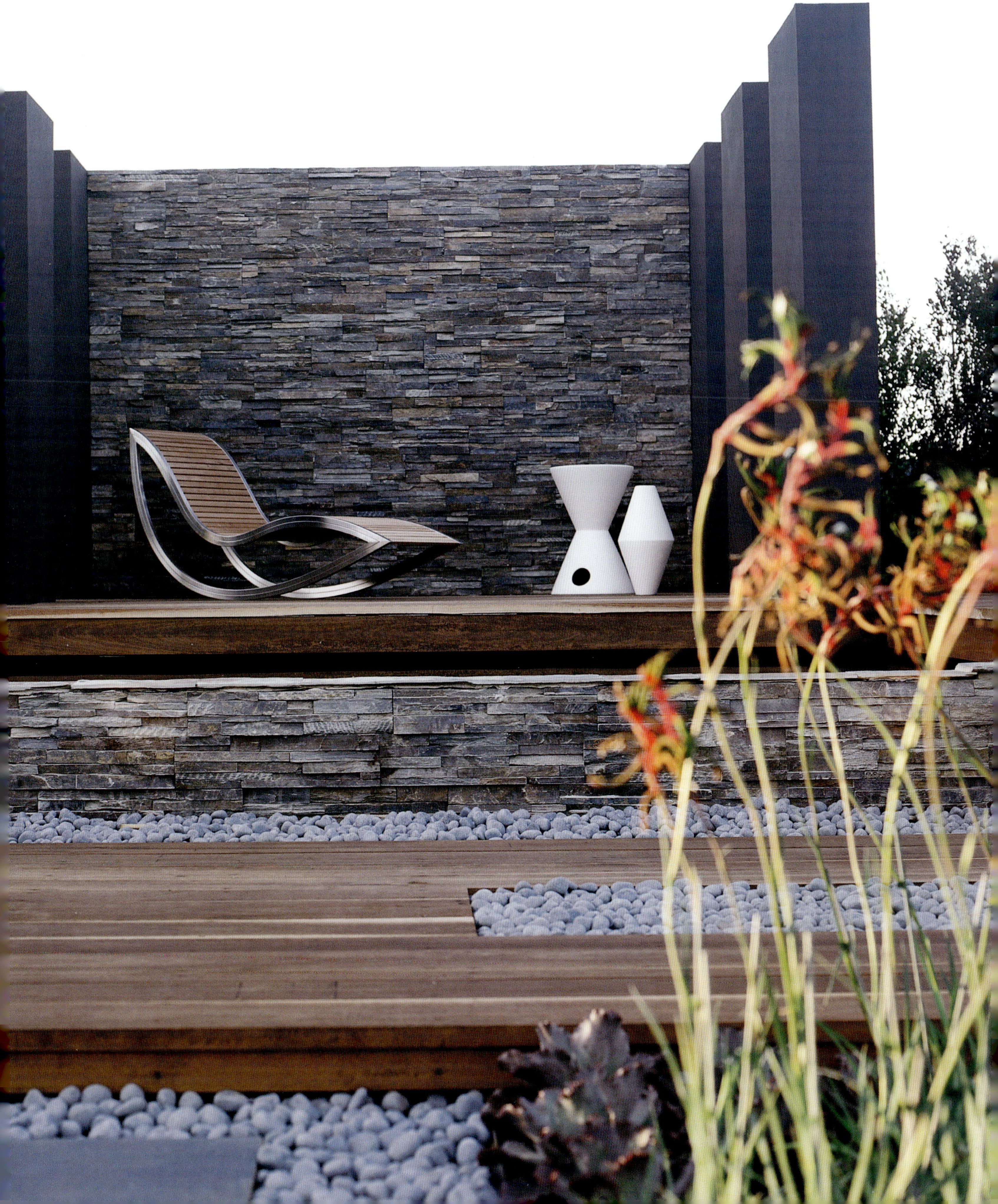

THE RESULT

This garden displays elements of contemporary design. I wanted it to be something real so that it didn't feel out of reach for the average gardener and would therefore inspire visitors. The planting is relaxed although architectural and forms a balance with the organic textures in the materials used in the display.

OPPOSITE A contemporary garden in full bloom.

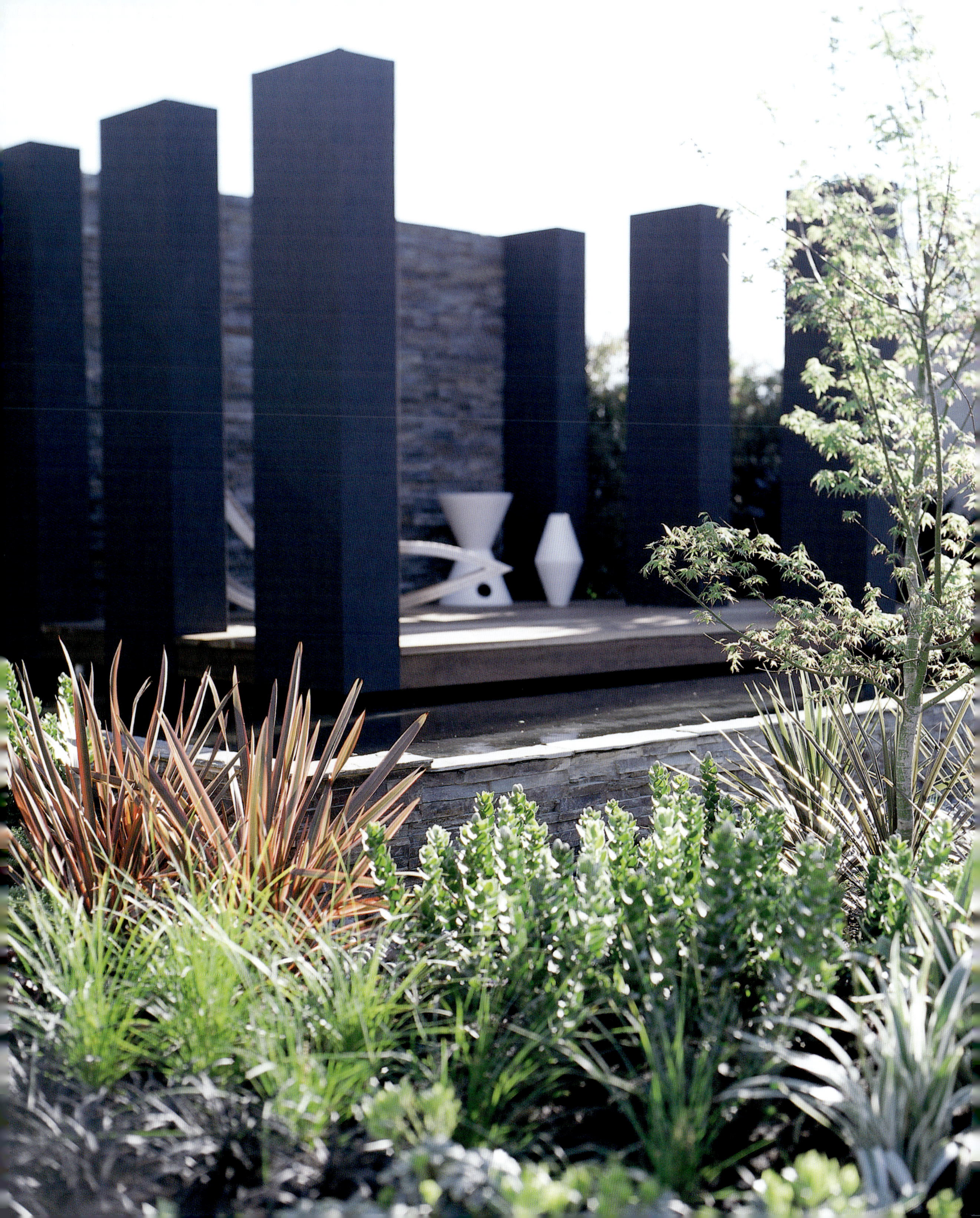

3 Living Symmetry

17 Wildes Meadow – A *belle* Garden

51 Naturally Distinctive

57 Urban Elegance

65 Stone and Greenery

99 Integrated Living

109 Echoes of Light

113 Sultry Fusion

29 Contemporary Comforts

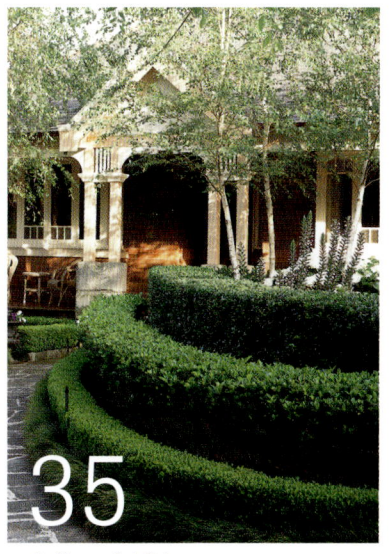

35 A Graceful Edge

43 Mission Possible

73 Plane Sailing

79 Visual Enlightenment

83 Garden of Eden

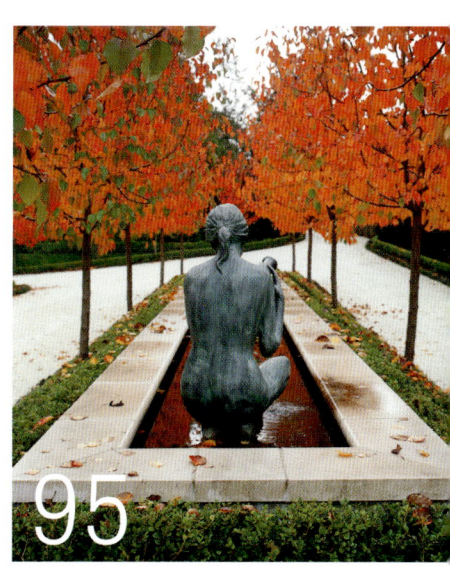

95 Manchurian Drive

119 A Classic Reflection

123 Poise and Beauty

131 Contemporary Australian Design in a Bush Setting

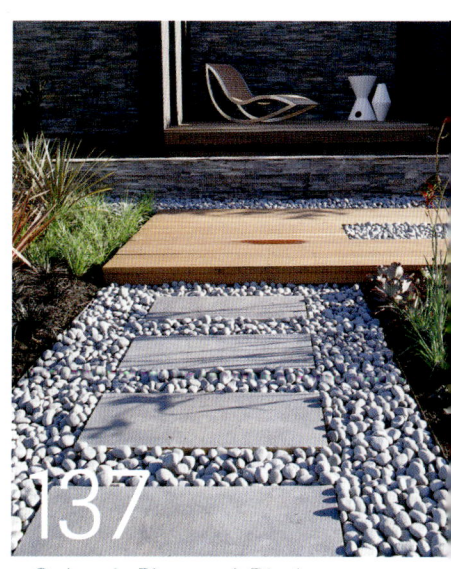

137 Sydney in Bloom – A Display Garden in Sydney's Domain

INDEX

A
Acanthus mollis 36
Acer palmatum (Japanese maple) 35, 138
   'Sango Kaku' (coral bark maple) 11, 100
   A. palmatum dissectum 'Seiryu' 79–80
Acorus gramineus 'Variegata' (Japanese sweet flag) 11
African daisy (*Arctotis* x *hybrida*) 52
agapanthus (*Agapanthus orientalis*) 84, 88, 120
Agave attenuata 54, 102, 126
Ajuga reptans 'Jungle Giant' 100
Anemone x *hybrida* (Japanese windflower) 36
Arctotis x *hybrida* (African daisy) 52
arum lily (*Zantedeschia aethiopica*) 36, 88
ash *see* golden ash; Raywood ash
autumn crocus (*Zephyranthes candida*) 68, 90
aviary 67–8
axis 7, 11, 18, 58, 100
azalea (*Rhododendron* 'Alba Magna') 36

B
balconies, penthouse 123–7
Bambusa lako (Timor black bamboo) 29–30, 114
bay tree 7
bench 7, 11, 62, 68, 77, 88, 102
birch (*Betula*)
   B. nigra 'Tropical Birch' 114
   silver birch (*B. pendula*) 11, 22, 36, 39, 90
bird-of-paradise flower (*Strelitzia regina*) 114, 120
black locust (*Robinia pseudoacacia* 'Umbraculifera') 88, 90
black mondo grass (*Ophiopogon planiscapus* 'Nigrescens') 138
blue gum (*Eucalyptus saligna*) 90
box
   perceived overuse of 61
   see also English box; Japanese box
Bradford pear (*Pyrus calleryana* 'Bradford') 39–40
bricks, second-hand 73
bromeliad 126
bush germander (*Teucrium fruticans*) 8
Buxus (box)
   microphylla var. *japonica* (Japanese box) 11, 18, 21, 36, 39, 54, 57–8, 66, 69, 74, 77, 88, 90, 95, 96, 119, 120
   sempervirens (English box) 7, 8, 11, 18, 21, 57–8, 74, 88

C
Callitris rhomboidea (native conifer) 132
Camellia 88, 90
   C. japonica 68
   C. japonica 'Nuccio's Gem' 84
   C. sasanqua 58, 62, 67–8
   C. sasanqua 'Plantation Pink' 65
   C. sasanqua 'Setsugekka' 36
children's garden 102, 104
Chinese elm (*Ulmus parvifolia*) 12, 22, 35, 62, 110
circular drive 8, 95–6
cobblestone wall 113–14
concept gardens 130–41
contemporary gardens 29–32, 51–4, 79–81, 99–105, 131–4
coral bark maple (*Acer palmatum* 'Sango Kaku') 11, 100
Cordyline
   C. nigra 138
   'Red Sensation' 11
country gardens 3–23
courtyard gardens 58
   entertaining area 109–10
   function plus aesthetics 29–32
   Japanese 4, 11
   penthouse 123–7
   privacy 43, 44, 108–9, 119–21
   tropical 113–116
   with a view 119–21, 123–7
crab apple (*Malus* sp.) 18, 35
Crassula ovata (friendship tree) 138
creeping juniper (*Juniperus horizontalis*) 22
crepe myrtle (*Lagerstroemia indica*) 35
croquet lawn 18, 21
cypress (x *Cupressocyparis leylandii* 'Leighton Green') 4, 7, 8, 11, 17, 21, 39, 44, 49, 51, 54, 61–2

D
dam 12, 22
Daphne odora 36
decked area 29, 32, 44, 138
directional planting 66, 88
display garden 136–41
double crab apple (*Malus ioensis* 'Plena') 18
driveway 8, 11, 12, 33, 83–4, 95–6
Duranta repens 'Sheena's Gold' 114

dwarf date palm (*Phoenix roebelinii*) 120
dwarf mondo grass (*Ophiopogon japonica* 'Nana') 4, 7, 11, 54, 58, 62, 84, 113
dwarf port wine magnolia (*Michelia figo* 'Coco') 100
dwarf red bougainvillea 54
dwarf star jasmine (*Trachelospermum asiaticum*) 35, 36, 49, 68

E
Echeveria sp. 8, 11, 58
elm *see* Chinese elm; variegated elm
English box (*Buxus sempervirens*) 7, 8, 11, 18, 21, 57–8, 74, 88
entertainment area 29, 39, 43, 44, 46, 49, 54, 102, 109–10
Eriostemon myoporoides (long-leaf wax flower) 18
espaliered trees 18
established trees 8, 35, 65, 67, 83
Eucalyptus
   E. caesia 'Silver Princess' 132
   E. mannifera (red-spotted gum) 22
   E. saligna (blue gum) 90
evergreen dogwood 22

F
family garden 57–62
Federation house 35–40, 99–105
fescue grass (*Festuca* sp.) 8, 18
foliage for colour 8, 12, 18, 22, 30, 36, 40, 49, 52, 77, 79–80, 96
fountain 8, 35–6, 68, 88, 95–6
fountain grass (*Pennisetum alopecuriodes*) 100
Fraxinus (ash)
   F. angustifolia 'Raywood' (Raywood ash) 12
   F. excelsior 'Aurea' (golden ash) 4, 7, 8
French lavender (*Lavendula dentata*) 21
friendship tree (*Crassula ovata*) 138
front entrance 51–2, 65–9, 73–5, 79–80, 100
front path 65–6, 73–4

G
garden furniture 7, 11, 12, 29, 32, 46, 62, 68, 77, 88, 102, 113
garden rooms *see* rooms
Gardenia augusta 'Florida' 36, 68, 100
gates 12
golden ash (*Fraxinus excelsior* 'Aurea') 4, 7, 8

gravel 96, 104
groundcover 22, 88

H
Hebe 100
   H. albicans 138
   'Lake' 8
Hedera canariensis (large-leaf ivy) 61, 84, 88
hedges
   box 8, 11, 21, 39, 57–8, 69, 74, 119, 120
   cypress 4, 7, 39, 61–2
   windows in 4, 7, 11, 12, 49
Helleborus orientalis 36
house
   blending indoors with out 32
   lines of sight from 4, 7, 11
   placement in garden 3, 4
   softening lines of 36, 52, 79
Howea forsteriana (Kentia palm) 120
Hydrangea macrophylla 36

I
illusions 49, 52, 58, 79–81, 84, 104, 110
Impatiens balsamina (white balsam) 88
Iris
   blue 8
   I. ensata (yellow Japanese iris) 39
Isolepis nodosa (New Zealand rush) 100
Italian lavender (*Lavandula stoechas*) 7, 68

J
Japanese box (*Buxus microphylla* var. *japonica*) 11, 18, 21, 36, 39, 54, 57–8, 66, 69, 74, 77, 88, 90, 95, 96, 119, 120
Japanese courtyard 4, 11
Japanese maple (*Acer palmatum*) 35, 138
   coral bark maple (*A. palmatum* 'Sango Kaku') 11, 100
   A. palmatum dissectum 'Seiryu' 79–80
Japanese sweet flag (*Acorus gramineus* 'Variegata') 11
Japanese windflower (*Anemone* x *hybrida*) 36
jasmine *see* dwarf star jasmine; star jasmine
Jekyll, Gertrude 88
Juniperus (juniper)
   J. chinensis 'Keteleerii' 95
   J. horizontalis (creeping juniper) 22
   J. virginiana 'Spartan' (pencil cedar) 11, 58, 61, 109–10, 126

K
Kalanchoe sp. 126
Kentia palm (*Howea forsteriana*) 120

L
Lagerstroemia indica (crepe myrtle) 35
landscaper rose 7
large-leaf ivy (*Hedera canariensis*) 61, 84, 88
lavender (*Lavandula*) 4
   L. dentata (French lavender) 21
   L. stoechas (Italian lavender) 7, 68
lawn 8, 18, 35, 62, 84, 88, 90, 102, 104–5
layered plants 36, 52, 90
lilly pilly (*Syzygium australe* syn. *paniculatum* 'Elite Form') 67, 68, 80, 114, 120
linden (*Tilia cordata*) 22
lines of sight 4, 7, 11
Liriodendron tulipera (tulip tree) 22, 104
Liriope muscari 'Evergreen Giant' 66, 90, 102, 110
lobelia 68
Lomandra longifolia 'Tanika' 100, 132
London plane tree (*Platanus* x *hybrida* syn. *P.* x *acerifolia*) 8, 74, 84
long-leaf wax flower (*Eriostemon myoporoides*) 21
Lutyens, Sir Edwin 88

M
Macartney rose (*Rosa bracteata*) 8, 11
Magnolia grandiflora 83, 90
   'Little Gem' 102
Malus (crab apple) 35
   M. ionensis 'Plena' (double crab apple) 18
Manchurian pear (*Pyrus calleryana*) 39–40, 77, 96
materials
   matching house 32, 54, 73, 126
   suiting landscape 134
Mediterranean garden 90
Metrosideros thomasii (New Zealand Christmas Bush) 52, 54
Michelia figo 'Coco' (dwarf port wine magnolia) 100
mirror 21, 110
mondo grass *see* black mondo grass; dwarf mondo grass
mop top robinia 88
mosaic tiles 54
Murraya paniculata (orange jessamine) 36, 68–9, 74, 84, 88, 90, 95, 119

N
native conifer (*Callitris rhomboidea*) 132
native grasses 21, 132
native red turpentine (*Syncarpia glomulifera*) 90, 104
New Zealand Christmas Bush (*Metrosideros thomasii*) 52, 54
New Zealand flax (*Phormium*) 21
   P. 'Bronze Baby' 52
   P. 'Chief' 138
   P. 'Dwarf Burgundy' 54, 80
New Zealand rush (*Isolepis nodosa*) 100

O
octagonal garden 7, 8, 11
olive tree (*Olea europea*) 52
Ophiopogon
   O. jaburan 8
   O. japonicus 'Nana' (dwarf mondo grass) 4, 7, 11, 54, 58, 62, 84, 113
   O. polaniscapus 'Nigrescens' (black mondo grass) 138
orange jessamine (*Murraya paniculata*) 36, 68–9, 74, 84, 88, 90, 95, 119
outdoor eating area 54
outdoor furniture 7, 11, 12, 29, 32, 46, 62, 68, 77, 88, 102, 113

P
parterre 4, 7, 21
paths 8, 22, 35, 52, 65–6, 73–4, 104
pavers 11, 39–40, 46, 54, 66, 72, 102, 109, 110, 113, 132
pear *see* Bradford pear; Manchurian pear; silver pear; snow pear
pebbles 11, 32, 52, 79, 102
pebbled wall 49
pencil cedar (*Juniperus virginiana* 'Spartan') 11, 58, 61, 109–10, 126
Pennisetum alopecuriodes (fountain grass) 100
penthouse balconies 123–7
perennials 18, 21
perfumed plants 68–9
periwinkle (*Vinca minor* 'Alba') 11
perspective 52, 67–8
Phoenix roebelenii (dwarf date palm) 120
Phormium (New Zealand flax) 21
   'Bronze Baby' 52

'Chief' 114, 138
'Dwarf Burgundy' 54, 80
planter boxes 29–30, 44, 49, 54, 102, 114
planting
   architectural plants 21, 80
   for colour 18, 52, 114
   directional 66, 88
   layered 36
   limiting varieties 4
   Mediterranean style 7
   perfumed 68–9
   perennials 18, 21
   repetition 54, 68, 84, 120
   seasonal interest 36
   for shade 36
   to soften walls 138
Platanus x *hybrida* syn. *P.* x *acerifolia* (London plane tree) 8, 74, 84
pleaching 7, 8, 18, 74, 77, 83–4
Plectranthus argentatus (silver plectranthus) 36
pond 30, 77
   in circular drive garden 95–6
   'floating' in courtyard 32, 35–6
   in Japanese courtyard 11
   lining 52, 54, 68
   linking house and garden 79
   perfumed planting 68–9
   raised 68, 95–6
   as 'Wow' factor 52
poplar (*Populus deltoides*) 4, 12
pots 11, 54, 88, 126
privacy 43, 44, 108–9, 119–21
purple-leafed bromeliad (*Vriesea imperialis*) 126
Pyrus (pear)
   P. calleryana (Manchurian pear) 39–40, 77, 96
   P. calleryana 'Bradford' 39–40
   P. nivalis (snow pear) 7, 46, 49, 100
   P. salicifolia (silver pear) 21

R
Raywood ash (*Fraxinus angustifolis* 'Raywood') 12
red-spotted gums (*Eucalyptus mannifera*) 22
reflective pond 32
Rhododendron 'Alba Magna' (azalea) 36
Robinia pseudoacacia 'Umbraculifera' (black locust) 88, 90
rooms
   massed planting 4
   small rooms in large gardens 18, 36

unifying 4, 7, 62
varying content 36
rose (*Rosa*) 21
   landscaper 7
   Macartney (*R. bracteata*) 8, 11
   rugosa 8
rosemary (*Rosmarinus officinalis* 'Blue Lagoon') 7

S
salt-tolerant plants 51, 52
salvia 21
shade, plants for 36
silver birch (*Betula pendula*) 11, 22, 36, 39, 90
silver pear (*Pyrus salicifolia*) 21
silver plectranthus (*Plectranthus argentatus*) 36
slatted screen 102
sloping site 43–9, 57, 61, 102
snow pear (*Pyrus nivalis*) 7, 46, 49, 100
soil, volcanic 17
stairs 22, 65–6
star jasmine (*Trachelospermum jasminoides*) 39, 62, 96, 110, 119, 120
stepping stones 4, 7, 8, 11, 22, 32, 46, 52, 57–8, 68, 138
stone sphinxes 88
Strelitzia reginae (bird-of-paradise flower) 114
succulents 8, 11, 51, 54, 126, 138
sunken garden 4, 11–12, 99–100
sweet viburnum (*Viburnum odoratissimum*) 21, 49, 66, 67, 68, 69, 77, 100, 102
swimming pool 43, 44, 68–9, 102
Syncarpia glomulifera (native red turpentine) 90, 104
Syzygium australe syn. *paniculatum* 'Elite Form' (lilly pilly) 67, 68, 80, 114, 120

T
tank garden 22
tennis court screen 22
terrace 46, 54, 88, 88, 102, 104–5
Teucrium fruticans (bush germander) 8
Thuja plicata (Western red cedar) 22
Tilia cordata (linden) 22
Timor black bamboo (*Bambusa lako*) 29–30, 114
Trachelospermum (jasmine)
   T. asiaticum (dwarf star jasmine) 35, 36, 49, 68
   T. jasminoides (star jasmine) 39, 62, 96, 110, 119, 120
Tradescantia discolor 114

transition zones 83, 100
trees, existing 8, 35, 65, 67, 83
tropical courtyard 113–116
tulips 21
tulip tree (*Liriodendron tulipera*) 22, 104

U
Ulmus (elm)
   U. parvifolia (Chinese elm) 12, 22, 35, 62, 110
   U. variegata (variegated elm) 11
underplanting 8, 11, 39
urns 8, 11, 65–6, 68, 88, 119–20
   Anduze 77, 90

V
variegated elm (*Ulmus variegata*) 11
vegetable garden 21–2
Viburnum odoratissimum (sweet viburnum) 21, 49, 66, 67, 68, 69, 77
   'Emerald Lustre' 100, 102
views, enhancing 18, 29, 65–9, 119–21, 123–7
Vinca minor 'Alba' (periwinkle) 11
Vriesea imperialis (purple-leafed bromeliad) 126

W
walls 11, 29, 44, 49, 113–14, 126, 134
water channel 52
water feature 39, 49, 54, 61–2, 79–81
water wall 30, 32, 90, 114, 134
weed prevention 49
Western red cedar (*Thuja plicata*) 22
white balsam (*Impatiens balsamina*) 88
windy site 7, 17–18, 51–4
woodland areas 12, 90
'wow' factor
   circular drive garden 96
   front garden 51–2

X
x *Cupressocyparus leylandii* 'Leighton Green' (cypress) 4, 7, 8, 11, 17, 21, 39, 44, 49, 51, 54, 61–2
Xylosma congestum 61

Y
yellow Japanese iris (*Iris ensata*) 39

Z
Zantedeschia aethiopica (arum lily) 36, 88
Zephyranthes candida (autumn crocus) 68, 90